The British Trauma Film

The British Trauma Film

Psychoanalysis and Popular British Cinema in the Immediate Aftermath of the Second World War

Adam Plummer

BLOOMSBURY ACADEMIC
NEW YORK • LONDON • OXFORD • NEW DELHI • SYDNEY

BLOOMSBURY ACADEMIC
Bloomsbury Publishing Inc
1385 Broadway, New York, NY 10018, USA
50 Bedford Square, London, WC1B 3DP, UK
29 Earlsfort Terrace, Dublin 2, Ireland

BLOOMSBURY, BLOOMSBURY ACADEMIC and the Diana logo are
trademarks of Bloomsbury Publishing Plc

First published in the United States of America 2023
Paperback edition published in 2024

Copyright © Adam Plummer, 2023

For legal purposes the Acknowledgments on p. ix constitute
an extension of this copyright page.

Cover design: Eleanor Rose
Cover images: Dead of Night, 1945, from left: Ralph Michael, Googie Withers, segment
'The Haunted Mirror,' dir. Robert Hamer © Everett Collection; Background image © Shutterstock

All rights reserved. No part of this publication may be reproduced or
transmitted in any form or by any means, electronic or mechanical, including
photocopying, recording, or any information storage or retrieval system,
without prior permission in writing from the publishers.

Bloomsbury Publishing Inc does not have any control over, or responsibility for,
any third-party websites referred to or in this book. All internet addresses given
in this book were correct at the time of going to press. The author and publisher
regret any inconvenience caused if addresses have changed or sites have ceased
to exist, but can accept no responsibility for any such changes.

Library of Congress Cataloging-in-Publication Data
Names: Plummer, Adam (Independent researcher) author.
Title: The British trauma film : psychoanalysis and popular British cinema
in the immediate aftermath of the Second World War / Adam Plummer.
Description: New York : Bloomsbury Academic, 2023. |
Includes bibliographical references and index. |
Summary: "Explores how psychoanalytic ideas of trauma, anxiety, sexual difference,
and subjectivity influence 1940s British cinema"– Provided by publisher.
Identifiers: LCCN 2022042751 (print) | LCCN 2022042752 (ebook) |
ISBN 9798765100479 (hardback) | ISBN 9798765100516 (paperback) |
ISBN 9798765100486 (epub) | ISBN 9798765100493 (pdf) |
ISBN 9798765100509 (ebook other)
Subjects: LCSH: Motion pictures–Great Britain–History–20th century. |
Psychic trauma in motion pictures. | Psychoanalysis and motion pictures.
Classification: LCC PN1993.5.G7 P55 2023 (print) | LCC PN1993.5.G7
(ebook) | DDC 791.43094109/045–dc23/eng/20221103
LC record available at https://lccn.loc.gov/2022042751
LC ebook record available at https://lccn.loc.gov/2022042752

ISBN:	HB:	979-8-7651-0047-9
	PB:	979-8-7651-0051-6
	ePDF:	979-8-7651-0049-3
	eBook:	979-8-7651-0048-6

Typeset by Integra Software Services Pvt. Ltd.

To find out more about our authors and books visit www.bloomsbury.com
and sign up for our newsletters.

Contents

Illustrations	vi
Acknowledgments	ix
Introduction	1
1 Althusser and Foucault, Psychoanalysis as Ideology and Discourse, and the Place of the British Trauma Film in British Immediate Post-War Cinema	17
2 "Broken Attachments and Traumatic Repetition": Psychoanalytic Perspectives on Loss, Trauma, Anxiety, and the Fragmentation of the Family Unit in *The Halfway House*	45
3 "The Perpetual Recurrence of the Same Thing": The Compulsion to Repeat the Trauma *ad Infinitum*, Male Anxiety, Sexual Difference and Motherhood, and the Interplay between Subjectivity and Objectivity in *Dead of Night*	79
4 "What Does a Woman Want?": Childhood Trauma, Female Desire, and Female Subjectivity in *The Seventh Veil* and *Madonna of the Seven Moons*	119
5 "The World Is Full of Neurotics": The Traumatized Serviceman, the Collapse of Maternal and Paternal Functions, and the Effects of Post-War Cultural Malaise in *They Made Me a Fugitive* and *Mine Own Executioner*	159
Concluding Remarks	199
Bibliography	207
The British Trauma Film—a Filmography	216
General Filmography	218
Index	221

Illustrations

2.1	*The Bells Go Down*: Tommy and Fire Officer MacFarlane seconds before the chimney collapses	51
2.2	*In Which We Serve*: The survivors of the sinking of *The Torrin*	52
2.3	*The Halfway House*: Oakley, Fortescue, Alice, and Richard and Jill French at the séance	59
2.4	*The Halfway House*: "Jim, c'est toi?"	59
2.5	*The Halfway House*: Alice and we realize that Rhys is really a ghost	62
2.6	*The Halfway House*: Gwyneth pays close attention to her father's words	65
2.7	*The Halfway House*: Then the incendiaries begin to fall. "In the corner, over there"	66
2.8	*The Halfway House*: The terrible nature of Rhys and Gwyneth's deaths: Rhys surrounded in flames	67
2.9	*The Halfway House*: The exact moment that the bombs have fallen	67
2.10	*The Halfway House*: Gwyneth just before the conflagration	68
2.11	*The Halfway House*: The incendiaries sparking behind and in front of her	69
2.12	*The Halfway House*: The shattering of peace, innocence, love, purity, and the family unit	69
2.13	*The Halfway House*: Will the war be won or lost? The loss of Tobruk on the twenty-first of June 1942	74
3.1	*Dead of Night*: Joan and Peter Cortland: "What shall we do tonight? Dress up – spend lots of money?"	87
3.2	*Dead of Night*: A London skyline unmarked by the Blitz	87
3.3	*Dead of Night*: Henry Moore's *Figure in a Shelter*	89
3.4	*Dead of Night*: Grainger reliving his trauma	91
3.5	*Dead of Night*: "Just room for one inside, sir"	93
3.6	*Dead of Night*: Any bus conductor on any day in normal life	94
3.7	*Dead of Night*: Jimmy and Sally: "Nobody else could have such a silly nose"	98
3.8	*Dead of Night*: Sally as mother to the phantom Francis Kent	102

3.9	*Dead of Night*: Walter Craig hits Sally "savagely, viciously"	103
3.10	*Dead of Night*: Peter's first vision in the mirror	107
3.11	*Dead of Night*: "Hmmm, handsome couple"	109
3.12	*Dead of Night*: Joan threatened with her extinction	115
4.1	*The Seventh Veil*: Francesca with Dr. Larsen: "Would you like to go back to school and be happy again?"	123
4.2	*The Seventh Veil*: Francesca's childhood traumas	124
4.3	*The Seventh Veil*: Orphaned and abandoned: Francesca and Nicholas	125
4.4	*The Seventh Veil*: Nicholas and his absent mother	132
4.5	*The Seventh Veil*: Francesca's re-entry into the paternal order	134
4.6	*The Seventh Veil*: Francesca chooses Nicholas	136
4.7	*Madonna of the Seven Moons*: Maddalena as the "sweet little maiden" Red Riding Hood	140
4.8	*Madonna of the Seven Moons*: "I want you to take this prayer book, for your comfort"	141
4.9	*Madonna of the Seven Moons*: The "excess" of Maddalena's libido: The third of October 1919 and the sixteenth of June 1920	142
4.10	*Madonna of the Seven Moons*: The aftermath of Maddalena's rape	145
4.11	*Madonna of the Seven Moons*: Guiseppe with Dr. Ackroyd: "It may have been a shock during her childhood"	147
4.12	*Madonna of the Seven Moons*: The reproduction of the means of reproduction	154
4.13	*Madonna of the Seven Moons*: Angela and Evelyn: "I'm taking no risks!"	155
4.14	*Madonna of the Seven Moons*: The price of Maddalena/Rosanna's transgressions	157
4.15	*Madonna of the Seven Moons*: "Goodbye Maddalena, my beloved wife"	157
5.1	*They Made Me a Fugitive*: Narcy and his henchmen at the Valhalla	163
5.2	*They Made Me a Fugitive*: Clem, the "bloke out of the R.A.F.," with Ellen and Narcy	164
5.3	*They Made Me a Fugitive*: Narcy's state of abjection	167
5.4	*They Made Me a Fugitive*: Sally realizes Narcy's capacity for evil	168
5.5	*They Made Me a Fugitive*: Sally's world shifting on its axis	168
5.6	*They Made Me a Fugitive*: Mrs. Fenshaw as Ferenczi's "mechanical automaton"	173

5.7 *They Made Me a Fugitive*: The barbarities that human beings are capable of: Mrs. Fenshaw murders her husband — 174

5.8 *They Made Me a Fugitive*: Carmen Mory, the "Black Angel" of Ravensbrück — 177

5.9 *Mine Own Executioner*: Adam Lucian: "My mother was his wife" — 183

5.10 *Mine Own Executioner*: Adam re-living his wartime trauma in the psychoanalytic setting — 184

5.11 *Mine Own Executioner*: Adam's Oedipal fixation — 185

5.12 *Mine Own Executioner*: Felix on Bab's couch: "Close your eyes, and talk, anything that comes into your head" — 190

5.13 *Mine Own Executioner*: "Don't let him see you as a vague or shadowy figure." Molly in the apartment — 191

5.14 *Mine Own Executioner*: Deeply buried elements of the traumatic event return in dreams and waking visions — 191

5.15 *Mine Own Executioner*: Pat and Felix: "It will always be you who will suffer for it" — 197

Acknowledgments

This book is the product of research carried out over the last ten or so years in the Film Departments at Queen Mary University of London and King's College London and in the Psychoanalysis Unit at University College London.

I would like to give special thanks to Queen Mary for the financial award that initially made the project possible, and to Lucy Bolton, Charles Drazin, and Libby Saxton of Queen Mary, who afforded me encouragement and support that far exceeded their responsibilities. I am grateful to them for their distinct contributions to this book, and for their limitless insight and guidance. I would also like to thank Caroline Bainbridge and Andrew Spicer who were so generous with their advice during my time at Queen Mary and after.

I am indebted to Lawrence Napper for his support during my early research into the influence of war trauma on British cinema at King's College London. I would also like to thank Christine English and Jonathan Sklar of University College London. Without them, and many others in UCL's Psychoanalysis Unit, the psychoanalytic aspects of this book would have remained tentative and underdeveloped. My thanks must go also to the indefatigable staff at the British Film Institute and the British Library.

I am extremely grateful to everyone at Bloomsbury who have made the process of bringing this book into being such a pleasure, most particularly Katie Gallof for her unfailing support for this project from the beginning.

Lastly, I could not have undertaken, and far less completed, this book without the unquestioning help, encouragement, and generosity of my family as a whole, and of my wife, Anna, and my daughters, Clementine and Eloise, in particular.

Introduction

A number of films made in Britain in the immediate aftermath of the Second World War clearly evidence the central role that psychoanalysis had come to play within British culture by the mid-1940s. These films engage with a range of psychoanalytic thinking both formally and narratively; they centralize characters suffering from traumatic neurosis, anxiety, amnesia, paranoid delusions, and schizophrenia, and they sometimes foreground psychoanalyst figures and psychoanalytic processes. In this book, I examine British cinema's post-war engagement with psychoanalysis from a critical theory perspective, drawing principally from the work of Louis Althusser and Michel Foucault. In adopting this approach, I make no claim for or against the truth of psychoanalysis, nor is this book a contribution to psychoanalytic film theory. Instead, I am proposing that because psychoanalysis was central to the ambient culture in Britain at this time, a critical examination of the psychoanalytic elements of these films is key to understanding their themes, their formal and narrative structures, and the positions, opinions, and worldviews that are embedded within them.

In the Ealing Studios production *Dead of Night* (Alberto Cavalcanti, Charles Crichton, Basil Dearden, Robert Hamer, 1945), a group of guests staying at a country house for the weekend recount their experiences of the supernatural to a psychoanalyst, Dr. Van Straaten. One of their number, a confident young woman Joan Cortland, tells a story that revolves around a gift she has given some time before to her then fiancé, Peter. This turns out to be an ornate Chippendale mirror in which Peter gradually begins to see visions of a room of a much earlier period. This is later revealed as the scene of its previous owner's murder of his wife and his subsequent suicide. The previous owner, Francis Etherington, a man of "dominating character, arrogant, reckless, handsome and of a violent temper," has been rendered immobile as the result of a tragic accident. As the story unfolds, Peter becomes increasingly listless as he somehow begins to identify with Francis Etherington's past traumatic experience. The film is careful to differentiate between the "reality" of the mirror's reflection as it appears to Joan, and the "fantasy" of Peter's traumatic visions, but this distinction begins to blur in the story's final sequence. Believing Joan to have been unfaithful to him, Peter attempts to strangle her as they struggle in front of the mirror, and, as she is held in his grasp, Joan too, for a second, sees Peter's vision, before smashing the mirror and breaking the spell. In having Joan share Peter's traumatic vision, *Dead of Night* challenges the viewer's presumption of Joan's "normality" and Peter's "abnormality," and any belief that the viewer might hold of a dividing line existing between reality and fantasy and the internal and external psychical worlds.

Dead of Night is one of the six British films of the mid-1940s that I examine in detail in later chapters. The others are *The Halfway House* (Basil Dearden, 1944), *The Seventh Veil* (Compton Bennett, 1945), *Madonna of the Seven Moons* (Arthur Crabtree, 1945), *They Made Me a Fugitive* (Alberto Cavalcanti, 1947), and *Mine Own Executioner* (Anthony Kimmins, 1947). My reasons for choosing these particular films are made clear in Chapter One. However, I introduce *Dead of Night* at this point because its Haunted Mirror story clearly evidences three of the various areas of psychoanalytic thinking that I argue are formative to the themes and structures of many British films in the immediate post-war period.

The first is associated with the effects of traumatic wartime experience. The figure of Peter chimes with other haunted male characters in British films of the mid-1940s that Andrew Spicer has grouped together as examples of the "post-war psychotic damaged man."[1] Spicer draws our attention to the tormented and yet passive, sexually repressed and "feminized" facets of these characters who would have been recognized, metaphorically, as traumatized veterans in need of understanding and compassion.[2] Ideas surrounding the effects of traumatic experience had found cultural purchase during the interwar years as a result of the public's engagement with books and articles by theorists such as Freud, Sándor Ferenczi, Karl Abraham, and Ernst Simmel, who were seeking to account for the connection between traumatic events and their consequences on the individual and the wider society.

The second is related to sexual difference. The figure of Joan is typical of the presentations of strong female characters in British productions of this time who often act as counterpoints to their variously distressed and vulnerable male figures. New ideas surrounding motherhood, sexual relationships, female sexual

---

[1] Andrew Spicer, *Typical Men: The Representation of Masculinity in Popular British Cinema* (London and New York: I.B. Tauris, 2001), pp. 175–7.
[2] Andrew Spicer, *Sydney Box* (Manchester and New York: Manchester University Press, 2006), p. 54.

development, and feminine psychology were circulating widely in Britain by the 1930s, motivated and supplemented by the numerous published writings of post-Freudians such as Melanie Klein and Karen Horney on the centrality of the role of the mother to the healthy development of children.

The third is connected to new ideas surrounding subjectivity and objectivity. I have argued that in making it clear that Joan shares Peter's traumatic vision, *Dead of Night* calls into question the idea that a strict border exists between the internal and external psychical worlds. Psychoanalytic object relational thinking defines the human being as existing precisely in this dual world of internal and external relationships. It specifies the individual's need to interact with other people as taking the central position in human development, and it becomes visible in these films' increasingly subjective and self-reflexive modes of address that run counter to the essentially realist nature of British early wartime cinema. These object relational influences emerge from a widespread popular engagement with the published work of Freud and Klein, radio broadcasts by Donald Winnicott, and articles in popular journals by Susan Isaacs. These theorists were concerned with how the internal world of the individual is constructed, and how it is formed by, and interacts with, the often-traumatic individual subjective experience of external reality. As Lavinia Gomez has summarised with precision, within object relations theory:

> Our inner world is a changing dynamic process, with some fixed and some more fluid patterns, both conscious and unconscious. These dynamics influence how we experience external reality and are themselves influenced by our experience of external reality.[3]

The starting point of this book is an observation that many British films made in the mid-1940s display forms of narration and stylistic representation that set them apart from early wartime productions and films made in the relative security of the late 1940s and 1950s. These differences came to exist as the result of the influence that Freud and his followers were exerting over British culture generally at this time, and it is by means of this engagement that British cinema was able to confront certain forces that had by now begun to weigh heavily on the British population. Perhaps the foremost of these were the profound collective emotional fallout resulting from the traumatic experience of the war, and anxieties emerging from the destabilization of British society's pre-war dominant social formations. It was by means of its interaction with

---

[3] Lavinia Gomez, *An Introduction to Object Relations* (London: Free Association Books, 1997), p. 2.

psychoanalysis that British cinema discovered a vocabulary that enabled it to describe these issues in a way that had resonance for its contemporary audiences, while at the same time providing safe spaces where the processing of their wartime experiences could begin.

But how can British cinema at this time, or indeed cinema at any time, be thought of as having anything to contribute to the processing of psychological trauma and anxiety on an individual or collective level?

The Art of Trauma

In a paper published in the mid-1990s exploring the effects of trauma on victims of the Holocaust, psychiatrists Dori Laub and Daniel Podell point to what they call the "art of trauma" as being able to act as an antidote to the annihilation of memory which occurs in the traumatized as a result of their disastrous experiences.[4] As Laub and Podell make clear, because of the radical break that occurs in the traumatized between experience and language, victims often cannot find categories of thought or words to articulate what they have suffered to others and even to themselves. Indeed, because of their extreme closeness to the traumatic event, the survivors of trauma may not even be able to recall the event at all. Instead, deeply buried elements of the event return in dreams, waking visions, or repetitious debilitating enactments in their daily lives, as they are often condemned to compulsively repeat the original event seemingly *ad infinitum*. The struggle of the traumatized to find ways to live with the anxietal effects of their pasts is therefore profoundly difficult. According to Laub and Podell, the freeing of victims from the shackles of trauma involves their confronting resultant latent memories which are encrypted within the mind of the individual or the collective society, and it is only by bringing these memories into the present that is it possible to begin to know the trauma and move beyond it.

The authors provide examples of works of art across many media forms that achieve this facing of traumatic memories by means of a certain kind of artistic representation. Works of art such as these

> inevitably contain a latent but powerful address that requires the viewer or reader to become engaged in a dialogue of his own with the trauma. Such works

---

[4] Dori Laub and Daniel Podell, "Art and Trauma," in *The International Journal of Psycho-Analysis* 76 (1995), pp. 991–1005.

of art reveal much in indirect ways: often, the most meaning can arise from the empty spaces, silences and omissions within them (e.g. pauses in oral testimony, or physical holes in paintings). Indeed, some artistic forms can *point* to 'that sphere', the psychological loci that harbour the deepest effects of trauma—those which are the most personal and particular to the individual. In essence, it is only through its indirect and dialogic nature that the art of trauma can come close to representing the emptiness at the core of trauma while still offering the survivor the possibility of repossession and restoration.[5]

(Laub and Podell's italics)

An essential element of the art of trauma is, therefore, the *indirect* indication of past traumatic events via oblique representation, and its purpose is not necessarily to come to an "objectively real" depiction of the traumatic event itself, but instead to create a safe representational space wherein the remembrance of the traumatic experience can begin, if only haltingly, to occur. The authors point to *Shoah* (Claude Lanzmann, 1985) as a film that motivates a powerful affect in its audiences not in direct representation, but instead in subtle, indirect ways. This nine-hour documentary comprises interviews with survivors, perpetrators, bystanders, and other witnesses of the Holocaust. A safe representational space is created in *Shoah* precisely

through the *absence* of photographs or pictures of the atrocities of the Holocaust, which are normally found in documentaries. An empty landscape, an architectural model, a studio replica are as close as Lanzmann will come to a direct representation of the event. Indeed, the force of the film lies in its silences—in words that merely echo real sound and in gestures that only mimic past movements.[6]

(My italics)

The establishment of this safe space allows for profound emotional resonances to be set in motion within its viewers, and this, in turn, allows normal emotional perspective to be left behind, and a new emotional perspective to be formed from where the victims can become to understand the trauma's impact on their lives.

But if we are to think of the British films of the mid-1940s as being capable of providing safe representational spaces for the processing of the psychological traumas and anxieties of the war, what empirical evidence is there that these films provoked these types of profound emotional resonances in their audiences?

[5] Ibid., p. 993.
[6] Ibid., p. 996.

Mass-Observation and the Emotional Experience of Cinema-Going in Britain in the 1940s

Between 1937 and the mid-1960s, the British social research project Mass-Observation aimed to record everyday life through posing questions to a volunteer panel of respondents and through anonymously recording conversations and behaviors on the street and at public events. In August 1950, Mass-Observation asked its panel of respondents whether they had ever cried in the cinema, and, if so, whether they were ashamed of this. Three months later, an analysis of its findings was published in the popular newspaper *The Daily Herald*.[7] In their assessment of the original replies to these questions, Sue Harper and Vincent Porter provide a fascinating insight into the feelings and emotions of British cinema audiences in the immediate post-war period.[8] The original Mass-Observation report is based on 318 replies, 125 from women and 193 from men, most of whom were between the ages of twenty and forty. The panel was also heavily skewed toward the middle class and administrative professions. In statistical terms, the responses of the panel are therefore of only limited value and are not representative of the British population as a whole. But importantly, these responses do provide an insight into the emotional reactions of a significant number of people to the experience of watching films in Britain in the period in question.

It is perhaps unsurprising that, in general, the women in the sample admitted crying more easily in films than the men. They made it clear time and again that they were rarely ashamed of this, and they were readily forthcoming on the nature of the emotional release that they felt whilst watching films. For example, a 26-year-old artist stated that: "The first film I ever saw had me in howls and I've never stopped since." In similar terms, a housewife aged forty-eight stated that:

> I never feel ashamed and get mad when my husband reminds me "it's only a story" and so on. I marvel that people can go through dry-eyed. But I don't consider the film satisfying if I haven't had a good cry.[9]

Even more revealingly, a sixty-year-old housewife recounted that:

> When I get to the stage when I let go I am in a completely remote world—I've stepped clear into the picture I watch. One rather amusing incident happened

---

[7] *The Daily Herald*, 18 November 1950.
[8] Sue Harper and Vincent Porter, *Weeping in the Cinema in 1950: Reassessment of Mass-Observation Material* (Mass-Observation Archive: University of Sussex Library, 1995).
[9] Ibid., p. 5.

when a friend and I went to see *To What Red Hell* with Sybil Thorndike. We had cried bitterly. We called into a shop in the road leading from the cinema. The elderly confectioner peered through the window and asked, has there been a big funeral? Everyone passing looks as though they have been crying. We explained it was the big picture showing at the cinema on the corner and she said decidedly "I *must* go and see it".[10]

In their answers, some of the males who were questioned did admit to crying whilst watching films. However, many more, while conceding that they did often respond emotionally to films, strove to distinguish these reactions from those that they observed in women by emphasizing the control that they were able to command over their feelings. For example, one civil servant, aged thirty-nine, made it clear that "I know I cry in the pictures—or at least will go as far as a man will before he gains control of himself." Another, a 36-year-old research economist, claimed that "I cannot remember having cried in a film … I have been educated to regard it as rather effeminate." Many men explained in their answers that they resolved the dilemma they felt was posed by their emotional reactions to films by taking charge of the choice of films that they went to see. For example, many echoed the answer of one respondent who answered that "I never cry in pictures because I don't go to pictures that make me cry." Sometimes, men even sought to consciously lower their emotional response to films by imagining how they would appear to other members of the audience if they surrendered to their feelings. Other male respondents recounted reminding themselves of the artificiality of the cinematic experience whilst watching certain films in order to distance themselves from the emotional content. Thus, a 34-year-old instrument maker admitted that, while seated in the cinema, "I am always bringing myself back to earth with a mental reminder that it is 'only a film.'"

Further insights can be gained from the responses by looking more deeply into the statistics themselves. In answering Mass-Observation's questions, both the female and male respondents referenced a wide range of pre-war, wartime, and post-war films, and many of the answers certainly attested to the affective experience that viewing these films produced in their audiences. However, within the context of this book, what is most interesting is the change in female and male responses that seems to have occurred during the wartime period.

The total number of films cited by both sexes across all age groups is broadly the same; 109 in the case of women and 114 in the case of men. When the films

[10] Ibid., pp. 5–6.

are split into those produced in the pre-war, wartime, and post-war periods, the total number of films cited in each period is again similar between women and men, twenty-five, thirty-two, and fifty-two, respectively for women, and twenty-eight, thirty-three, and fifty-three, respectively for men. Post-war films therefore seem to have produced a far greater emotional response in their audiences than pre-war and wartime films. Even more revealing, as Harper and Porter point out, is that this correlation between female and male responses breaks down in the case of the films made in the post-war period when the responses are divided into age ranges.

Again, perhaps unsurprisingly, women between the ages of thirty-six and forty cited four times as many films from this period as making them cry compared to the men in the same age range. However, what is surprising is that men between the ages of thirty-one and thirty-five named 50 percent more films than the women in the same age group as provoking these responses, and men between the ages of twenty-six and thirty named twice as many as the women in the same age group. While it could be argued that these last two differences are reflective of the higher number of men than women in the sample, Harper and Porter consider instead that:

> This imbalance does not justify the changes between each age [range]. The number of postwar films cited by younger men, and the higher number of films cited overall by the older female respondents, means that the younger men in this sample, those who grew to maturity—and probably fought—during the war years, wept more easily than those who were older.[11]

Two conclusions may be drawn from the Mass-Observation survey that have direct relevance for this book. The first is that a great many women and men did feel the act of viewing films at this time often an intensely emotional experience, whether they felt themselves able to display this openly or not. The second is that the intensity of this experience seems to have increased markedly during the period of wartime, and the magnitude of this increase was dependent on the respondents' age and their sex. This increase is most striking in the case of men who were likely to have had direct exposure to the war, and both factors point toward a connection between the heightened experience of watching films and the profound psychological effects of the war itself.

The end of the war in Europe in the early summer of 1945 had initiated a period in which the British public was compelled to confront the traumas and

[11] Ibid., p. 21.

anxieties not only of many returning servicemen, but of significant numbers of the civilian population who were living with the individual and collective effects of the Blitz, the fragmentation of family units, the effects of traumatic bereavement, the mass evacuation of children, and the harsh economic constraints that had by now come to be a factor in everyday British life. In addition, the British public soon came to realize that many of the structures which had bound society together in the face of the common enemy had disappeared with the onset of peacetime. The social historian David Kynaston reports that even amidst the euphoria of the VE day celebrations on the eighth of May 1945, some had begun to feel the discomfort of imminent change from a condition that had become familiar during the war. For example, Kynaston quotes the painter and writer Denton Welch as commenting at this moment that: "There were awful thoughts and anxieties in the air—the breaking of something—the splitting apart of an atmosphere that had surrounded us for six years."[12]

Three months later, the war in the Pacific would be brought to an end by the dropping of the atomic bombs on Hiroshima and Nagasaki, and although the British public's reactions to these events are enormously diverse and therefore difficult to quantify, there is little doubt that the advent of the atomic age brought with it a general feeling of insecurity and in some cases even one of moral crisis.[13] The Nuremberg Tribunal would commence in November 1945 and would last for almost a year, during which time the extent and consequences of the Holocaust would gradually become clear to the British public.

Over the course of the next eighteen months, more than four million British servicemen would be demobilized, and for most the transition from active service to civilian life would be far from easy. Often their pre-war jobs were no longer open to them; many were suffering from various forms of traumatic psychopathology, and advice and support were often not readily available. The strains on marriages were severe; husband and wife had often not seen each other for months or even years on end, and with many women having taken over absent servicemen's jobs in the workplace during the hostilities, there was little chance of a return to the pre-war *status quo*, and traditional gender roles would need to be renegotiated.[14]

A third of British homes had been damaged and a quarter of a million destroyed during the war, and the economic difficulties of this period, which

[12] David Kynaston, *Austerity Britain 1945–51* (London: Bloomsbury, 2007), p. 16.
[13] Mass-Observation, "Atomic War?," in *Peace and the Public* (London, New York, and Toronto: Longmans, Green and Co., 1947), pp. 8–13.
[14] Kynaston, pp. 97–100.

resulted partly from the withdrawal of the American Lend-Lease contract in August 1945 meant that little could be done in the way of reconstruction in the short term. The recently elected Attlee government now embarked on a program of radical social and economic reforms that would transform many aspects of British life, including the nationalization of major industries and public utilities, the creation of the Welfare State, and the decolonization of large parts of the British Empire. Rationing, price controls, and production controls were maintained and sometimes even tightened, with the consequence that increasing numbers of consumers and producers felt compelled to find ways to circumvent the regulations.[15] Many normally law-abiding people thus became criminalized, and the black market "spiv" and the juvenile delinquent now emerged as recognizable social types. During the months that followed the divorce rate and crime rate would soar, the economy would deteriorate further, and to make matters worse, the winter of 1946/7, which became popularly known as the "big freeze," would be the worst in more than fifty years.

The Percolation of Psychoanalysis within British Culture in the First Half of the Twentieth Century

The diverse detrimental effects of the experience of the war and its aftermath find expression in British cinema at this time by means of its engagement with the "new psychiatry" of psychoanalysis. The key questions to be addressed at this stage are why did psychoanalysis come to have such resonance for the British population at this particular moment, and how did it come to provide the vocabulary which some elements of British cinema would adopt in the immediate post-war period to enunciate these effects? To answer these questions, it becomes important to delineate the ways in which psychoanalysis had come before this period to occupy a position of prominence within British culture.

As Robert Hinshelwood has noted, psychoanalysis had achieved a foothold in Britain in the early years of the twentieth century at a moment of tumult; the characteristics of which would strongly determine its various points of access. Britain's position of global economic dominance, which had been established partly as a result of the Industrial Revolution of the late eighteenth

---

[15] Ina Zweiniger-Bargielowska, *Austerity in Britain: Rationing, Controls, and Consumption 1939–1955* (Oxford: Oxford University Press, 2000), pp. 151–3.

and early nineteenth centuries, had, by the second decade of the twentieth century, come to be increasingly threatened by the new methods of mass industrial production which had been established in other countries, most notably America and Germany. Meanwhile, the confident expectations of social and economic progress that those in power in the Victorian era had based on the application of the sciences were beginning to lose momentum, with the consequence that many of the long-established assumptions that had underpinned the predominance of European culture were becoming increasingly unsure.[16]

At the same time, changes to the status of women in British society had at last begun to achieve momentum, and the first phase of the move toward female emancipation, which since the middle of the nineteenth century had involved incremental gains in the rights of women to employment, education, property ownership, and enfranchisement, would come to its initial conclusion with the passage of the Representation of the People Act in 1918. As a result of these changes, established attitudes to sexual relations and the position that women held in the family unit, and the position that the family unit occupied within society, were beginning to be discussed openly and were often being called into question.

The trade union movement and the general belief in a right to education were becoming widely established, and, through the increasing economic importance of the professions, the middle classes were beginning to encroach on the positions of power that had hitherto been the territory of the aristocracy. In addition, Britain's relationships with foreign powers were becoming increasingly strained, and in some areas of the world, most notably in Russia and Germany, revolution and social unrest were once again beginning to rise to the surface after being contained in Europe for more than a century.[17]

Hinshelwood identifies several different cultural locations in which psychoanalysis became influential in Britain in the atmosphere of change that characterized the first two decades of the twentieth century.

The first was established via the wide contemporary interest in the scientific investigation of spiritualistic phenomena that was being pursued in Britain by institutions such as the Society for Psychical Research. Various influential members of the Society, most notably F. W. H. Myers and Henry Sidgwick,

---

[16] Robert Hinshelwood, "Psychoanalysis in Britain: Points of Cultural Access, 1893–1918," in *Psychoanalysis and Its Borders*, ed. by Giuseppe Leo (Lecce: Frenis Zero Press, 2012), p. 241.
[17] Ibid., pp. 241–2.

claimed that Freud's theories of repression and the unconscious that he had developed from his studies of the dissociative states of hysteria supported their own case for the scientific proof of the existence of the spirit world.[18]

The second was opened by those who were campaigning at this time for changes in social attitudes toward sexuality. The doctor and writer Havelock Ellis, for example, saw similarities in Freud's theory of sexual repression to his own widely published theories surrounding sexuality, narcissism, auto-eroticism, and childhood sexual development.[19]

At the same time, the application of psychoanalysis was gaining popularity in the areas of clinical psychiatry and the new experimental science of psychology. The psychiatrist and psychologist W. H. R. Rivers famously and successfully adapted a form of psychoanalytic psychotherapy during the First World War for the treatment of victims of shell-shock at the Craiglockhart Military Hospital in Edinburgh,[20] while in the field of psychology Rivers and others drew upon psychoanalysis to support their research into a new scientifically based empirical form of psychology that distinguished itself from both philosophy and neuroscience.[21]

Meanwhile, in the realm of literature, Freud's theories were attracting writers who saw the value of their application to understanding human emotions and motivations and even the creative process itself. Authors connected to the Bloomsbury Group such as Adrian Stephen, Lytton Strachey, Virginia Woolf, and Joan Riviere engaged with Freud's works in diverse ways and thus ensured the circulation of psychoanalytic ideas throughout metropolitan radical political circles.[22] Another Bloomsbury member, James Strachey, would eventually translate Freud's complete works into English, and these would be published after the war by Virginia and Leonard Woolf's Hogarth Press.[23]

Finally, in the sphere of education, Freud's ideas concerning the developmental stages of children were beginning to inform the "progressive" and "permissive" systems of learning that sought to privilege children's free development both within the school system and as future members of society.[24] Hinshelwood

---

[18] Ibid., pp. 244–7.
[19] Ibid., pp. 247–50.
[20] Ibid., pp. 250–4.
[21] Ibid., pp. 255–8.
[22] Gregorio Kohon, *Introduction to The British School of Psychoanalysis: The Independent Tradition*, ed. by Gregorio Kohon (New Haven and London: Yale University Press, 1986), pp. 46–7.
[23] Hinshelwood, "Psychoanalysis in Britain," pp. 258–64.
[24] Ibid., pp. 264–9.

concludes that it is the multivalent nature of Freud's work that enabled it to engage with so many sites in the vast and varied British cultural domain, and that would ensure its place in British language and create "an eventually vibrant new dialogue: a psychoanalytic dialogue" in the years to come.[25]

While the first two decades of the twentieth century saw psychoanalytic thinking gaining a foot-hold in many corners of the British cultural milieu, Graham Richards argues that it was the Great War, and the changes that this wrought in all aspects of British life, which would ensure that the dissemination of psychoanalytic ideas would effectively become complete in Britain by the 1930s.[26] Richards reports that within a few years after the end of the war a "fashionable craze" for psychoanalysis had taken hold in the popular consciousness; driven by a wave of popular texts written by psychoanalysts and their sympathizers on diverse subjects such as war trauma and neurosis, childhood problems and education, dream analysis, criminal psychology, religion, and female and male sexuality. According to Richards, the public's fascination with these psychoanalytic ideas was fueled by a widespread dissatisfaction with the existing social order and a demand "for new ideas on all topics, as if the dominant pre-war world-views could not be abandoned fast enough."[27] Writing in 1921, D. H. Lawrence caricatured the public mood of the moment when he observed that:

> By this time psychoanalysis had become a public danger. The mob was on the alert. The Oedipus Complex was a household word, the incest motive a commonplace of tea-table chat. Amateur analyses became the vogue. 'Wait till you've been analysed,' said one man to another, with varying intonation. A sinister look came into the eyes of the initiates—the famous, or infamous, Freud look. You could recognize it everywhere, wherever you went.[28]

What Richards feels to have been the motivational factor in the outstanding success of psychoanalysis in Britain during this period was a convergence of the psychological needs of a substantial section of the population with the appearance of a system of ideas that promised to meet these needs. Whilst the emergence of psychoanalysis in British culture in the first two decades of the twentieth century had been located at the intersection of the moves toward modernity,

---

[25] Ibid., pp. 278–9.
[26] Graham Richards, "Britain on the Couch: The Popularization of Psychoanalysis in Britain 1918–1940," in *Science in Context* 13:2 (2000), p. 183.
[27] Ibid., p. 199.
[28] D. H. Lawrence, *Psychoanalysis and the Unconscious* (Mineola, NY: Dover Publications, 2005), p. 3.

female emancipation, new ideas surrounding sexuality, and the interrogation of established ideas surrounding established religion that Hinshelwood has described, Richards proposes that, although these issues certainly endured, "they were all transformed by the experience of the war itself."[29] In similar terms, Dean Rapp argues that

> the serious interest in psychoanalysis was stimulated primarily by its use as a treatment during the war. As the popular scientific magazine *Discovery* would explain: "thanks largely to its successful application to shell-shock cases [psychoanalysis] took the public by storm towards the end of the war."[30]

The popular appeal of psychoanalysis in the 1920s and 1930s can be defined, therefore, as being rooted more than anything else in the experience of the Great War, and precisely in the enduring traumatic effect that the war had inflicted on the British population.

The experience of the treatment of shell-shock during and after the First World War would lead to a re-evaluation of all the basic beliefs of psychiatric practice in Britain, both in civilian life and in the armed forces.[31] Many lessons were learned from the findings of the War Office Committee of Enquiry into Shell Shock, which met for the first time in 1920, and which concluded in 1922 that "it is clear to us that during 1916 and 1917 the question of the condition of the nervous system of the recruit did not receive adequate consideration."[32] As the psychoanalyst and historian Pearl King has observed, by the early years of the Second World War, psychoanalytic and other psychological practices had been integrated into many aspects of the war effort.[33] Soon after war had been declared, Anna Freud and Dorothy Burlingham opened the Hampstead War Nurseries in response to the social and emotional upheaval that was being faced by children who had been traumatized by the Blitz or separated from one or both parents. At the same time, the psychoanalysts Donald and Clare Winnicott were working on the problems of caring for difficult and disturbed children suffering from

---

[29] Richards, "Britain on the Couch," p. 221.

[30] Dean Rapp, "The Reception of Freud by the British Press: General Interest and Literary Magazines 1920–1925," in *Journal of the Behavioural Sciences* 24 (1988), pp. 191–2. Rapp quotes from the December 1921 edition of *Discovery*.

[31] Anthony Richards, "The British Response to Shell Shock: An Historical Essay," in *Report of the War Office Committee of Enquiry into "Shell-Shock"* (London: Imperial War Museum, 2004), p. iv.

[32] *Report of the War Office Committee of Enquiry into "Shell-Shock"* (London: Imperial War Museum, 2004), p. 166.

[33] Pearl King, "Activities of British Psychoanalysts during the Second World War and the Influence of Their Inter-Disciplinary Collaboration on the Development of Psychoanalysis in Great Britain," in *International Review of Psycho-Analysis* 16:15 (1989), pp. 15–33.

the effects of evacuation.³⁴ Meanwhile, the British Psycho-Analytical Society was becoming involved in planning for the medical and child-care services which would be needed in the post-war period to address the widespread dislocation of life that the war had caused.

Faced with the problems that resulted from mass conscription, the armed forces had realized that there was a need for skilled psychological help with the process of the selection of personnel, appointing consultant psychiatrists for the Navy, the Air Force, and the Army. Psychological testing and psychiatric interviews were sanctioned by the Army Council, and the first experimental War Office Selection Board was established for the vetting of officer recruits and staffed by psychoanalysts W. R. Bion, Jock Sutherland, and Eric Wittkower, and the psychologist Eric Trist.³⁵

In 1944, the psychoanalyst A. T. M. Wilson was appointed to investigate the psychiatric problems that ex-prisoners of war might face on their return to Britain and during their re-integration into civilian life; as a result of his report twenty Civil Resettlement Units were established, and approximately 50,000 men would pass through them over the following two years.³⁶ The wartime consultant psychiatrist to the Army, John Rawlings Rees, reported soon after the war had ended that psychoanalytic or other psychological methods had also been widely deployed during the war in the fields of training, the boosting of morale, discipline, education, psychological warfare, and the treatment of the psychotic and psychoneurotic symptoms of war trauma.³⁷

By the end of the Second World War, because of the developing public engagement with psychoanalysis that Hinshelwood, Richards, King, Rapp, Rees, and others have described, and because of the exposure of the population to a wide variety of psychoanalytic wartime interventions, psychoanalytic knowledge had come to be firmly ingrained within many areas of British day-to-day life and so assimilated within many aspects of British culture. But what are the processes by which the cultural appropriation of knowledge occurs, and what roles had psychoanalysis come to play within British culture and specifically within British cinema by the mid-1940s? To provide a conceptual model capable of addressing these questions, it becomes necessary to think of the proliferation of psychoanalytic knowledge within British culture at this time in relation to Althusser's idea of ideology and Foucault's idea of discourse.

---

³⁴ Ibid., p. 18.
³⁵ Ibid., p. 24.
³⁶ Ibid., p. 26.
³⁷ John Rawlings Rees, *The Shaping of Psychiatry by War* (New York: W. W. Norton, 1945), pp. 77–117.

1

Althusser and Foucault, Psychoanalysis as Ideology and Discourse, and the Place of the British Trauma Film in British Immediate Post-War Cinema

Althusser: Ideology, the Reproduction of the Relations of Production, and the Ideological State Apparatuses

Althusser's essay "Ideology and Ideological State Apparatuses" was published in the wake of the civil unrest that left Paris paralyzed in the summer of 1968, quickly becoming central to what Fredric Jameson has termed the "heated polemics and ideological battles that characterized the Marxisms of the 1960s and 1970s."[1] Althusser proposes that what we normally think of as ideological beliefs, positions, or worldviews never exist only in the consciousness of the individual, but are supported, reinforced, and reproduced by the apparatuses of state power. Althusser's argument is developed from the classical Marxist principle that the structure of every capitalist society is constituted by unities that exist on two levels. At the base is the infrastructure, which contains the productive forces and the "means of production," and above this rests the superstructure, which contains the "repressive" state apparatuses such as the government, the army, the police, and the courts. What Marx terms the "means of production" are the material components that taken together form the processes of production, as well as the labor power that is needed to keep the processes of production running smoothly.

According to Marx, the idea of the "state" is synonymous with the superstructure, and to maintain its position of power over the infrastructure it must make certain that the means of production, at the same time as being

---

[1] Fredric Jameson, Introduction to "Ideology and Ideological State Apparatuses," in *Lenin and Philosophy and Other Essays* (New York: Monthly Review Press, 2001), p. vii.

productive, are also themselves able to be reproduced. The reproduction of the means of production is achieved mostly at the level of the corporation; the responsibility of which is to ensure that the raw materials and fixed installations needed for production are replenished and replaced. The corporation must also provide its labor force with the means with which to reproduce itself, for example, by providing sufficient wages to pay for the housing, food, and clothing necessary to ensure that the worker is able to return to work day after day.[2] Althusser builds on Marx's theory by proposing that it is not enough merely for the state to ensure the labor power has the material conditions to ensure its reproduction; it must also make certain it has the potential to fulfill the different requirements expected of it within the socio-technical division of labor. While a certain amount of the education needed to achieve this potential is provided at the corporate level by means of training and apprenticeships, according to Althusser, this is largely achieved outside the sphere of the company by means of the state's educational apparatus.[3]

But what are young workers taught within this educational apparatus? Certainly, to read, to write, and to add, as well as other skills that are directly useful to be able to fulfill the different roles they will come to occupy later in life within the system of production. In addition to these skills, claims Althusser, workers are also taught the rules of good behavior, morality, and civic and professional conscience:

> To put this more scientifically, I shall say that the reproduction of labour power requires not only a reproduction of its skills, but also, at the same time, a reproduction of its submission to the rules of the established order, i.e. a reproduction of submission to the ruling ideology for the workers, and a reproduction of the ability to manipulate the ruling ideology correctly for the agents of exploitation and repression, so that they, too, will provide for the domination of the ruling class "in words."[4]

For Althusser then, the process of the reproduction of the labor force can be revealed as having at its core not only the reproduction of its skills, but also the reproduction of its subjection to the rules and practices of the ruling ideology itself. To reconcile the concept of ideological subjugation with Marx's proposal that society is composed of infrastructure and superstructure, Althusser

---

[2] Louis Althusser, "Ideology and Ideological State Apparatuses," in *Lenin and Philosophy and Other Essays* (New York: Monthly Review Press, 2001), pp. 85–92.
[3] Ibid., pp. 87–8.
[4] Ibid., p. 89.

introduces the idea that the superstructure, instead of being made up solely from the repressive state apparatuses, should be thought of as also containing disparate entities that he terms the "ideological state apparatuses." These entities present themselves in the form of other distinct and specialized institutions that include the educational system and the systems of the different churches, the family unit, the political parties, the trade unions, and the various forms of the arts and the media. But what should we think as constituting the difference between these ideological state apparatuses and the repressive state apparatuses Marx has described such as the army, the courts, or the police?

While the repressive apparatuses exist within the public domain and are unified by their common membership of the institutions of government, the unity of the ideological apparatuses as a body is not so immediately visible because they *seem to exist*, for the most part, only within the personal domain. Moreover, while Marx considers the repressive apparatuses to function mostly by means of repression and violence, Althusser claims that the ideological apparatuses function, predominantly, by means of the diverse influences that the superstructure exerts by means of culture:

> What unifies their diversity is precisely this functioning, insofar as the ideology by which they function is always in fact unified, despite its diversity and its contradictions, *beneath the ruling ideology*, which is the ideology of "the ruling class".[5]
>
> (Althusser's italics)

Althusser argues that while in the Middle Ages the church represented the one dominant ideological state apparatus, concentrating as it did the religious, educational, and cultural functions, in modern social formations these functions have devolved to the school system as well as to other ideological apparatuses such as the systems of communication and culture.

What is the function of these modern-day ideological state apparatuses? According to Althusser, *all* ideological state apparatuses, whatever they are, contribute to the same result, that is the reproduction of the *relations* of production that the state relies on for its survival. In other words, although the aim of these various apparatuses is to achieve the "training" of the population and to ensure that the population has the potential to fulfill the roles that have been assigned to them within the division of labor, their purpose is to ensure that the asymmetry of the power relations that exists between superstructure

[5] Ibid., p. 98.

and infrastructure is maintained and reproduced. Each of the ideological state apparatuses contributes toward this purpose in the way that is proper to it, for example, the political apparatus by subjecting individuals to the political state ideology, and the communications and the cultural apparatuses, Althusser claims, by "cramming every citizen with daily doses of nationalism, chauvinism, liberalism, and moralism."[6]

As well as describing the aims and functions of the ideological state apparatuses Althusser reflects on the nature of ideology itself, presenting the idea that the defining feature of all ideologies is their demand for beliefs that exist outside the realm of normal consciously held ideas. He argues that these beliefs become ingrained in the popular consciousness by virtue of their "obviousness":

> It is indeed a peculiarity of ideology that it imposes (without appearing to do so, since these are "obviousnesses") obviousnesses as obviousnesses, which we cannot *fail to recognize* and before which we have the inevitable and natural reaction of crying out (aloud or in the 'still, small voice of conscience'): "That's obvious! That's right! That's true!"[7]
>
> (Althusser's italics)

Althusser proposes that this type of reaction signifies the existence of a system by which ideology works to claim an "individual" as a "subject," arguing that this system operates by means of a process he terms "interpellation" or "hailing." In order to illustrate this system, he uses the everyday example of a policeman who calls out to a member of the public "Hey, you there!":

> Assuming that the theoretical scene I have imagined takes place in the street, the hailed individual will turn around. By this mere one-hundred-and-eighty-degree physical conversion, he becomes a *subject*. Why? Because he has recognized that the hail was 'really' addressed to him, and that "it was *really him* who was hailed" (and not someone else). Experience shows that the practical telecommunication of hailings is such that they hardly ever miss their man: verbal call or whistle, the one hailed always recognizes that it is really him who is being hailed.[8]
>
> (Althusser's italics)

In this way, according to Althusser, ideology interpellates individuals as subjects, but instead of defining this as occurring because of the individual's gradual

---

[6] Ibid., p. 104.
[7] Ibid., p. 116.
[8] Ibid., p. 118.

exposure to specific ideological influences, Althusser proposes instead that we have all, always, lived in ideology. For Althusser then, ideology exists, as Freud describes the unconscious as existing, trans-historically and eternally, and thus individuals are "always-already" interpellated as subjects because they "*are always-already subjects*" (Althusser's italics).[9]

Althusser's work is of importance to this book in two distinct ways. First, his re-thinking of the Marxist theory of superstructure to include the functions of the ideological state apparatuses provides a starting point for understanding how these films operate to restore the "normality" of the female and male subject following the traumatic experience of the war. This process of normalization most often involves the restoration of dominant political, social, and sexual practices, most specifically by means of their attempts to re-establish "normal" female and male sexual productivity in their conclusions. Second, Althusser's description of how by a process of interpellation ideology claims the individual as a subject provides a conceptual framework for how psychoanalytic knowledge comes to be communicated by these films to their audiences for specific ideological purposes sometimes outside the audiences' own realm of consciously held ideas, and sometimes even outside the conscious intentions of the films' authors.

Foucault: Knowledge, Discourse, Immanence, and the Multiplicity of the Relations of Power

Foucault proposes that knowledge circulates within culture by means of sequences of signs, figures, marks, or traces that exist in both written and spoken form, and he names these sequences "statements."[10] Statements that may meaningfully be grouped together because of their interest in the same subject, their derivation from the same place of origin, or their association with the same institutional apparatus, Foucault terms discourses. The word "discourse" describes groupings of statements that are freely dispersed and redistributed, and that belong to a single system of formation, such as one relating to medicine, or sexuality, or psychiatry. According to Foucault, an historical analysis of the discourses that have existed at a particular time should question them as to their

---

[9] Ibid., p. 119.
[10] Michel Foucault, *The Archaeology of Knowledge* (London and New York: Routledge, 2002), pp. 89–98.

mode of existence, what it means for them to have come into being, and what can be learned from the fact that they appeared when and where they did. An evaluation of the conditions necessary for a particular discourse to be able to form, express, and redistribute a given system of thought within a particular period can reveal something of what Foucault terms that period's "cultural unconscious" or "episteme."

Foucault's system for examining the cultural infiltration of knowledge can be considered as being informed by psychoanalysis in that it admits the possibility of unconscious mental functioning; however, it defines this as operating not within the psyche of an individual, but instead on a collective cultural level. As Lisa Downing explains, in employing the term "unconscious," Foucault is referring to

> hidden, inaccessible rules, codes and beliefs that have effects in the world; but effects which appear as facts of nature. However, it is distinct from psychoanalysis insofar as it does not offer interpretations or propose "cures" for misguided beliefs based on unconscious phantasy. It simply describes what it uncovers or lays bare, as the metaphor of "archaeology" would suggest.[11]

For Foucault then, discourse operates both within and outside the awareness of the author of the statement, and the systems of communication that provide the means of expression of the statement. Thought of in these terms, psychoanalysis becomes in Britain by the mid-1940s not only a distinctive form of psychological treatment and a model for psychological functioning, but also an historical discourse, a factor that is both consciously and unconsciously appropriated by British culture, and in the context of cinema, one that is endlessly redistributed in different arrangements by the films in which it forms a constituent part.

Foucault also argues that the relationship between knowledge and discourse is influenced by the dominant systems of power that are coercive on the population at specific historical moments. What Foucault is proposing is therefore different to the structural model of power that Marxist critical theorists such as Althusser have put forward to describe the mechanisms of coercion that hold sway over the individual within society. As we have already established, Althusser considers that power is wielded within a hierarchical system of control operated by both the "repressive State apparatuses" (the army,

---

[11] Lisa Downing, *Michel Foucault* (Cambridge, New York, Melbourne, Madrid, Cape Town, Singapore, São Paulo, Delhi, Tokyo, and Mexico City: Cambridge University Press, 2008), p. 10.

the police, or the courts) and the "ideological State apparatuses" (the family, schools, or the media) working together in "very subtle or tacit combinations."[12] Althusserian theory, therefore, adopts the view that consciously or unconsciously held ideological positions, opinions, or worldviews are always supported and reinforced by the apparatuses of the state, and that power is first and foremost derived from the institutions of government. While Foucault accepts this to be true, he believes that power should be understood *also* "in the first instance as the multiplicity of force relations immanent in the sphere in which they operate and which constitute their own organization."[13] In the words of Lisa Downing again, Foucault's model of the relations of power should therefore be defined

> in stark opposition to earlier theories of power, such as the dyadic model of the Hegelian Master-Slave dialectic or the Marxist critique of class oppression which borrowed from it, in which the proletariat is the 'single locus of great Refusal' and the bourgeoisie the single oppressor.[14]

Power, according to Foucault, can be understood as being not just the preserve of a group of institutions intended to ensure the subservience of the citizens of a given state, but also as one attributed to a complex strategical situation in a particular society. For Foucault then, power should be understood not as something *always* exercised from above, as is suggested by Althusser, but instead as a force that emerges at innumerable points within culture in the interplay of non-egalitarian and mobile relations. Nor is it something that is necessarily imposed onto different types of knowledge relationships, economic processes, or sexual relations, but a factor *immanent* to those relationships and arising as the result of the divisions, fault-lines, and asymmetries found *within* them. An analysis of the psychoanalytic discourses existing in British cinema at this time should, therefore, be sensitive not only to the normalizing ideological messages of these films that come from above, but also to the *multiplicity* of the relations of power that defined what discourses were able to circulate at this time, the form that those discourses were permitted to take in these specific films, and who in these films was awarded the ability to enunciate or receive the statements that constituted those discourses.

---

[12] Althusser, "Ideology and Ideological State Apparatuses," p. 98.
[13] Michel Foucault, *The Will to Knowledge: The History of Sexuality* (London: Penguin Books, 1978; repr. 1998), p. 92.
[14] Downing, *Michel Foucault*, p. 90.

Using Critical Theory to Understand the Role of Psychoanalysis in British Cinema in the Immediate Post-War Period

Foucault's work, just as much as Althusser's, is central to how this book accounts for the multiplicity of functions that psychoanalysis performs in many British films of the mid-1940s. My interest in the psychoanalytic elements of these films is based therefore not on *psychoanalysis as psychoanalysis* but on *psychoanalysis as ideology* and *psychoanalysis as discourse*. I am not employing psychoanalytic theory to understand these films. Instead, I am using a critical framework to understand how the ideological beliefs expressed by these films in psychoanalytic terms, and the psychoanalytic discourses embedded within these films, inform their engagements with the profound collective emotional effects of the war. The main purpose of this book is to discover *what is at stake in these engagements*; specifically, to understand how these films are molded by ideology and discourse in a way that enables them to begin to address the emotional fallout of the war *at the same time as* proposing what the structures of power could look like or should look like in a new post-war Britain.

The stresses within established power structures at this time are often presented in these films in terms of the problems that have come to exist in male and female relationships. Within these films' narratives, either or both are often marginalized by their supposed psychopathologies, and then returned—or, as we will see, not returned—to a state of "normality" in their conclusions. This passage from psychopathology to normality can be accounted for, to an extent, within an Althusserian model of subordination based on the commonly held idea of cinema as a cultural apparatus operating within a normative patriarchal value system. However, no less important to an understanding of these films is Foucault's description of how knowledge and power are elements not only wielded by a cultural apparatus to claim the individual as a subject, but also elements wielded by individuals in relation to that apparatus. This last factor provides a starting point for understanding the peculiarly oppositional and *fragmented* nature of these films, which often becomes obvious to us as viewers precisely because of the inability of these films to form coherent narrative scenarios or conclusions. No less important is how an engagement with Foucault's work can reveal the *subversive discursive forces* of these films, which often run counter to their own stated normative ideological beliefs and outside the will of their authors.

My close reading of six British films of this period draws heavily on Althusser's hierarchical concept of ideology and Foucault's concept of the discursive nature of power to reveal the different forms in which they recirculate generally accepted psychoanalytic knowledge. My conceptual model draws on both Althusserian and Foucauldian approaches because I believe that the positions, opinions, and worldviews that shape how these films engage with contemporary cultural concerns come to exist and operate within them as a result of both hierarchical *and* discursive influences. As Charles Barr has pointed out, in British cinema at this time:

> Often there is an eloquent and poignant disjunction between surface drama, as observed in talk and action, and interior drama, which may be conveyed through the eyes [...] and/or through expressive gaps in the film's narrative structure, creating a strong sense of something *other* that is being repressed, or sought in vain.[15]
>
> (Barr's italics)

Barr's idea of British films at this time containing disjunctions conveyed through expressive narrative gaps calls to mind Laub and Podell's claim that it is precisely the silences and omissions found within the art of trauma that allow the traumatized to become aware of and "know" the historical trauma itself. What we will discover in the chapters that follow is that in British films of this period these gaps, silences, and omissions operate multidimensionally; to form protected spaces where the processing of trauma and anxiety can begin, as part of an hierarchical system designed to ensure the normalization of the female and male subject, and also under the influence of other discursive systems that are *immanent* to the films themselves that motivate often very different worldviews and provide contrasting messages for their audiences.

Both Althusser and Foucault emphasize how knowledge comes to circulate and have influence *unconsciously* on a collective cultural level. In the context of this book, this idea enables an understanding of how psychoanalysis informs the opinions and worldviews of these films sometimes outside the awareness of their authors. However, there are also levels at which psychoanalysis is *consciously* appropriated by the films' authors, most obviously in their decision to exploit the popularity that psychoanalysis was enjoying with the British public.

For example, Sydney Box, the producer of *The Seventh Veil*, attributed that film's financial success primarily to the central space that psychoanalysis and war

---

[15] Charles Barr, "Introduction: Amnesia and Schizophrenia," in *All Our Yesterdays: 90 Years of British Cinema* (London: BFI Publishing, 1986; repr. 1996), p. 25.

neurosis occupy in the film's narrative. In his autobiography, Box explained that the original idea for the story of *The Seventh Veil*

> grew out of one of Verity's War Office documentaries, *The Psychiatric Treatment of Battle Casualties*. This was an enthralling and often heartrending subject that gave me my first insight into the theory and practice of psychiatry. It was this insight that gave *The Seventh Veil* its extraordinary appeal to its audiences—that and the fact that the time of its appearance was so right. Psychiatry was a novelty in those days [...] and its use as a storytelling device was new to the screen. Within a year or two, of course, psychiatrists were popping up in every other movie, but when *The Seventh Veil* appeared they were unheard of, and there is no doubt that our picture benefitted considerably from what Jung liked to call synchronicity.[16]

In similar terms, Derek Collett, the biographer of *Mine Own Executioner* author Nigel Balchin states that

> it was probably the topicality of psychoanalysis that proved to be the prime factor in ensuring the success of *Mine Own Executioner*. In 1945, the discipline was still regarded in the media as a new and exciting one, with public interest in it being stimulated and sustained by the movie industry.[17]

There is little doubt that in Britain in the 1940s, just as in America, opportunities abounded for novelists, screenplay writers, and film producers to exploit at an economic level the public's interest in psychoanalysis. Therefore, an assessment of the ideological and discursive influences of psychoanalysis on the formal and narrative systems of films of this period should consider these industrial factors, at the same time as acknowledging the signs, figures, marks, and traces of psychoanalytic knowledge that may have existed outside authorial control.

It is the films of this period that orientate themselves around culturally ingrained psychoanalytic ideas that I group together and term "British trauma films." I adopt this term to describe a category of films drawn from a range of different genres which have a common preoccupation with the neurotic or psychotic *effects* of the war. These effects are sometimes obvious to us as viewers but at the same time often not acknowledged by their central characters or directly within their narratives. These factors render these films different from the documentary-inflected British films made in the early years of the war such

---

[16] Sydney Box, *The Lion That Lost Its Way*, ed. by Andrew Spicer (Lanham, MD, Toronto, and Oxford: The Scarecrow Press, 2005), p. 49.
[17] Derek Collett, *His Own Executioner: The Life of Nigel Balchin* (Bristol: Silverwood: 2015), p. 166.

as *In Which We Serve* (Noël Coward and David Lean, 1942), *Went the Day Well?* (Alberto Cavalcanti, 1942), *The Bells Go Down* (Basil Dearden, 1943), and *San Demetrio London* (Charles Frend, 1944). Films such as these certainly centralize traumatic *events* and the lead-up to these events, but they are often less inclined to confront the devastating personal or collective psychical consequences that these events have had for the individual or for the wider society. A list of British trauma films is included at the end of this book, and what I am interested to explore is how films such as these—far from merely importing "pop-Freudian characterizations"[18]—build their narrative themes and narrative and formal systems around often complex psychoanalytic ideas toward specific remedial and ideological ends.

Throughout this book, the contemporary psychoanalytic discourses that influence the component parts of these systems are referred to as "historical psychoanalytic discourses." When these discourses are found to have entered a cultural medium such as cinema, they are defined as either "narrative psychoanalytic discourses," "cultural psychoanalytic discourses," or "ideological psychoanalytic discourses." A narrative psychoanalytic discourse is formed when psychoanalytic ideas, psychoanalyst figures, or psychoanalytic processes appear explicitly *in* a film's narrative. When psychoanalytic concepts are appropriated by these films as part of their formal or narrative structures, this is referred to as a cultural psychoanalytic discourse. Narrative or cultural discourses that are employed by the films to express certain positions, opinions, or worldviews are designated as ideological psychoanalytic discourses.

The textual analyses that follow in later chapters also rely heavily on psychoanalytic ideas of trauma and anxiety, and I employ these in the way that they might have been understood by the general population in Britain in the mid-1940s. The word "trauma" is used to describe an episode defined by its intensity and the disorder it brings to the victim's psyche. The term is used to refer to a specific detrimental event, and the effect of that event is defined as a neurosis or a psychosis. The word "anxiety" is used to describe a type of neurosis caused either by the mobilization of a defensive strategy designed to avoid trauma ("signal anxiety") or by the detrimental effect that the trauma has on the victim ("automatic anxiety"). The films I analyze in later chapters often do not represent the neurotic or psychotic effects of the war explicitly, indeed in many it appears as if the war has never happened at all. Building on Barr's idea that these

---

[18] James Naremore, *More than Night: Film Noir in Its Contexts* (Berkeley, Los Angeles, and London: University of California Press, 1998), p. 9.

films can be found to display expressive gaps, and on Laub and Podell's idea that the art of trauma is defined by its empty spaces and omissions, what I want to explore is how these films seem to activate an operation of fragmentation within their various structures, which has as one of its results an initiation of alternative modes of expression that either *disavow* the existence of the war completely, or that *displace* these traumatic effects onto others that are less threatening.

The idea of cinematic fragmentation calls to mind the post-Freudian work of Sándor Ferenczi, Klein, and Anna Freud, who think of mental fragmentation as a defensive mechanism operating in circumstances where the individual, when faced with the threat or consequence of trauma, does not consciously acknowledge that threat or consequence at all. In similar terms, in this group of films, the detrimental events that constitute past traumatic experience often come to be disavowed or displaced, and the neurotic or psychotic effects of trauma become apparent only by reading between the lines of narrative and film form. Within Freudian thinking, displacement is the process often observed in dreams, whereby the traumatic intensity of an experience is liable to be detached from it and attached instead to ideas which are less threatening but are nevertheless related by a chain of associations. So, in many British films of the immediate post-war period, the traumatic event itself is often omitted, and the neurotic or psychotic effects of trauma are displaced onto symptoms easily recognizable within classical generic paradigms such as obsessional behaviors, dysfunctional familial relationships, dysfunctional sexual relationships, criminal behaviors, or the perception of supernatural phenomena.

While all British trauma films have as their common denominator a preoccupation with the consequences of traumatic experience, the nature of engagement with the cause of the trauma changes over time. In the early films, the original traumatic event is often omitted from the narrative or only mentioned by the films' characters briefly and with great reluctance. In the later films, the moment that has constituted the seat of the trauma becomes clearer, and often it is the revisiting of this moment that becomes the driving force of their narratives and the basis of their remedial processes. Examples of British trauma narratives can be found in many different types of films that found popularity with audiences at this time. These films operate either explicitly, in building their narratives around the psychopathologies of their distressed central characters and around psychoanalyst figures or psychoanalytic processes, or implicitly in that they are narratively or formally structured with reference to culturally accepted psychoanalytic knowledge.

In his history of Ealing Studios, Barr proposes that Ealing's output during the 1940s, rather than being grouped under the headings "pre-war," "wartime," and "post-war," could more productively be classified in the categories "up to 1941," "1942–3," and "1944–8." Assessing the films that fall into the third of these classifications, Barr observes that

> the crisis of the war having passed or at least shifted to more distant locations, attention turns to what happens afterwards, specifically to ways of learning from the experiences of the war, consolidating social changes, carrying over the discovery of unity and solidarity into the postwar world.[19]

In similar terms, in her assessment of the effects of the Second World War on Hollywood cinema, Kaja Silverman argues that several films made between 1944 and 1947 attest "with unusual candor to the castrations through which the male subject is constituted."[20] Silverman points out that in many of these films

> the "hero" returns from World War II with a physical or psychic wound which marks him as somehow deficient, and which renders him incapable of functioning smoothly in civilian life. Sometimes the veteran also finds himself strangely superfluous to the society he ostensibly protected during the war; his functions have been assumed by other men, or—much more disturbingly—by women.[21]

Both Barr and Silverman are proposing that certain films made in Britain and America between 1944 and 1947—or 1948—address the individual traumatic experience of the war *and* the social discontinuity that this experience has initiated in the wider population. Therefore, for the purposes of this book, it is argued that the "immediate aftermath" of the war began approximately a year before the end of the war as the detrimental effects of the war came to achieve widespread cultural recognition, and ended three or four years later, as British cinema finally began able to look ahead toward the post-war future.

As will become clear to the reader from the film analyses that follow, the part that psychoanalysis plays at this time in British culture generally and in British cinema specifically is often complex and sometimes oppositional. On the most obvious level, psychoanalysis provides these films with a language that enables them to describe the trauma of the war and provide safe spaces

---

[19] Charles Barr, *Ealing Studios* (London: Studio Vista, 1993), p. 50.
[20] Kaja Silverman, "Historical Trauma and Male Subjectivity," in *Male Subjectivity at the Margins* (New York and London: Routledge, 1992), p. 52.
[21] Ibid., p. 53.

for their audiences to begin to process their own experiences. On another level, psychoanalysis operates in terms that are far more complex; sometimes working toward the reinforcement or restoration of the dominant relations of social, political, or sexual power by means of the normalization of the subject, and at other times in ways that call into question the relations of power themselves. The relationship that these films have with psychoanalytic knowledge and the psychoanalytic processes is therefore often extremely ambivalent. This ambivalence manifests itself most obviously in the unresolved nature of these films' narrative scenarios and conclusions, and what renders these films often incapable of achieving narrative closure is precisely the traumatic nature of the context in which they were made.

Psychoanalytic Discourse as a Factor in Established Approaches to Hollywood Film Noir and the Hollywood Woman's Film of the 1940s

While very little attention has been paid to the emergence of psychoanalysis as an influence on 1940s British films, the same cannot be said for 1940s Hollywood films. Indeed, this was recognized even as far back as the mid-1950s by the French critics Raymond Borde and Etienne Chaumeton in *A Panorama of American Film Noir*, the first book-length study of Hollywood film noir. Here, the authors propose that the identifying sign of film noir is its interest in moral ambivalence and criminal violence, and that the contradictory complexity of the situations which these films lay out combine to give their public a shared feeling of insecurity:

> All the works in this series exhibit a consistency of an emotional sort; *namely the state of tension created in the spectators by the disappearance of their psychological bearings*. The vocation of film noir has been to create *a specific sense of malaise*.[22]
>
> (Borde and Chaumeton's italics)

Borde and Chaumeton's definition starts from their assessment of the particular impression that these films make on the viewer, in contrast to later commentators who tend to focus on how the narrative themes or stylistic structures of these films differ from other types of films. The authors propose that while the

---

[22] Raymond Borde and Etienne Chaumeton, *A Panorama of American Film Noir* (San Francisco: City Lights Books, 2002), pp. 18–19.

immediate source of film noir is the hard-boiled detective novel, its wider historical context—police corruption, connections between the underworld and politics, large-scale drug trafficking, and widespread prostitution—also plays a significant part. They also emphasize the importance of cultural influences such as Surrealism, German Expressionism, prewar Hollywood gangster and horror films, and psychoanalysis. They state that the hard-boiled detective novels of Dashiell Hammett and Raymond Chandler were undoubtedly influenced by psychoanalytic concepts, and that the cultural proliferation of psychoanalytic practices during the 1930s and 1940s exercised an even greater influence on the scriptwriters, dialogue writers, and producers who would adapt their novels for the screen.

Psychoanalysis is proposed as manifesting itself in these films in two distinct ways, "explicitly" in films such as *Spellbound* (Alfred Hitchcock, 1945) and *The Snake Pit* (Anatole Litvak, 1948) which are devoted to the description and explication of a case history, and "implicitly" in films with a "psychological atmosphere" borrowed from the psychoanalytic "theory of affectivity," such as *Leave Her to Heaven* (John M. Stahl, 1945) or *Gilda* (Charles Vidor, 1946). The authors also consider that it is as a result of their engagement with psychoanalysis that detective films generally have been furnished

> with many features of a noir psychology. To begin with, it has underlined the irrational character of criminal motivation: the gangster is a neurotic whose behavior can be fully understood only in utilitarian terms; aggressiveness, sadism, and masochism are self-serving; the interest, or love of, money is often only a cover for libidinal fixation or infantile conflict.[23]

They argue that the "cynicism" in the views of Freud also accords well with the strangeness and moral ambivalence of the noir series because:

> Psychiatry no longer believes in traditionally defined good or evil. It knows that criminal behaviour patterns often hide self-destructive reactions or guilt complexes, while moral conscience (the super-ego) is linked to the instincts it represses by means of an entire network of complicity.[24]

Finally, they suggest that censors of the time were able to push back the limits of what it was permissible to show because psychoanalysis imbued the films' explanations of their characters' actions with a scientific guarantee of validity.

---

[23] Ibid., p. 19.
[24] Ibid., pp. 19–20.

The idea that psychoanalysis might have influenced the thematic preoccupations of Hollywood film noir was taken up by the British critic Raymond Durgnat in an article published in 1970, "Paint It Black: The Family Tree of Film Noir." Here, Durgnat argues that, while crime or criminals provide the real or apparent narrative focus in all film noir, the series might be defined by certain dominant motifs which the films have in common. While he does not mention the influence of psychoanalysis on noir's narrative themes directly, Durgnat implies its influence by expressing three of these motifs in distinctly psychoanalytic language. For example, in a section on "Portraits and Doubles," he describes the tone of the films as being "somber, claustrophobic, deadpan and paranoid. In the shaded light it is often just a little difficult to tell one character from another." In another on "Sexual Pathology," he develops Borde and Chaumeton's idea of film noir being characterized by a sense of ambivalence when he states that: "The yin and yang of puritanism and cynicism, of egoism and paranoia, of greed and idealism, deeply perturbs sexual relationships, and *film noirs* abound in love-hate relationships ranging through all states of intensity." In similar terms, in a section on "Psychopaths," Durgnat declares that the films often centralize male characters with a tragic flaw, such as James Cagney's in *White Heat* (Raoul Walsh, 1949) whose actions are the result of his "raging Oedipus Complex."[25]

Alan Silver and Elizabeth Ward's *Film Noir: An Encyclopedic Reference to the American Style* was published in 1979, listing over two hundred examples made between the beginning of the Second World War and just after the Korean conflict. The authors argue that the characteristics of these films are straightforward in that they are

> contemporaneous, usually urban, and almost always American in setting. The few exceptions involve either urban men in a rural locale or Americans abroad. There is a narrative assumption that only natural forces are at play: extraordinary occurrences are either logically elucidated or left unexplained—no metaphysical values are adopted. Finally, the noir cycle's consistent visual style is keyed specifically to recurrent narrative patterns and character emotions. Because these patterns and emotions are repeatedly suggestive of certain abstractions, such as alienation or obsession, it may seem that film noir is overly dependent on external constructions such as Existentialism or Freudianism.[26]

---

[25] Raymond Durgnat, "Paint It Black: The Family Tree of the *Film Noir*," in *The Film Noir Reader*, ed. by Alain Silver (New York: Limelight, 2004), pp. 47–50.

[26] Alain Silver and Elizabeth Ward, *Film Noir: An Encyclopedic Reference to the American Style* (New York: The Overlook Press, 1979), p. 3.

The authors provide examples of how the obsessions of noir's male characters with its femme fatales are often purely sexual and therefore "patently Freudian," and they state that the "overtly Freudian" aspects of these relationships construct a sequence of narrative events that typify the noir vision.[27]

The idea that psychoanalysis might operate as a narrative and cultural discourse within dominant power systems was proposed in the 1980s by scholars investigating the Hollywood woman's film of the 1940s. For example, in *The Desire to Desire*, Mary Ann Doane suggests that a medical discourse is activated in these films that results in their psychoanalyst figures being able to read the symptoms of their psychopathological central female characters, and so reveal "the essential kernel of truth" which escapes the unqualified eye:

> Breakdowns and instability in the representation of female subjectivity are evident in all types of the woman's film. But in films of the medical discourse they receive a special twist. For these incoherencies and instabilities do not remain unseen or unrecognized by the texts; on the contrary, they are recuperated as the signs of illness or psychosis. In this way, the purported subject of the discourse, the woman, becomes its object, and her lapses and difficulties in subjectivity are organized for purposes of medical observation or study.[28]

Doane also points out that psychoanalysis fits easily within the structure of classical Hollywood narrative by providing an enigma (what is wrong with the character and what has caused her symptoms), a justification for the classical device of repetition (the compulsion to repeat the original trauma), and a final solution (the cure, usually by returning to the original scene of the trauma). Doane concludes that in the way this scenario plays out the practices of the psychoanalyst come to resemble those of the detective.[29]

Frank Krutnik explores the representation of masculinities in Hollywood film noir in his 1990s study, *In a Lonely Street*. He observes how the influence of psychoanalysis on noir resulted in overtly subjectivized dramas of crime and passion which differed markedly from the more "controlled" modes of address of hard-boiled fiction. This manifests itself within these films' narratives in their psychological verisimilitude, in their preoccupation with the representation

---

[27] Ibid., p. 5.
[28] Mary Ann Doane, "Clinical Eyes: The Medical Discourse," in *The Desire to Desire: The Woman's Film of the 1940s* (Basingstoke and London: Macmillan Press, 1987), p. 44.
[29] Ibid., p. 47.

of often "perverse" sexualities, and in their use of psychoanalyst figures in the service of male rationality and patriarchal cultural authority. Krutnik also pertinently points out that there is an intriguing paradox at work in regard to the representation of psychoanalyst figures:

> On the one hand, the depiction of psychoanalysis as a rationalist 'science' has as its aim the eradication of disorder and deviance. On the other hand, psychoanalysis serves the function of bringing out a complex and patently destabilising undercurrent of excessive and disordered desires which elude easy rationalisation. These ultimately have to be contextualised in a "world beyond reason" and ascribed to the "mysterious force" of Fate.

Krutnik also employs a Freudian framework to interrogate how Hollywood noir reveals an obsession with internally divided male figures who are alienated from culturally permissible parameters of masculine identity and desire, concluding that these films frequently offer an engagement with problematic masculine identities while at the same time finding themselves unable in their conclusions to fully embrace or sanction such subversive potentialities.[30]

In comparison to these earlier studies that emphasize the influence of psychoanalysis on film noir, more recent commentators have tended to foreground other factors. For example, in a study published in 2002, Andrew Spicer lists as film noir's main cultural influences: hard-boiled crime fiction, the gangster film, Gothic romance, German Expressionism, Weimar cinema, German émigré filmmakers, French Poetic Realism, American expressionist films of the 1930s and early 1940s, but not psychoanalysis. However, he does consider psychoanalysis a persistent theme in its preoccupation with schizophrenia, psychosis, and disturbed sexuality, alongside existentialism, urban angst, and social themes such as law and order and corruption. Spicer thinks of the main narrative strategies of noir to be the voice-over, flashbacks (either confessional or investigative), subjective camerawork, and dream states; however, he does not point to psychoanalysis as being an influential force behind why these strategies came to be used by film makers, or why they were attractive to audiences at this particular time.[31] Remarkably, James Naremore hardly mentions psychoanalysis at all in *More Than Night: Film Noir and Its Contexts*, considering it to appear in these films only in the form

---

[30] Frank Krutnik, *In a Lonely Street: Film Noir, Genre, Masculinity* (London and New York: Routledge, 1991), pp. 45–55.
[31] Andrew Spicer, *Film Noir* (Harlow, Essex: Longman/Pearson Education, 2002), pp. 5–19, 64–83.

of "pop-Freudian" characterizations, and important only in connection to noir's visual and narrative traits along with low-key photography, images of wet city streets, and romantic fascination with femmes fatales.[32]

As this brief survey demonstrates, the practice of investigating the psychoanalytic elements of Hollywood films of the 1940s is well-established, and I acknowledge the impact of this body of work on my approach to British films made in the same period. Borde and Chaumeton's definition of film noir as based on the particular impression that these films make on their audiences has been particularly influential on my belief that British films of this time had particular remedial value for their audiences, and Doane's and Krutnik's ideas have been influential on how I have defined the British trauma film as operating within dominant power systems. However, what is striking is how the nature of these previous engagements changes over time. While the earlier studies acknowledge the importance of other cultural influences on Hollywood film noir while devoting most of their attention to the influence of psychoanalysis, in the later studies most attention is given to other cultural influences and relatively little to psychoanalysis. Just as in the clinical setting emphasis had shifted in the 1980s away from psychoanalysis and toward other therapeutic practices such as cognitivism, emphasis shifted in film studies in the 1990s away from critical approaches based on psychoanalysis to other approaches. Because the majority of the studies of 1940s British cinema were written after this change had taken place, it is perhaps unsurprising that there has been a lack of attention to the influence of psychoanalysis on British films made at this time. This lack is one of the things this book is intended to address.

The Place of the British Trauma Film in the Landscape of British Immediate Post-War Cinema, and Connections between the British Trauma Film and British Film Noir

Over the next four chapters, I analyze six films made in Britain in the mid-1940s, *The Halfway House*, *Dead of Night*, *The Seventh Veil*, *Madonna of the Seven Moons*, *They Made Me a Fugitive*, and *Mine Own Executioner*. These have been chosen to provide a sample of the different types of popular films made at this time whose narrative themes and narrative and formal structures were

---

[32] Naremore, *More than Night*, p. 9.

influenced by psychoanalysis. But are these merely isolated examples of films that were influenced in this way, or can common ground be found between these films and other films that this period of British cinema produced? Or, to put this a different way, could my critical approach to these particular films also have relevance to the broader range of films made in Britain at the same time? To answer these questions, it becomes important to place these films in the wider context of British immediate post-war film production.

In *Realism and Tinsel*, Robert Murphy argues that the general tendency of critics to take only the realist films of the 1940s seriously has led to a failure to appreciate a wide range of films that were made under other influences. Murphy maps out the field of immediate post-war British cinema with five cycles of films, costume dramas, contemporary melodramas, gangster films, morbid thrillers, and comedies, while admitting that these are to an extent arbitrary in that some films do not fit comfortably into any category and others fit into more than one. However, his account does provide a valuable survey of the different types of films that were popular in Britain at this time. I provide only a short synopsis of Murphy's findings before turning to how Murphy and others have thought of some of these films as examples of British film noir. The intention of both assessments is to establish whether a connection can be found between the specific films that I examine in the chapters that follow, and those that others have categorized in different ways.

Murphy defines the costume drama as the most popular type of film made between the end of the war and 1950; its scope ranging from "creaking epics like *Bonny Prince Charlie* to Tod Slaughter's *The Curse of the Wraydons*, from respectful adaptations of Dickens and Shakespeare to bodice-ripping exploitation films like *Idol of Paris*." The dominant studio for the wartime production of costume films was Gainsborough, where studio head Maurice Ostrer had produced *The Man in Grey* (Leslie Arliss, 1943) and *Fanny by Gaslight* (Anthony Asquith, 1944). These were followed after the war by *The Wicked Lady* (Leslie Arliss, 1945), *Caravan* (Arthur Crabtree, 1946), and *The Magic Bow* (Bernard Knowles, 1946), but when Ostrer's role was taken over by Sydney Box, emphasis was switched elsewhere and only five more costume dramas would be made in the next four years. The first three, *The Man Within* (Bernard Knowles, 1946), *The Brothers* (David MacDonald, 1947), and *Jassy* (Bernard Knowles, 1947) were financially successful, but the last two, *The Bad Lord Byron* (David MacDonald, 1949) and *Christopher Columbus* (David MacDonald, 1949), were box office failures. Meanwhile, at Ealing the tendency to move away from documentary-inflected realist films produced in the early war years such as *The Halfway House* and *Dead of Night* led the studio to produce four costume dramas, *Pink String and Sealing Wax* (Robert Hamer, 1946), *The Life and Adventures of Nicholas Nickleby* (Alberto Cavalcanti, 1947), *The Loves of Joanna Godden* (Charles Frend, 1947), and *Saraband for Dead Lovers* (Basil Dearden, 1948). Adaptations of literary classics were also popular, and David Lean followed the success of *Brief Encounter* (1945) with *Great Expectations* (1946) and *Oliver Twist* (1948). Meanwhile, Filippo Del Guidice's Two Cities Films, which had been responsible for the wartime realist films *In Which We Serve* and *The Way Ahead* (Carol Reed, 1944), produced Lawrence Olivier's *Henry V* (1944) and *Hamlet* (1948), and then three costume films, *Carnival* (Stanley Haynes, 1946), *Beware of Pity* (Maurice Elvey, 1946), and *Hungry Hill* (Brian Desmond Hurst, 1947).[33]

Turning his attention to contemporary melodramas, Murphy argues that while wartime examples such as *Millions Like Us* (Sidney Gilliat and Frank Launder, 1943) and *The Gentle Sex* (Leslie Howard, 1943) featured women who discover hidden resources, they tended to be passive recipients of their good or bad fortune. In contrast, in post-war films such as *The Years Between* (Compton Bennett, 1946), Powell and Pressburger's *I Know Where I'm Going* (1945) and *Black Narcissus* (1947), and *The Courtneys of Curzon Street* (Herbert Wilcox, 1947) they struggle more actively with their destiny. *The Years Between* describes the problems of re-integration; and post-war stresses are also the subject of Alexander Korda's *Perfect Strangers* (1945) and *A Girl in a Million* (Francis Searle, 1946). Gainsborough had released two contemporary melodramas at the end of the war, *Love Story* (Leslie Arliss, 1944) and *Madonna of the Seven Moons*, following these with *They Were Sisters* (Arthur Crabtree, 1945) and *Root of All Evil* (Brock Williams, 1947), after which the studio turned mainly to comedies and action pictures. Murphy points out that there are similarities between the two best-known contemporary melodramas of the period, *The Seventh Veil* and *Brief Encounter* (David Lean, 1945), in that both their central female figures suffer breakdowns and both their narratives unfold in flashback. Both films also share the common theme of a woman having to choose between two men, as do Powell and Pressburger's *I Know Where I'm Going* and Herbert Wilcox's *I Live in Grosvenor Square* (1945).[34]

---

[33] Robert Murphy, *Realism and Tinsel: Cinema and Society 1939–48* (London and New York: Routledge, 1989), pp. 120–45.
[34] Ibid., pp. 99–119.

Murphy traces the beginning of the spiv cycle to Gainsborough's late wartime *Waterloo Road* (Sydney Gilliat, 1945) in which Stewart Granger plays a small-time South London gangster Ted Purvis: "with his flash suit, his loud tie, his easy money, and his dangerous charm he is easily recognized as the screen's first spiv." The film was almost universally praised by the critics and was followed by British National's *Appointment with Crime* (John Harlow, 1946), Alliance's *Dancing with Crime* (John Paddy Carstairs, 1947), and the low budget offering *Black Memory* (Oswald Mitchell, 1947). Alliance also made *They Made Me a Fugitive* starring Trevor Howard as former serviceman Clem Morgan who becomes involved with a gang of black marketeers. This film drew a barrage of criticism from the critics who found it "horrifyingly well-made" but unnecessarily brutal and lacking in moral perspective, but it became one of the top box office pictures of 1947 along with Ealing's *It Always Rains on Sunday* (Robert Hamer, 1947) and the Boulting Brothers' *Brighton Rock* (John Boulting, 1948). Five more spiv films would be released the following year, Gainsborough's *Good-Time Girl* (David MacDonald), *Night Beat* (Harold Huth, 1948), *The Flamingo Affair* (Horace Shepherd, 1948), *A Gunman Has Escaped* (Richard M. Grey, 1948), and *Noose* (Edmond Greville, 1948).[35]

Borrowing a phrase coined by contemporary film critic Arthur Vesselo, Murphy terms as "morbid films" those that have in common "an unpleasant undertone, a parade of frustrated violence, an inversion and disordering of moral values, [and] a groping into the grimier recesses of the mind."[36] Murphy defines these as featuring men physically or mentally damaged by war, men on the run, and murder mysteries. However, he also includes several supernatural films as morbid films, such as Gainsborough's *A Place of One's Own* (Bernard Knowles, 1945), British National's *Latin Quarter* (Vernon Sewell, 1945), Ealing's *The Halfway House* and *Dead of Night*, and Alliance's *Daughter of Darkness* (Lance Comfort, 1947). Films about ex-service men faced with problems of post-war adjustment such as *They Made Me a Fugitive, Good-Time Girl, Night Beat*, and *The Flamingo Affair*, which Murphy has already placed in the spiv cycle, are also placed in the first sub-grouping of morbid films. But while *A Matter of Life and Death* (Michael Powell and Emeric Pressburger, 1946) features David Niven as a brain-damaged pilot, it is excluded as a morbid film because "it is difficult to see him as psychologically disturbed," while *Mine Own Executioner* and Powell

---

[35] Ibid., pp. 146–67.
[36] Arthur Vesselo, quoted in ibid., p. 168.

and Pressburger's *The Small Back Room* (1949) are included because of their "lighting style and general atmosphere." *They Made Me a Fugitive* also appears again in the men on the run sub-grouping, which also includes *Take My Life* (Ronald Neame, 1947), Gainsborough's *My Brother's Keeper* (Alfred Roome, 1948), and Carol Reed's *Odd Man Out* (1947). Murphy observes that the films in his murder mystery sub-grouping are usually about good men led astray such as Robert Newton's signalman in *Temptation Harbour* (Lance Comfort, 1947), James Mason's embittered surgeon in *The Upturned Glass* (Lawrence Huntington, 1947), and Eric Portman's barber/hangman in *Daybreak* (Compton Bennett, 1948). Similarly, the acid-bath killer played by Robert Newton in *Obsession* (Edward Dymytrk, 1949) is trapped in a loveless marriage, and John Mills's character in *The October Man* (Roy Ward Baker, 1947) is wrongly accused of murder.[37]

Murphy's section on comedies has less relevance for this book because, as he points out, relatively few British comedies were made between 1945 and 1949. Even Ealing, the studio "synonymous with comedy" released none at all in 1945 or 1946, and only one in 1947, *Hue and Cry*, and one in 1948, *Another Shore*, both directed by Charles Crichton.[38]

I have stated that the six films analyzed in later chapters have been chosen to represent the different types of films made at this time that were influenced by psychoanalysis. While they were not chosen on the basis of Murphy's or any other commentators' categories, five out of the six films do figure in three of Murphy's categories, the exception being *Madonna of the Seven Moons*. While this film is not strictly speaking a historical costume drama, its elaborate costumes and sets, uncertain temporal and spatial location, and romantic storylines enable it to be categorized both as a costume drama *and* a contemporary melodrama. Also, because Gainsborough was the dominant studio for both costume dramas and contemporary melodramas it was considered important to include one of their films. Because *Madonna of the Seven Moons* is in many ways typical of Gainsborough's costume and contemporary output, because its release date places it in the middle of the Gainsborough series, and because of its particular interest in schizophrenia, it was chosen over the others.

The Seventh Veil and *Brief Encounter* were the obvious choices in the contemporary melodrama category; the former was chosen over the latter

[37] Murphy, *Realism and Tinsel*, pp. 168–90.
[38] Ibid., pp. 191–218.

mainly because of the more explicit nature of its central character Francesca's psychopathology and its use of the psychoanalytic setting as a narrative mechanism; however, *Brief Encounter* and several other examples could easily have been chosen. *They Made Me a Fugitive* is the central film in all studies of the spiv series and so was an easy choice, but many others show signs of psychoanalytic influence, particularly *It Always Rains on Sunday* and *Brighton Rock*. *Dead of Night* and *Mine Own Executioner* figure prominently in Murphy's account of the morbid film and many other films he mentions could have been chosen. However, because *Dead of Night* clearly evidences the influence of so many different psychoanalytic influences, and because of *Mine Own Executioner*'s explicit interest in war trauma and the psychoanalytic process, these films have been included. I have not analyzed any comedies, mainly because so few were made at this time, but *Hue and Cry* does contain isolated examples of children who show signs of traumatization and also suggests how re-enactments of trauma in children's games might begin a process of healing, and so it was a candidate for inclusion. Because of the importance of *The Halfway House* as the first British film to show the effects of war trauma and traumatic bereavement, it was felt that this film was a good starting-point for investigation.

While in *Realism and Tinsel* Murphy approaches this period by categorizing the different types of films made, Murphy and others also have considered how many films of this time from different categories might be grouped together as examples of British film noir because of their common thematic qualities. In a later article, Murphy states that:

> As film noir is a critical category constructed to deal with a specific group of Hollywood films, it would be surprising to find its characteristic traits fully mirrored in British films. But if one defines noir in terms of films that reveal the underbelly of society, expose baser emotions, concentrate on melodramatic events and represent the world as turbulent and often unjust, then a substantial portion of British cinema falls within its scope.[39]

The idea of a British film noir was originally put forward by William K. Everson in two essays published in *Films in Review* in 1987, and this was developed into a body of work by other commentators such as Murphy, Tony Williams, Raymond

---

[39] Robert Murphy, "British *Film Noir*," in *European Film Noir*, ed. by Andrew Spicer (Manchester and New York: Manchester University Press, 2007), p. 84.

Durgnat, and Andrew Spicer over the following decades.[40] Each of these authors notes that the various films they define as displaying noir tendencies are bound together less by stylistic similarities than by commonalities of theme, and each finds different ways of categorizing them. Murphy provides four headings, films about men damaged psychologically often by the war such as *They Made Me a Fugitive*, *Daybreak*, and *Mine Own Executioner*, films characterized by a combination of "shabby realism and film noir melodrama" including *The October Man*, *Temptation Harbour*, films concerned with crime and punishment, for example *They Made Me a Fugitive* and *Brighton Rock*, and "international interventions" such as *The Third Man*. On the other hand, Andrew Spicer divides the films into four sub-cycles: "Gothic melodramas that continued the exploration of Victorian hypocrisy" including *Pink String and Sealing Wax*, *Jassy*, and *Kind Hearts and Coronets* (Robert Hamer, 1949) and literary adaptations such as *Great Expectations* and *Nicholas Nickleby*; "psychological thrillers that probed the mental traumas produced by the war" such as *Mine Own Executioner*, *The October Man*, and *The Small Back Room*; "crime thrillers that investigated the social upheavals and discontents" including *Dancing with Crime*, *They Made Me a Fugitive*, *Brighton Rock*, and *The Third Man*; and "semi documentaries which, like their American counterparts, were an unstable mixture of social realism and noir melodrama" such as *It Always Rains on Sunday* and *Good Time Girl*.[41]

There is certainly an overlap between the films that Murphy and Spicer consider as examples of British film noir and some of the films that I group together as British trauma films, and it is also true that the problems of re-integration and the post-war crime wave are themes common to both sets of films. The key difference is that the sub-cycles suggested by Murphy and Spicer, although different, both exclude significant areas of British post-war film production. For example, neither Murphy or Spicer can find a place in any for the Gainsborough melodramas, and many other costume dramas and contemporary melodramas that together make up the majority of the films made at this time are similarly excluded. I am not suggesting this as being wrong; my point is only that the British trauma film as a category is different from British film noir in

---

[40] Tony Williams, "British Film Noir," in *Film Noir Reader* 2, ed. by Alain Silver and James Ursini (New York: Limelight Editions, 1999), pp. 243–69, Raymond Durgnat, "Some Lines of Enquiry into Post-war British Crimes," in *The British Cinema Book*, ed. Robert Murphy (London: BFI Publishing, 2001), pp. 135–45, Spicer, *Film Noir*.

[41] Spicer, *Film Noir*, pp. 182–91.

its definition, and also that it has the potential to include a greater variety of films precisely because the influence of psychoanalysis was so pervasive in the immediate post-war period.

Chapters Two, Three, Four, and Five consist of my textual analyses of the films I have chosen from a critical theory perspective. In Chapter Two, "Broken Attachments and Traumatic Repetition," I examine representations of the effects of war trauma on the family unit in *The Halfway House*, an Ealing Studios release from the summer of 1944. Here, I compare the narrative structure of one segment of this film to the narrative structure of two other films released earlier in the war, placing the film's framing narrative alongside psychoanalytic cultural discourses connected to reccurring dreams and the disastrous circular enactments that plague the victims of trauma in their everyday lives. Then, I examine the unusual temporal narrative dislocation by means of which *The Halfway House* widens out its trauma narrative from the individual sphere to the wider society.

In Chapter Three, "The Perpetual Recurrence of the Same Thing," I provide a close critical analysis of Ealing's *Dead of Night*, released immediately after the end of the war in September 1945. In the first section, I demonstrate the film's formal and narrative uses of the strategies of disavowal, displacement, and compulsive repetition in its representations of trauma and traumatic neurosis. In the second section, I examine the film's interest in female and male sexual development, and its interaction with psychoanalytic discourses related to sexual difference and motherhood. In the third section, I scrutinize the film's relationship with psychoanalytic object relations theory, and particularly its employment of Freud's idea of projection in paranoia, and Ferenczi's and Anna Freud's idea of the identification with the aggressor, to call into question that boundaries exist between subjectivity and objectivity and reality and fantasy.

Chapter Four, "What Does a Woman Want?", explores discourses of childhood trauma, female desire, and female subjectivity in the enormously successful Sydney and Muriel Box production *The Seventh Veil* and Gainsborough's *Madonna of the Seven Moons*, both released in 1945. The section on *The Seventh Veil* begins with an assessment of the parts played by early detrimental experiences and the predisposition to traumatic neurosis in the childhoods of its central figures, Francesca and Nicholas. I proceed to explore how psychoanalysis provides a framework for the film's narrative, and how it is integral to the film's ideological re-inscription of the *status quo* of sexual relationships in its conclusion. In the section on *Madonna of the Seven Moons* that follows, I trace that film's engagement with childhood sexual trauma, the discourse of schizophrenic psychosis, and the pathologization of female desire, before proceeding to examine what is at stake in the ambivalent and fragmented nature of the film's narrative irresolution.

In Chapter Five, "The World Is Full of Neurotics," I examine two films made toward the end of the period in question, *They Made Me a Fugitive* and *Mine Own Executioner*, to show how both engage with the traumatized serviceman and the crisis of the male subject in more literal terms than the earlier films in the sample. In the section on *They Made Me a Fugitive*, produced by the Anglo-American company Alliance, I begin by examining how the opposite but complementary figures of Clem and Narcy provide the means for the recirculation of contemporary discourses surrounding the effect of traumatic events and individual and collective moral responsibility. I proceed to explore how various characters in the film function within wider discourses that describe a neurotic collapse of both paternal and maternal functions in the atmosphere of Britain's post-war cultural malaise. Finally, in the section on British Lion's *Mine Own Executioner*, I begin by exploring the nature of the traumatized war veteran Adam's psychical affliction, and the film's unusual proposition that Oedipal fixation is the cause of his traumatic psychosis. I continue to examine the film's broadening of the scope of male affliction, and the consequences of both Adam's and the psychoanalyst figure Felix's psychopathological impulses toward destruction and self-destruction. Finally, I assess *Mine Own Executioner*'s proposition that the British collective traumatic experience of the Second World War has initiated an ideological breakdown in the cultural systems of communication, and its suggestion that a solution to this dilemma may be found within the interpersonal processes of psychoanalysis.

2

"Broken Attachments and Traumatic Repetition"

Psychoanalytic Perspectives on Loss, Trauma, Anxiety, and the Fragmentation of the Family Unit in *The Halfway House*

Introduction

In his history of Ealing Studios, Charles Barr proposes the 1944 film *San Demetrio London* as marking a turning point in their wartime production. Barr states that:

> From 1940 to *San Demetrio* almost all the films dealt, directly or indirectly, with the fighting of the war; the emphasis then changes. […] The crisis of the war having passed or at least shifted to more distant locations, attention turns to what happens afterwards, specifically to ways of learning from the experiences of the war, consolidating its social changes, carrying over the discovery of unity and solidarity into the postwar world.[1]

San Demetrio tells the story of a British Merchant Navy oil tanker shelled by enemy action, set ablaze, and then being brought home from the mid-Atlantic by the remnants of her crew. The group includes men from different social classes and different parts of the British Isles, but despite having to endure extreme hardship, they all pull together and demonstrate great courage, resourcefulness, and self-sacrifice. Released two months after *San Demetrio* in April 1944, Ealing's *The Halfway House* is in some ways like that film in that it describes traumatic wartime *events* at the same time as doing its bit for the war effort by promoting ideas of community, duty, and social responsibility. However, while *San Demetrio* can usefully be thought of as indicating the end of the era when British cinema was only concerned with fighting the war, I would like to propose

---

[1] Charles Barr, *Ealing Studios* (London: Studio Vista, 1993), p. 50.

The Halfway House as the film that signals the beginning of a new era, one where British cinema became able to acknowledge the traumatic *effects* of the war, specifically the damage that had been done to the family unit by bereavement, and anxieties that had emerged in the British population at a time when it was uncertain whether the war would be won or lost.

In their assessments of *The Halfway House*, most commentators have paid attention to the film's ideological messages that promote the war effort, and these are undoubtedly productive. However, what is remarkable is that the film's interest in war trauma and wartime anxieties has received very little attention. This is surprising for three principal reasons. First, because such prominence is awarded by the film to the story of Alice Meadows and her husband Harry and the profound consequences that the death of their son Jim has had on their relationship. Second, because the film's framing story which outlines the fate of the inn's landlord Morgan Rhys and his daughter Gwyneth seems so firmly rooted in contemporary psychoanalytic discourses surrounding the effects of trauma and the significance of repetitious behavior in the processing of traumatic affect. Third, because the film is so careful to orientate the backward-looking narrative structure of its framing story around two moments in the war that undoubtedly had implications for how long the war would last and what the war would cost in human lives. Therefore, rather than concentrating on how *The Halfway House* operates ideologically to promote the war effort and ensure the reproduction of the family unit, the focus of this chapter is on other relations that exist within the fabric of the film, which on close scrutiny reveal what the film has to say about the damage that the war had by now inflicted on the family unit, and by extension on the whole of British society.

I look first at the narrative arrangements of two films released slightly earlier in the war, *The Bells Go Down* and *In Which We Serve*, comparing these to the various parts of *The Halfway House* that concern the bereavement of Alice and Harry Meadows. Then, I examine the film's framing story of Morgan and Gwyneth Rhys, positioning the factors that are at stake here alongside contemporary psychoanalytic discourses surrounding the circular nature of reccurring dreams and obsessional behaviors that occur in daily life. Lastly, I examine the expressive dislocation that is created by the unusual temporal structure of the film's framing story, arguing that it is precisely this dislocation that enables *The Halfway House* to widen out its various trauma narratives from the private to the public sphere, and so to lay bare the ramifications of both individual and collective British traumatic wartime experience.

Synopsis of *The Halfway House*

The action of *The Halfway House* takes place over the evening of the twentieth of June and the whole day of the twenty-first of June 1943. At the beginning of the film, we are introduced to a diverse group of characters, all of whom seem to have lost their way in life. These characters converge from various parts of the country on the Halfway House, a secluded inn situated near the village of Cwmbach deep in the Welsh countryside.

In Cardiff, a famous conductor David Davies (Esmond Knight) is directing a symphony orchestra in a state of obvious physical and mental exhaustion. After the concert, his doctor states that because of his ill-health he will be dead in three months if he does not cancel his forthcoming British Council tour of Lisbon and Madrid. His dresser suggests the Halfway House as somewhere for him to be able to rest for a few days; however, his doctor informs him that the inn has been destroyed in an air raid some time before.

The next day, at the Inner Temple in London, Richard French and his wife Jill (Richard Bird and Valerie White) discuss the terms of their impending divorce with their solicitor; however, their resourceful teenage daughter Joanna (Sally Ann Howes) overhears the conversation and contrives to achieve her parents' reconciliation by bringing them together at the inn.

At Parkmoor Prison, Captain Fortescue (Guy Middleton) has just finished his sentence for embezzling funds from his regiment. The prison governor, an ex-Army colonel, tries to persuade him to re-join as a private soldier. Instead, Fortescue declares that he is determined "to get his money's worth," but before this he will enjoy a cycling holiday in Wales. On his way there, he joins up with an old friend, a black marketeer William Oakley (Alfred Drayton) who has driven from London for a fishing trip, intending to stay at the Halfway House where he has been a frequent visitor in the years leading up to the war.

At a Welsh port, Captain Harry Meadows and his French wife Alice (Tom Walls and Françoise Rosay) are mourning the death of their son Jim, who has been killed in a German torpedo attack exactly one year before. This tragedy has forced the couple apart emotionally, but Alice is able to find some comfort in her study of spiritualism.

Lastly, at Bristol Temple Meads station, Margaret (Philippa Hiatt) is reunited with her Irish fiancé Terence (Pat McGrath) after he has returned from working for the Irish government in Lisbon. However, their relationship is threatened by Terence's support of his country's neutrality in the war and his request that

Margaret should join him when he takes up a Secretaryship with the Irish Legation in Berlin.

Later that day, after all the guests have arrived at the inn, they sit down at dinner together along with the landlord Morgan Rhys and his daughter Gwyneth (Mervyn and Glynis Johns). During the meal, we learn that Harry Meadows is the ex-captain of the *Minerva*, a munitions ship that was sailing with a transatlantic convoy when it was torpedoed, and that he had prematurely issued the order to abandon ship. As a result, he feels himself a coward. Rhys announces to the group that the inn had been bombed during a German air raid exactly one year before, and that it burned to the ground. After dinner, Alice persuades Jill to assemble the guests for a séance, and when they have joined hands together, it seems at first glance that Alice has succeeded in contacting her dead son. To the anger of many of the party, her husband disrupts the proceedings, but afterward the couple find themselves able to express their emotions to each other, and they are reunited in their grief.

The guests come to the gradual realization that both Rhys and Gwyneth have returned as ghosts after being killed when the inn was destroyed in an air raid one year before, and that somehow time has been turned back to that point. Rhys explains to them that this has happened so that the guests could have a few hours in which to change their minds and hearts.

As the evening draws in, the sound of aircraft engines overhead signals that the air raid is about to begin all over again. However, the closeness of mortal danger motivates in each of the guests the courage necessary to confront the various issues that have brought them to the inn, and they leave reconciled to their responsibilities to their families and the war effort. At the end of the film, the bombs begin to fall and Rhys, Gwyneth, and the inn itself, are once again consigned to the flames.

Traumatic Events without Consequences: British Cinematic Engagements with Psychological Trauma in the Early Years of the War

Toward the end of *The Halfway House*, as the guests gather for the last time, Jill French asks the landlord Morgan Rhys what will happen next and why they have been brought together. Rhys replies:

> Perhaps you couldn't see the way you were going. Perhaps you needed a pause in time. A pause to stand still and look at yourselves and your difficulties. You

have had a few hours given back to you from life. A few hours in which to change your minds and hearts.

One of the results of this pause in time is that, by the end of the film, its characters can renounce any self-centered preoccupations that they may have had previously and embrace their responsibilities to the war effort and their families. Even at the beginning of the film, David Davies is committed to a British Council morale raising tour of Lisbon and Madrid. Richard French is a squadron leader in the RAF, his wife Jill is in the Red Cross, and Margaret is an officer in the Women's Royal Navy Service. At the end of the film, Margaret's Irish fiancé Terence will give up his intention to work in Berlin for the Irish Legation and will instead join the fight against Germany, Fortescue will apply to re-join his old regiment, Harry Meadows will declare his determination to return to service in the Merchant Navy, and even William Oakley will do his bit for the war effort by renouncing his activities as a black marketeer and stating his resolve to serve his time in prison.

The few hours that the group has had together at the Halfway House have also served to promote the reproduction of the family unit. So, Richard and Jill French are able to resolve their differences to the joy of their daughter Joanna and the three leave the inn reunited ("The three of us together again. Together for always"). Harry and Alice Meadows are reconciled in their grief for the loss of their son, and the barrier of Irish neutrality that had stood in the way of Terence and Margaret's marriage is removed by his promise to take up arms against the common foe.

The ideological worldview of *The Halfway House* is therefore clearly laid out, and it is this that has been the focus of most critical attention. For example, Alan Burton and Tim O'Sullivan consider that the film reworks its source material, a 1940 play by Peter Ogden with a pre-war setting called *The Peaceful Inn*, "for a wartime agenda and the characters are led to a full awareness of their roles and responsibilities in the conflict."[2] In similar terms, Wheeler Winston Dixon sums the film up as "very transparently a propaganda piece,"[3] and it was most likely the obviousness of these ideological messages that contributed to Charles Barr dismissing the film in his 1977 history of Ealing Studios as "a dismal

---

[2] Alan Burton and Tim O'Sullivan, *The Cinema of Basil Dearden and Michael Relph* (Edinburgh: Edinburgh University Press, 2009), p. 63.
[3] Wheeler Winston Dixon, "*The Halfway House*," in *Liberal Directions: Basil Dearden and Postwar British Culture*, ed. by Alan Burton, Tim O'Sullivan, and Paul Wells (Trowbridge: Flicks Books, 1997), p. 110.

experience [...] arid, abstract, statuesquely posed and declaimed," although he would recalibrate this position somewhat in later editions.[4] If the film is thought about only in relation to these particular messages, then it would seem right to place it alongside *San Demetrio London* in the category of Ealing films made in the early years of the war that deal principally with fighting the war through promoting ideas of community spirit, self-sacrifice, and social responsibility. However, what I want to propose is that there are other elements at play in *The Halfway House* that enable it to be placed just as much in the category of British trauma films made later in the war, and immediately after the war, which were beginning to find ways to confront the traumatic consequences of the war that by now were taking their toll on the British population.

Two examples will suffice here to show how earlier wartime films that include traumatic episodes tend to incorporate these into their narrative systems. Ealing Studios' *The Bells Go Down*, like *The Halfway House* directed by Basil Dearden but released almost a year earlier in May 1943, tells the story of four unemployed men who volunteer to join the Auxiliary Fire Service in the East End of London at the beginning of the war. These are an irrepressibly chirpy cockney Tommy Turk played by the comedian Tommy Trinder, an older Spanish Civil War veteran Brookes, a young newlywed Bob Matthews, and a petty thief Sam. The first part of the film outlines their training at the hands of their senior officer Ted Robbins and District Fire Officer MacFarlane, and, after they have completed their training, the four are promoted to serve with the National Fire Brigade. The second part unfolds over the final thirty-eight minutes of the film's eighty-five-minute running time as their National Fire Brigade unit fights several fires over two nights of the September Blitz of 1940. An effective combination of location shooting, studio reconstruction, process photography, and model work, this long sequence is intensely dramatic, culminating in Tommy and Fire Officer MacFarlane being trapped on a balcony of the maternity wing of St. John's Hospital where Bob's wife Nan has just given birth to their son. Nan and the baby are saved, but now Tommy and Officer MacFarlane look upwards from the balcony to see that the unsupported wall and enormous chimney that towers over them are on the point of collapse (Figure 2.1). As they share a cigarette, a shot from their perspective shows the entire structure beginning to come down on top of them, and they die engulfed in flames and fallen masonry. Later, at the Christening of Bob and Nan's son, which is attended by most of the surviving

---

[4] Barr, *Ealing Studios*, p. 52. Barr adds a retrospective to the 1993 edition, pp. 185–6.

Figure 2.1 *The Bells Go Down*: Tommy and Fire Officer MacFarlane seconds before the chimney collapses.

characters including Tommy's mother Ma Turk, the couple inform the attending vicar that they would like him to be named Tommy.

The independent British Lion production *In Which We Serve*, written and produced by Noël Coward, who also starred in the film and co-directed with David Lean, was released in September 1942 and tells the story of the *Torrin*, a Royal Navy destroyer. The opening segments of this film also have a marked documentary quality when they show the ship being built, launched, and trialed at sea at full power. The *Torrin* is then seen in action with a flotilla of other ships during the Battle of Crete, taking part in a successful night attack on German transport ships and destroyers. However, the next day, the *Torrin* is attacked by a formation of German bombers and dive bombers, and, after she has received several direct hits, the ship's captain Kinross gives the order to abandon ship. A group of men manage to swim to a float, and they somehow hang on to it, although some are wounded, and all are exhausted and covered in oil (Figure 2.2). Over the course of the next few hours, the men are repeatedly machine-gunned by the German planes that roar overhead; those who are wounded are hauled

Figure 2.2 *In Which We Serve*: The survivors of the sinking of *The Torrin*.

onto the float and those that die are set adrift. The film's interwoven storylines are now told in a series of flashbacks, as four of the characters, Captain Kinross, Chief Petty Officer Walter Hardy, Ordinary Seaman Shorty Blake, and a young stoker, think about their families and the events that have led them to this point in their lives. Shorty and the young stoker are killed along with several others, but Captain Kinross, Walter Hardy, and almost half of the rest of the *Torrin*'s crew survive their ordeals and they later resolve to take up the battle against Germany again with even stronger heart.

In both films the key traumatic episodes, in *The Bells Go Down* the deaths of Tommy Turk and Officer MacFarlane in the conflagration at the hospital, and in *In Which We Serve* the plight of the men stranded at sea, act as what I am going to call *terminal events* in each film's narrative arc. These moments, precisely because of the extreme dramatic tension that they are likely to instill in the viewer, result in a freezing of the path of the films' narratives and a closing out of the possibility of any further narrative exposition. So, in *The Bells Go Down* the sequence in which Tommy and Officer MacFarlane are killed in the flames occurs almost at the end of the film, followed only by a ninety-second sequence that shows Ma Turk, Ted Robbins, Brookes, and Sam, at the Christening of Bob and Nan's baby, and then a single shot of the street market outside that brings the film back to where it began. At the Christening, Ted Robbins tentatively approaches Ma Turk saying: "Hello Ma, I haven't seen you since—since the fire. I was up there, you ought to feel proud," to which Ma Turk replies: "I do." A long tracking shot then follows Ma Turk as she moves to join the others at the font. Only at one brief point of this shot do we see Ma Turk's face; her expression does certainly betray her intense emotion, but this emotion seems to be held in check by a resolve that Tommy's death should not have been in vain.

In contrast, the narrative arc of *In Which We Serve* places its key traumatic episode near the beginning of the film, but this structural inversion renders this moment no less of a terminal event. The main stories that make up the large part of the film's narrative are told in a series of flashbacks, and then, in the final few minutes, the film returns to the present when the survivors of the sinking of the *Torrin* are picked up by another Allied ship. After this moment, Captain Kinross is seen going below deck to attend to those of his men who are wounded and dying, and only three brief sequences follow this section. In the first, Shorty Blake's mother and his wife Freda learn of Shorty's survival. In the second, a telegram arrives at the house of Captain Kinross that informs his wife, Alix, that he too is quite safe. In the third, Captain Kinross is seen addressing his men and informing them that they will be sent to replace men killed in other ships and expressing his confidence that they will all re-join the war with greater resolve.

As in *The Bells Go Down*, the traumatic episode of *In Which We Serve* has effectively frozen the narrative at the point of trauma, allowing only the minimum of further narrative exposition, and allowing no examination of the effects that this terrible episode must have had on those who experienced it directly, or of the toll that it must have taken afterward on their loved ones.

While the key traumatic episodes of *The Bells Go Down* and *In Which We Serve* act as the climactic moments in the films' presents that may only be followed by brief moments of narrative exposition, in *The Halfway House* the traumatic episodes that the film describes are ordered as having happened in the film's past; initially given less narrative focus, but later revealed as having disastrous consequences for everything that comes to take place in the film's present. Here, and in British trauma films generally, the traumatic episode acts not as a terminal event but instead as an *initiating event*, one that drives the story forward from the point when the trauma happened to the point when the consequences of the trauma begin to unfold.

The Effects of Traumatic Experience: Profound Mourning and Extreme Traumatic Mourning in the Story of Alice and Harry Meadows

At the planning stage of *The Halfway House*, the story of Alice and Harry Meadows had been the least important part of the film, but this segment was completely rewritten after the celebrated French actress Françoise Rosay had agreed to pay the part of Alice. Rosay had recently escaped from German-occupied France via North Africa to Britain, where her friend, the Ealing director and *Halfway House* associate producer, Alberto Cavalcanti, introduced her to studio head Michael Balcon. T. E. B. Clarke, an Ealing apprentice screenwriter at the time, was instructed to build up the story and infiltrate it into the film without upsetting the balance of the script.[5] Clarke would later contribute the Golfing Story to *Dead of Night* and write the screenplay for several of the Ealing comedies, and as a result of Clarke's revisions, the story now occupies the center ground within the film's multiple narratives, contributing greatly to the general feel of the film in a way rivalled only by the framing story of the ghostly innkeeper Rhys and his daughter Gwyneth.

Near the beginning of *The Halfway House*, we find Alice at her home in a Welsh port town. She has recently escaped from German-occupied France, leaving behind not only the country of her birth but also her family and her house in Saint-Malo. She is now living in Britain with her husband Harry, who has not long ago retired after a twenty-one-year career as a ship's captain, serving for the last three years with the Merchant Navy Convoys. We learn that Alice and Harry's son Jim, a Royal Navy officer, has been killed exactly one year before when his ship was sunk in a German torpedo attack. In her grief, Alice has turned to spiritualism for comfort, and she has persuaded Harry that they should leave their present home and buy a farm in a remote part of the country. Now, Alice is packing for the trip to the farm, and on the way there they will break the journey by staying for a night at the Halfway House. Moments later, Harry arrives home, and it becomes clear that Alice holds him responsible for persuading Jim to join the Royal Navy and, by extension, for Jim's death. When Harry protests that Jim always loved the sea, Alice replies:

> Yes, he loved the sea. He loved to sail his boat on summer days in Saint-Malo. Yes, he loved the sea. So, you think it was good that he should find how horrible war can make it? Yes, he loved the sea, so he must go to sea and …

---

[5] T. E. B. Clarke, *This Is Where I Came in* (London: Michael Joseph, 1974), pp. 144–7.

Harry tries to comfort Alice by putting his arms around her, but she shrugs him off saying: "Take your hands off me! Go away!"

On the journey to the Halfway House, the extent of Harry's reluctance to move to the farm becomes clear. When Alice says that they will need to replace the roof of the barn and buy another machine for making butter, Harry retorts: "Sure you think it's worth it? Just so you can stick yourself away in that godforsaken hole with nothing but chickens and cows for company?" Alice replies: "But I don't want company. Must I tell you that again? I want to be away from people who cannot understand how I feel." What is evident is that, in her belief of Harry's responsibility for Jim's death, Alice has turned away from Harry and the world in general and toward spiritualism for comfort. At the same time, Harry has turned away from Alice and toward the bottle. He says: "Alright, well, you stick to your spirits, and I'll stick to mine! Anyway, we've got to live somehow, and I don't care much what we do or where we do it." When they arrive at the inn, Harry inquires of Rhys whether there is a double room available, but Alice instead asks for two single rooms. When Harry asks if she is trying to make a fool of him in public, Alice replies: "*Je préfère être seul.*"

We have already seen that British films made in the early war period are inclined to position the lead-up to the traumatic episode at the center of the narrative, and that the dramatic effect of the episode itself tends to halt the narrative before any consequences are able to emerge. Conversely, in films made in the immediate aftermath of the war, the traumatic event is often removed from their present and buried in the past, referred to by the films and their central characters in passing and sometimes not mentioned at all. So, in *The Halfway House*, the events surrounding Jim's death are referred to only once, and very briefly, when Alice says to Rhys that "his ship was torpedoed one year ago this week." But the consequences that Jim's death has inflicted on Alice and Harry have been laid out by the film very clearly, and at length, in terms of their constantly being forced back to the tragedy, their inability to continue a loving physical relationship, and the incapacity of either of them to communicate clearly to the other what Jim's death has meant for them. Remarkably, in the case of Alice, this incapacity extends even to her refusal to enunciate the fact of Jim's death to Harry at all ("Yes, he loved the sea, so he must go to sea and …").

Alice's feelings of dejection have led her to a dependency on hopes that have been offered to her by spiritualism; specifically, her belief that she will be able to contact Jim again at some point in the future. As she later makes clear to Rhys: "Never shall I believe that I've lost him forever. I'm sure that one day, perhaps soon, he'll speak to me again from where he is now." In similar terms, Harry has become dependent on alcohol to be able to cover over both the loss of his son and his emotional and physical separation from Alice. The film makes it obvious that both have turned away from the attachments that they have built with each other over many years of being together and from any interest that they had previously in the outside world, and it is this turning away that threatens to diminish them as individuals and to have lasting implications for their marriage.

What is striking about these sections of *The Halfway House* is how they lay out the consequences that Jim's tragic death has had for Alice and Harry in terms that are so closely related to the symptoms of profound mourning that Freud describes in his paper "Mourning and Melancholia." Here, Freud points out the similarities between these types of symptoms and those that are to be found in "melancholia," which we would now call depression:

> Profound mourning, the reaction to someone who is loved, contains the same painful frame of mind, the same loss of interest in the outside world—in so far as it does not recall him—the same loss of capacity to adopt any new object of love (which would mean replacing him) and the same turning away from any activity that is not connected with thoughts of him. It is easy to see that this inhibition and circumscription of the ego is the expression of an exclusive devotion to mourning which leaves nothing over for other purposes or other interests. It is really only because we know so well how to explain it that this attitude does not seem to us pathological.[6]

According to Freud, after a death there always follows a prolonged period in which the attachments that the bereaved has formed with the loved one must be given up. This surrendering of the past may cause, in turn, a general withdrawal of attachments, and it is only after this period of withdrawal that the bereaved is able to re-form attachments with others. In cases such as these, the one who is grieving certainly understands that the original love object is lost and that this is a process that must be endured for a finite period. However, in cases of what Freud terms *extreme traumatic mourning* this process may be resolutely resisted, and the period of mourning drawn out to such an extent that

> a turning away from reality takes place and a clinging to the object through the medium of a hallucinatory wishful psychosis. Normally, respect for reality gains

---

[6] Sigmund Freud, "Mourning and Melancholia," in *The Standard Edition vol. XIV*, ed. by James Strachey (London: The Hogarth Press, 1957; repr. 1999), p. 244.

the day. Nevertheless its orders cannot be obeyed at once. They are carried out bit by bit, at great expense of time and cathectic energy, and in the meantime the existence of the lost object is psychically prolonged.[7]

In suggesting that a state of hallucinatory wishful psychosis can be found in cases of extreme traumatic mourning, Freud is proposing that such a high level of anxiety can exist in the mind of the bereaved that a belief and a disbelief in the loss of the loved object can run concurrently. Or, to put this a different way, there may be an *attenuation of belief* in the traumatically bereaved that leads to the borderline between belief and disbelief becoming blurred, and the psychical existence of the lost object becoming prolonged. This attenuation of belief, in effect a willingness of the traumatized to believe that is firmly held but that exists only on a precarious surface level is a recurrent preoccupation in British trauma films, and it will be a persistent object of investigation in the film analyses that follow in later chapters.

It has been useful to think of Freud's ideas of the profoundly bereaved withdrawing from the world and turning away from loved ones as having a discursive existence in how *The Halfway House* has formulated the early part of the story of Alice and Harry. But what becomes most influential from the film's séance sequence onward is how Alice's mourning becomes defined *as extreme and traumatic* precisely by means of the emphasis that is accorded to the attenuation of her belief in whether she has lost Jim forever. This becomes clear toward the end of the séance sequence when Alice's wish that Jim will one day speak to her again seems for a moment to come true.

After the guests have dined together with Rhys and Gwyneth just before the inn, and they, are once again consigned to the flames, Rhys invites them to sit in the garden where Gwyneth will bring them their coffee. Alice sits with Jill French, and she tells Jill that despite her belief in spiritualism she has never had the opportunity to communicate with Jim directly. Alice then reveals to Jill her desire to hold a séance, and she asks her to gather those guests that are interested. Later that evening, Alice is seated with Jill and Richard, Terence, Fortescue, and Oakley in a circle around a table in the drawing room; their hands are held palm down on the table and their fingers are touching. David Davies is playing the piano in the background and Harry sits in the shadows outside the circle. Alice demands whether there is "any visitor from the spirit world here with us tonight?," and, if here, that they should tell their name. The taps of the table seem

---

[7] Ibid., pp. 244–5.

to spell out the letter J, and Alice asks: "Jim, *c'est toi?*" Now, Alice hears what she believes to be Jim's voice, but her belief in Jim's presence is immediately shattered by the realization that what she thought was Jim's voice is merely the sound of a radio broadcast being played by Harry.

Harry's intervention in the séance has a profound effect on Alice and it is initially condemned by most of the others around the table; but this event will later lead to the couple at last being able to talk to each other about Jim's death. However, the unusual formal terms in which this sequence is laid out also serve to align the viewer with Alice's state of extreme traumatic mourning, specifically in the way that they motivate the viewer to share the precarious nature of Alice's belief in whether what she experiences in the séance is real.

What is initially certain to us in this sequence is that when Alice hears the voice, she believes it to be Jim's, but Alice's belief is immediately dashed by the realization that the voice is instead coming from the radio that is being played by Harry. At the point when Alice believes, we believe as well, partly because the film has been careful to suggest by the interplay of looks between Jill and Richard and between Fortescue and Oakley that they are not responsible for the taps of the table and therefore that the taps may be real. Our state of belief in Alice's psychical connection to Jim is augmented by the atmospheric piano playing of David Davies, and perhaps also by our desire that the voice is really Jim's for the sake of Alice, with whom we have by now built a great deal of sympathy. However, even at the point when we believe in this reality, the level of our belief has been attenuated by the film's unusual use of lighting, which transforms the feel that the sequence has for us exactly at the point when Alice asks whether any visitor from the spirit world is present.

Up until this moment, all of those sitting around the table, including Alice, have been lit with classical three-point lighting that has emphasized their three-dimensional shapes and therefore their state of realness. But from this point onward, Alice is predominantly lit with a direct high-key light, which has the effect of separating her from the rest of the group by accentuating her image and—at the same time—rendering it two-dimensional and so creating a feeling of unreality deriving specifically from her figure's lack of normal shape and perspective (Figure 2.3). Running counter to this, the intensity of the high-key lighting on Alice also emphasizes her serene rapture when she believes that she has at last contacted Jim and that this contact is real (Figure 2.4). The result of

Figure 2.3 *The Halfway House*: Oakley, Fortescue, Alice, and Richard and Jill French at the séance.

Figure 2.4 *The Halfway House*: "Jim, c'est toi?"

the ambiguity of these signals is that the level of the viewer's belief becomes aligned precisely with the ambiguity of Alice's belief, and we are turned just as easily as she is from a state of belief to one of disbelief when she realizes that the voice that she hears is not Jim's.

Part of what has led Alice and Harry's relationship to the point of catastrophe has been their being compelled to repeat the tragedy of Jim's death without this repetition being transformed into an act of remembrance that might move their relationship forwards. This dilemma is addressed, to an extent, when the overcoming of their reluctance to talk to each other about Jim' death begins to form the basis of their reconciliation. So, after the séance, Harry is at last able to say to Alice: "He's always with me Jim is. I know that I shouldn't have done what I did just now, but you see … you see Jim belongs to you and me. Still belongs." And, in similar terms, Alice is at last able to say to Harry: "I have been so miserable. It made me lose all reason. I didn't think how much you also were hurt."

The story of Alice and Harry Meadows has laid out in very affecting terms the state of ambiguity and complex emotional wounding that results from the trauma of personal loss. On a surface level, it does this by aligning us emotionally with the character of Alice as she endures the vicissitudes of her coming to terms with the consequences that Jim's death has had on her marriage. On a deeper level, the film achieves this by infiltrating the psychoanalytic ideas of profound mourning and extreme traumatic mourning into the fabric of Alice and Harry's relationship, and so it is able to expose the divisions and fault-lines that have resulted for them, and then align us with these ideas by means of its formal processes.

In demonstrating how Alice and Harry have broken the cycle of repetition by bringing the fact of Jim's death into the present, *The Halfway House* suggests that Alice and Harry have now begun the process of *working-through* the loss of their son in the psychoanalytic sense of getting over a painful experience by bringing it into speech and embracing a new situation. The psychoanalytic ideas of repetition and working-through also have discursive resonance in the sections of the film that describe the fate of the landlord Morgan Rhys and his daughter Gwyneth. However, unlike in the story of Alice and Harry, where the traumatic event itself is talked about only tentatively and lies buried in the past, here the traumatic event is spoken about very explicitly and then shown to us, and it therefore exists very much in the present.

The Effects of Traumatic Experience: Remembering, Repeating, and Working-Through the Trauma in the Story of the Landlord Morgan Rhys and His Daughter Gwyneth

Within the context of the film's framing story of Rhys and Gwyneth, two things that *The Halfway House* takes considerable trouble to define are, first, not only that they are *ghostly* but that they have *really returned as ghosts* after being killed one year before when the inn was destroyed in an air raid, and second, that their return has happened with the purpose of accomplishing certain specific objectives.

That Rhys and Gwyneth are ghostly is continually emphasized to the guests, and to us, in how they are differentiated from the guests by their serenity, their economy of movement, the rather stilted style of their vocal delivery, and the certainty of their worldviews, and it was perhaps these qualities that contributed to Charles Barr's dismissal of elements of the film as arid, abstract, statuesquely posed, and declaimed. However, the fact that they are not just ghostly but really ghosts becomes clear to the guests in the first half of the film during the various encounters that they have with them, and this knowledge is communicated to the viewer by the formal syntax that film employs in laying out these encounters. This is particularly obvious in the film's use of reverse shots, reaction shots, and point of view shots, and it is in how these shots are combined that the film provides a mechanism by which the certainty of this knowledge is shared almost at the same time, and in equal measure, by the film's characters and by us as viewers.

This structuring of shots can be seen at work in several sequences in the first half of the film; the first of which occurs near the beginning, just after Fortescue and Oakley's hair-raising ride down to the Halfway House on Fortescue's bicycle without brakes. When they arrive after their adventure, the inn appears to be deserted but the door is open, and so they enter, and Fortescue proclaims the place to be "a snug sort of billet." Now, while Oakley wanders off to find assistance, Fortescue sinks exhausted into a chair just inside the entrance. As he settles back, we see in a front-on medium shot his expression suddenly change from repose to surprise as he evidently thinks he sees someone or something in front of him. He says: "You weren't there a moment ago, were you? Or were you?" Then, a shot from his point of view reveals his vision to be the figure of Rhys whom Fortescue sees—*just as we are now also seeing*—gradually taking shape in front of his eyes.

That Rhys is really a ghost is reiterated in a sequence that occurs slightly later in the film, which delivers its message by neatly reversing the formal structure of this previous sequence. When Rhys brings Alice a cup of tea in her room soon after she and Harry have arrived at the inn, Alice shows Rhys a picture of Jim and reveals that he was killed when his ship was torpedoed one year ago this week. As they are talking, Rhys is positioned on the left-hand side of the frame and Alice is on the right, and between them is a full-length mirror in which we can see reflected the closed door to the room. Therefore, we are positioned between the mirror and the door. Now, Rhys excuses himself saying that the other guests will soon be arriving, and he walks in front of the mirror, past us, and toward the door. While we should be able to see Rhys's figure reflected in the mirror, instead we can see only the door opening and beginning to close seemingly on its own. Alice's gaze has been following Rhys as he moves toward the door behind us, but now she looks back at the mirror and she is amazed when she sees no sign of Rhys's reflection (Figure 2.5). Thus, the fact that Rhys casts no reflection in the mirror is revealed first to us, and then only moments later to Alice.

A similar structure is used slightly later in the film to instill the knowledge that Gwyneth is really a ghost. After Oakley has signed the register and discovered

Figure 2.5 *The Halfway House*: Alice and we realize that Rhys is really a ghost.

that the last guests to stay at the inn have left exactly one year before, Oakley and Fortescue sit at a table in the garden enjoying the sunshine and a glass of sherry. While Oakley stares into the distance, Fortescue is paying close attention to Gwyneth as she walks across the lawn followed closely behind by Joanna. Fortescue then becomes agitated at something, and he asks Oakley: "Hey! Do you see what I see?" Then, from Fortescue's point of view, we see that while Joanna is casting a shadow on the ground in front of her Gwyneth is casting no shadow at all.

But why does the film take such trouble to demonstrate almost simultaneously to the guests and to us the fact that Rhys and Gwyneth are not just ghostly but really ghosts?

One answer to this question can be found in the popularity of several British films made in the early part of the war that build their stories around ghostly figures that are ultimately proved to be merely people imitating ghosts. This is especially true of several British comedies made in the first two or three years of the war. For example, in the Gainsborough Pictures release *The Ghost Train* (Walter Forde, 1941) a disparate group of travelers who include a music hall performer Tommy Gander (Arthur Askey) are stranded overnight at a railway station that is reputed to be haunted by a ghostly train. Although the train certainly seems to be ghostly, only at the close of the film is it revealed that it has been made to appear thus by a gang of Nazi sympathizers who have made use of the station's reputation as a cover for a conspiracy to smuggle guns. In similar terms, in Ealing's Will Hay comedy vehicle *The Ghost of St. Michael's* (Marcel Varnel, 1941), an English private school is evacuated from the Home Counties to an ancient castle on the Isle of Skye, which is supposedly haunted by a ghostly bride. Here again, only in the last few minutes of the film is it revealed that what seemed to be a ghost was in fact an enemy agent bent on enabling German submarines to land on the island.

We have already established that the figures of Rhys and Gwyneth serve as the mediums through which the film's ideological messages are conveyed to the various guests and so on to the film's audiences. The knowledge that Rhys and Gwyneth are known at the mid-point of the film by the guests and by us to be really ghosts ensures that attention is firmly anchored to their messages and not diverted from these messages by our looking for clues that might prove or disprove the truth of Rhys and Gwyneth's story, and this knowledge increases the likelihood of the guests' and our subjectification to the ideological messages themselves. Or, to put this a different way, for these ideological messages to be meaningful, the attenuation of belief that has been fundamental to the conclusion of the story of Alice and Harry cannot be allowed to exist in this story without the validity of these messages being called into question. Thus, the certainty of belief in Rhys and Gwyneth's existence as ghosts has pointed us toward an understanding of the first of the specific purposes of their return from the dead. The motivation behind this is undoubtedly ideological; and the formation of our shared belief in their story has served to position us as viewers, in Althusser's words, beneath the film's ruling ideology. However, what I would like to argue is that our knowledge that Rhys and Gwyneth are really ghosts also serves later in the film to relocate the narrative of their story away from these ideological messages and toward another of the film's narrative systems that operate at the level of discourse to define the second of Rhys and Gwyneth's specific purposes.

That we accept Rhys and Gwyneth as being really ghosts means that we must also accept that they really died when the bombs fell on the inn one year before on the twenty-first of June 1942. The circumstances of their deaths become clear in the middle section of the film when Rhys tells the story of the destruction of the inn to the guests after they have gathered for dinner. In this section, Rhys describes their deaths as events that have happened in the past and, at the end of the film, we will witness these events again as they are presented as moments that exist in its present. However, now, in the middle of the film, Rhys and Gwyneth are standing at the head of the table facing the guests, and Rhys is telling the story and Gwyneth and the guests are listening, but our gaze is mostly on Gwyneth as she pays close attention to what her father is saying (Figure 2.6). Rhys recounts that, on the night when the bombs fell on the inn:

> Only Gwyneth and me is here, sitting at supper. Then in the distance we hear guns. It is the evening we hear on the news that Tobruk is fallen. And then, as though that wasn't bad enough, the old sirens start to bay like the hounds of hell themselves. Often, we had the old sirens but never any bombs. And we hear a plane moaning above the house. It is coming nearer and nearer, louder and louder. It is like the wind that comes before a storm. Suddenly, down it swoops, machine gunning the house. Breaking two windows upstairs and a bottle of whisky standing in the bar. Then all is quiet. But it isn't long before we hear it coming back. Hovering over the house like a bird of ill omen. And then the old bomb burst in the road, just by there in front. Then the incendiaries begin to fall. One comes through the ceiling, in the corner

Figure 2.6 *The Halfway House*: Gwyneth pays close attention to her father's words.

over there. Another through this window here. And one on the middle of the carpet. A great white fire with blue sparks. Until the whole house is burning and flaming to the skies.

As Rhys is describing how the incendiary bombs began to fall, the film cuts from showing Rhys and Gwyneth in a medium shot as he talks and she listens, to a series of closer shots from the perspective of the guests. So, now we see that the guests are seeing the exact place where the first bomb crashed through the ceiling (Figure 2.7), then, the window where the second bomb entered, and then, the exact place on the carpet where it landed and started to burn. As Gwyneth listens to her father's account, her expression changes from her accustomed calmness to one of distinct unease.

The reason for Gwyneth's unease becomes clear to us in a sequence at the end of the film when the guests have gathered for the last time. After Rhys has explained to them why they have been brought together at the inn, he says to them: "You would do well to get ready now, it is very near" and the guests understand that the bombing is about to start all over again and that they must prepare to leave, or their lives will be at risk. Now, we hear the

Figure 2.7 *The Halfway House*: Then the incendiaries begin to fall. "In the corner, over there."

German bomber that Rhys has described earlier in the film roaring very loudly overhead and then we see the first bomb explode in the road outside the inn and hear its deafening blast. There now follows a ten-second sequence made up of four shots that show us in no uncertain terms the terrible nature of Rhys and Gwyneth's deaths.

Each shot in this sequence lasts for exactly two seconds; each one dissolves into the next, and the brevity of the shots and the fact that no diagetic sound is used to overlay them render the sequence unlike anything that we have seen in the film before. The first is a close-up of Rhys; he is surrounded by flames and smoke and his face contorts in agony (Figure 2.8). The second is of the clock that we have seen previously hanging on the wall in the séance sequence coming down on top of us, or perhaps on top of Rhys, or on Gwyneth; its hands frozen at the exact moment that the bombs have fallen (Figure 2.9). The third is of Gwyneth, again in close-up. She is at first startled and then shocked as the incendiary bombs seem to spark behind her and in front of her and then ignite and surround her with flames. Then her face, like her father's seconds before,

Figure 2.8 *The Halfway House*: The terrible nature of Rhys and Gwyneth's deaths: Rhys surrounded in flames.

Figure 2.9 *The Halfway House*: The exact moment that the bombs have fallen.

contorts in agony (Figures 2.10 and 2.11). The fourth is of a china swan that breaks as it lands on the floor and is then crushed by the masonry that is falling from the inn's ceiling (Figure 2.12).

The uncompromising nature of the first and third shots in this sequence shocks us, given that up until now Rhys and Gwyneth have been ordered only as the calm and measured mediums through which the film's ideological messages are delivered, and we understand that the film has now shifted its gears. On the most obvious level, the second shot is representative of the destruction of the fabric of the inn; however, it also points toward the temporal disruption on which the wider narrative of the film is based. The fourth shot is a clear metaphor for the shattering of all that the figure of the swan normally represents, specifically peace, innocence, love, purity, and the sanctity of the family unit that the film has up until this moment taken such pains to protect and reproduce.

The disruption of normal time and space is also emphasized by the dissolves between the shots, and it is consequently unclear to us whether these events are occurring consecutively or simultaneously, or whether they are happening in one place or in different places. The dissolves therefore amplify the uncertainty

Figure 2.10 *The Halfway House*: Gwyneth just before the conflagration.

"Broken Attachments and Traumatic Repetition" 69

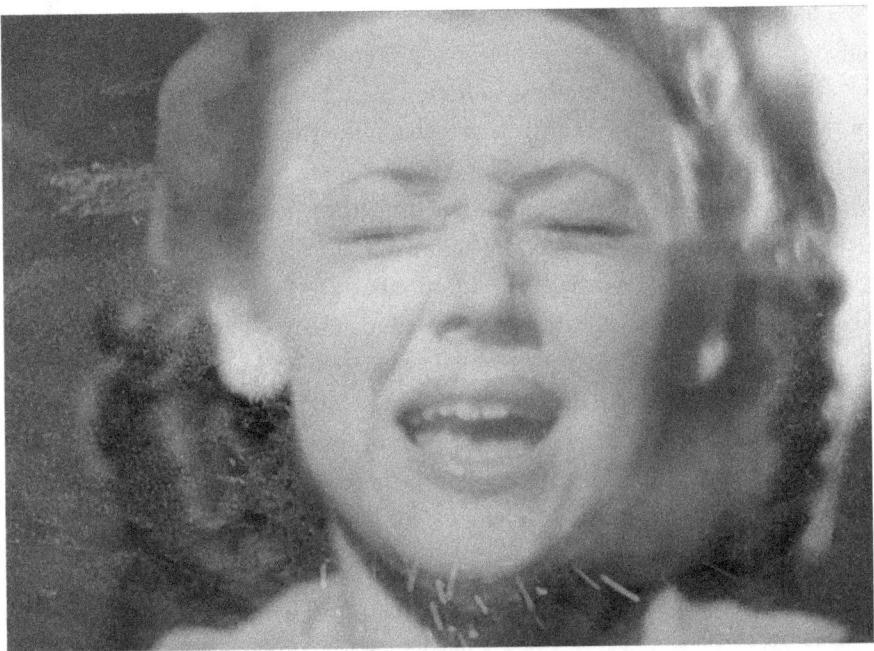

Figure 2.11 *The Halfway House*: The incendiaries sparking behind and in front of her.

Figure 2.12 *The Halfway House*: The shattering of peace, innocence, love, purity, and the family unit.

that has already been introduced by the content of the second shot, by calling into question whether these are objective presentations of what is being endured by Rhys and Gwyneth as they suffer in their final moments, or subjective presentations of the internal suffering that they themselves are experiencing at this moment. Taken as a whole, these four shots begin to make clear to us the second purpose of Rhys and Gwyneth's return from the dead, which is to demonstrate to us something of the nature of traumatic wounding itself.

The temporal and spatial dislocations that are experienced by Rhys and Gwyneth and also by us in this sequence are defined in terms that call to mind the work of Ferenczi, who, in his seminal paper on historical trauma, "Confusion of the Tongues between the Adults and the Child" describes the enormous confusion felt by the victim at the moment of trauma, and also the fracturing or "atomization" of the mental structure that can form after the event.[8] As psychiatrist and psychoanalyst Jonathan Sklar explains:

> The idea [of atomization] came from Ferenczi's thinking about a mind being unable to bear containing and holding on to the integration of thoughts, feelings, and history because of the intense painfulness of what would have to be known. Rather than just unconscious elements being split off, projected, and abandoned, in more severe pathology the mental structure itself fractures under the psychic strain and falls to pieces.[9]

That Rhys and Gwyneth are in this sequence not living the moment of their trauma but repeating it, as they have already repeated it when Rhys has told the story earlier, points toward the symptoms of mental wounding that Freud and others have argued remain even after the traumatic moment itself is over. In their examination of the lasting effects of traumatic moments on victims of the Holocaust, psychiatrists Dori Laub and Nanette Auerhahn find that:

> Because of the radical break between trauma and culture, victims often cannot find categories of thought or words to express their experience; they cannot articulate trauma even to themselves. Knowing—in the sense of articulation, analysis, elaboration and reformulation—requires the preservation or reclaiming of the internal other that is destroyed in situations of terror. Too close to the extreme experience, survivors are captive observers who can only

[8] Sándor Ferenczi, "Confusion of the Tongues between the Adults and the Child," in *Final Contributions to the Problems and Methods of Psychoanalysis* (London: Hogarth Press, 1933), p. 165.
[9] Jonathan Sklar, *Landscapes of the Dark: History, Trauma, Psychoanalysis* (London: Karnac, 2011), p. 67.

repeat it. Indeed, they may not even be able to remember it, except for the haunting, fragmented visual percepts that they cannot integrate affectively into their personality.[10]

But why should the victims of trauma, who, in their confusion, are unable to make sense of their experiences while they are happening or remember them or communicate them to others afterward, be compelled to repeat the experiences when the traumatic moment is passed? And why, within the specific context of this film, should Rhys and Gwyneth, and indeed us as viewers, be forced to endure the traumatic repetition of their deaths in the film not once but twice?

In "Remembering, Repeating, and Working-Through," Freud reports that some of his neurotic patients who have suffered from conflicts in their early childhoods do not remember them because they have been defensively repressed and so buried in the past. However, he also finds that the repressed elements of the conflicts have the tendency to return in their dreams and in debilitating obsessional behaviors that occur in their later lives. These elements have the tendency to emerge once again during the analytic treatment by means of the reactions motivated within the transference relationship that develops between the patient and the analyst. Writing specifically about what occurs in the analytic setting, Freud states that:

> We may say that the patient does not *remember* anything of what he has forgotten and repressed, but *acts* it out. He reproduces memory but as an action; he *repeats* it, without, of course, knowing that he is repeating it.[11]
>
> (Freud's italics)

Within the vicissitudes of the analytic process then, the analyst treats the conflict, which has hitherto been repressed by the patient *but that is now being repeated*, not as something that exists in the past, but as a present-day force able to be linked to the past through the dialogue that occurs between the analyst and the patient. As a result of the demonstration of this linkage by the analyst to the patient, over time, the conflict can begin to be confronted, and so the process of working-through and overcoming can begin.

---

[10] Dori Laub and Nanette Auerhahn, quoted in "Art and Trauma," in *The International Journal of Psycho-Analysis* 76 (1995), pp. 991–1005.

[11] Sigmund Freud, "Remembering, Repeating and Working-Through," in *The Standard Edition* vol. XII, ed. by James Strachey (London: The Hogarth Press, 1958; repr. 1999), p. 150.

In *Beyond the Pleasure Principle*, written a few years later in the aftermath of the First World War, Freud turns his attention from the neuroses of peacetime to those that have been caused by the traumatic events of that war. He argues that some light might be shed on the complexities of these types of illnesses by the study of the repetitious nature of the dreams of the victims:

> Now dreams occurring in traumatic neurosis have the characteristic of repeatedly bringing the patient back into the situation of his accident, a situation from which he wakes up in another fright. This astonishes people far too little. They think the fact that the traumatic experience is constantly forcing itself upon the patient even in his sleep is a proof of the strength of that experience: the patient is, as one might say, fixated to his trauma.[12]

However, Freud continues to argue that the tendency of the traumatized to repeat the traumatic event afterward in reccurring dreams or waking visions should be understood as resulting not just from a fixation on the traumatic event itself, but as a mental process that has the effect, over a period, of enabling these experiences to be assimilated into the psyche and therefore controlled. He illustrates how this process works by reporting an observation that he has made of his grandson, aged one and a half, who plays a game where he persistently throws away and then retrieves a wooden cotton reel after he has become distressed when his mother had briefly left the room:

> At the outset he was in a *passive* situation—he was overpowered by the experience; but, by repeating it, unpleasurable though it was, as a game, he took on an *active* part. These efforts might be put down to an instinct for mastery that was acting independently of whether the memory was in itself pleasurable or not.[13]
>
> (Freud's italics)

Thus, by means of his returning to the original traumatic event by representing it to himself metaphorically, just as those traumatized by war return to the traumatic event metaphorically in their dreams and waking visions, the child can turn a situation in which he was merely a victim into one in which he is able to take an effective part and thus gain mastery over the experience. Thought of in these terms, the second purpose of Rhys and Gwyneth's return from the dead can be understood as not only showing us something of the nature of traumatic

---

[12] Sigmund Freud, "Beyond the Pleasure Principle," in *The Standard Edition vol. XVIII*, ed. by James Strachey (London: The Hogarth Press, 1955; repr. 1981), p. 13.
[13] Ibid., p. 16.

wounding itself, but also demonstrating to us how the detrimental effects of trauma might be overcome by the revisiting the traumatic moment in memory, and then transforming those memories into words.

By infiltrating these psychoanalytic ideas into its framework, and by using Rhys and Gwyneth as metaphors for the traumatic experience of others, the film has provided some hope that it may eventually be possible for the victims of trauma to break the cycle of trauma and anxiety and move forwards in their lives. This story therefore speaks to those that have personal experience of trauma. However, *The Halfway House* also seeks to widen out this idea of remedial repetition so that it might have relevance on a more general societal level, and it does this by drawing our attention to two specific dates that are mentioned at various moments during the film. These are perhaps missed by viewers today, but they must have had great significance for the film's wartime audiences.

The Beginning of the End of Wartime Anxiety: The Twenty-First of June 1942 and the Twenty-First of June 1943

The Halfway House introduces the idea that returning to a traumatic past event might have benefits not just for certain individuals but for society in general by drawing the viewer's attention to two specific dates; the first of which defines the film's present, and the second the precise moment in the past to which the guests return when they arrive at the inn. As we have already seen, it is made clear early in the film that the film's present is the twenty-first of June 1943 when Oakley reads, and we in the same moment see, the entry in the inn's register of guests. The date in the past to which the guests return is made clear to us at various points during the narrative when we are shown objects that the guests have already noticed as being in some ways anachronistic. Two examples will suffice here to demonstrate how the knowledge of this earlier date is conveyed to the viewer.

Early in the afternoon, after all the guests have arrived at the inn, Richard and Joanna French are playing darts in the bar and Harry is leaning on the bar counter drinking a glass of whisky and watching them. After Joanna has won the game, Harry says to Richard: "I say, isn't today Friday June the twenty-first?," to which Richard replies: "Yes, of course." Then, Harry draws Richard and Joanna's attention to a tear-off calendar that is hanging on the wall next to the counter. So

Figure 2.13 *The Halfway House*: Will the war be won or lost? The loss of Tobruk on the twenty-first of June 1942.

that he can examine the calendar more closely, Richard takes it off the wall and he then exclaims: "That's last year's calendar. Look!" and, in a close-up, we are shown the calendar, and we can see that the date is Thursday the twenty-first of June 1942 (Figure 2.13).

Soon after this, Oakley, Fortescue, and David Davies are talking together in the seating area just inside the entrance to the inn; David Davies is sitting on a sofa reading a newspaper and he says: "How very odd. This paper's a year old, June the twenty-first 1942" and he reads out the paper's headline that states: "Rommel approaching Fort Capuzzo." Then, Fortescue notices that all the other newspapers that are laid out on a table behind the sofa are also a year old.

In the same way that the film has already provided proof to the guests that Rhys and Gwyneth are not just ghostly but really ghosts, the film is now providing proof to the guests not only that they have travelled back in time, but that they have travelled back specifically to the twenty-first of June 1942. Thus, where previously this proof has ensured that close attention to the film's ideological messages, here it ensures that close attention is paid to the significance of this specific date. While we already know that the twenty-first of June 1942 was when Rhys and Gwyneth were killed in the air raid, and that this was the week that Alice and Harry's son Jim was killed in action, the film proceeds to show why this date might have a wider significance.

The film makes the significance of this date clear at three specific moments. As we have already noted, the first of these occurs early in the film when David Davies reads out the headline to Fortescue and Oakley: "Rommel approaching Fort Capuzzo." The second is at the mid-point of the film as Rhys is telling the guests the story of the destruction of the inn when he makes clear that this happened on "the evening we hear on the news that Tobruk is fallen." The third is near the end of the film after Alice and Harry have made their peace with each other and they join the other guests in the drawing room. At this point, just as the clock is striking nine, Terence turns on the radio to listen to the news and the guests hear:

> This is the BBC Home and Forces Programme. Here is the news and this is Bruce Belfrage reading it. Tonight's bulletin from Cairo announces the fall of Tobruk in the early hours of this morning. Details are not yet to hand. The Eighth Army is now digging in on a line running between Fort Capuzzo and Halfaya Pass. Since our last bulletin, the Germans claimed to have pierced the outer defences of Sevastopol.

The surrender of Tobruk by the British Eighth Army on the morning of the twenty-first of June 1942 was the second largest capitulation by the British Army in the Second World War after the loss of Singapore three months earlier. On the night of the seventeenth of June, Winston Churchill had flown to Washington to meet President Roosevelt and settle certain important strategic issues including the joint development of the atomic bomb. On the morning of the twenty-first of June, he was with Roosevelt in his study in the White House when a telegram was put into the president's hands, who then passed it to Churchill without comment. According to Churchill's own account of this moment, the message said: "Tobruk has surrendered, with twenty-five thousand men taken prisoners." Churchill later wrote that:

> This was one of the heaviest blows I can recall during the war. Not only were its military effects grievous, but it had affected the reputation of the British armies. At Singapore eighty-five thousand men had surrendered to inferior numbers of Japanese. Now in Tobruk a garrison of twenty-five thousand (actually thirty-three thousand) seasoned soldiers had laid down their arms to perhaps one-half

of their number. If this was typical of the Desert Army, no measure could be put upon the disasters which impended in North-East Africa. I did not attempt to hide from the President the shock I had received. It was a bitter moment. Defeat is one thing; disgrace is another.[14]

The fall of Tobruk was utterly unexpected by Churchill and the War Cabinet. There is also plentiful evidence that when the news was relayed to the general public later the same day it gave rise in some to fears that the Allies would now lose the war, or, at the very least, that winning the war would take longer than had been expected and cost many more lives. It is also sure that the loss of Tobruk had major symbolic importance for the British people, not the least because it had been successfully defended against concerted Axis attack over the course of eight months the previous year. Over the weeks that followed, the enormity of the defeat would lead to fierce debate in the House of Commons, and the normally muted British press would demand that politicians and military leaders alike should answer for what had caused this immense military setback.[15]

So much for the significance of the twenty-first of June 1942 being presented as the film's past, but what are we to make of how the film also very specifically defines its present as the twenty-first of June 1943?

As I have already made clear, *The Halfway House* was shot in the summer of 1943 but not released until April 1944, and so the film's present can be thought of as more or less contemporary with the time that it was shot. Just as the twenty-first of June 1942 had great significance for the British population, the early summer of 1943 also had great import, in that in the general public's perception of the development of the war, by the second week of May 1943 the North African campaign had effectively ended when British and American troops marched into Tunis and an estimated 250,000 German soldiers surrendered their arms. With the Allies now in control of North Africa and the Mediterranean open to Allied traffic, attention could turn to the invasion of Sicily and beyond. Thus, by the middle of June 1943, by which time *The Halfway House* was in production, hopes were high that the tide of the war had finally turned.

---

[14] Winston Churchill, *The Second World War Volume IV: The Hinge of Fate* (London: Penguin Books, 1985, repr. 2005), pp. 343–4.
[15] For an in-depth account of the reaction to the Fall of Tobruk, see Karen Horne and David Katz, "The Surrender of Tobruk in 1942: Press Reports and Soldiers' Memories," in *Scientia Militaria* 44:1 (2016), pp. 190–208.

By removing the space of time between these two pivotal moments in the war, *The Halfway House* creates a temporal narrative dislocation that transports its guests and its viewers from the relative security of the summer of 1943 back to the darkest days of the war in the summer of 1942. For today's audiences, even if they are aware of the importance of the fall of Tobruk, the comparative feeling of safety that defined the summer of 1943 has largely been lost, and so this aspect of the film's meaning is diminished. However, for its contemporary audiences, even taking account of the time that had elapsed between the shooting and the release of the film, the fall of Tobruk undoubtedly still had great significance, and being returned to that moment must have been an uncomfortable experience.

When the guests have gathered for the last time, and just before they leave the inn as the bombing is about to begin all over again, Rhys says to the group:

> When you go away and walk up the road to Cwmbach, you will have spent the night in an inn. But if you look back from the crest of the hill, the Halfway House will not be here. Soon it will be as if you had never come at all. But if you remember, it will be as you remember a forgotten snatch of song. It will be a picture before your eyes gone before you realize it is there. Or an echo in the hidden places of your mind.

As the guests begin to climb over the pile of rubble that seems to be all that remains of the inn, each one takes their leave of Rhys and Gwyneth, and each declares in an internal monologue their resolutions for the future. The last to leave are Harry and Alice. Harry says: "I must get back to where I belong, back to the sea," and Alice says: "Later my son, not yet." Harry and Alice's time at the inn has afforded them the opportunity to revisit their traumatic pasts and communicate what they have suffered to each other, and, specifically in the case of Alice, this process has enabled her to finally understand that Jim is lost and must be given up, and that she must commit her future to Harry.

While each member of the group seems to be aware that, while the months ahead will not necessarily be easy for them, they can now look forward to a future less encumbered by the echoes of the past. In the same way, by transporting its contemporary audiences from the relative security of the summer of 1943 back to their own moment of collective anxiety in the summer of 1942, the film has provided a safe space within which they can confront their own traumatic pasts and, in time, also look forward toward to a brighter post-war future.

3

"The Perpetual Recurrence of the Same Thing"

The Compulsion to Repeat the Trauma *ad Infinitum*, Male Anxiety, Sexual Difference and Motherhood, and the Interplay between Subjectivity and Objectivity in *Dead of Night*

Introduction

Since the 1960s, many commentators have emphasized the importance of Ealing Studios' *Dead of Night* to the history of the British fantasy film, declaring it to be, for example, "Britain's first significant entry into the sphere of the supernatural,"[1] "the most important English supernatural thriller prior to the late 1950s,"[2] and "arguably the most famous ghost story ever produced within British cinema."[3] Over the last thirty or so years several commentators have approached the film from a psychoanalytic perspective; many proposing repression as underpinning the film's various preoccupations. The concept of repression dates from the earliest days of psychoanalysis when Freud was attempting to account for the amnesia of hysterical patients; he uses the term to describe a process by which unacceptable thoughts or memories are defensively excluded from the conscious and buried in the unconscious. Freud outlines three phases of repression: "primal repression," in which the internal drive impulses are denied or suppressed, "repression proper," or "after-pressure," in which affects, symptoms, and other mental derivatives of the drive impulses are repressed within the unconscious, and "the return of the repressed", in which

---

[1] Ivan Butler, *The Horror Film* (London: A. Zwemmer, 1967), p. 73.
[2] David Pirie, *A New Heritage of Horror* (London and New York: I.B. Tauris, 2008), p. 16.
[3] Peter Hutchings, *Hammer and Beyond: The British Horror Film* (Manchester and New York: Manchester University Press, 1993), p. 26.

these mental derivatives involuntarily irrupt into consciousness in the form of dreams, waking visions, and parapraxes.[4]

Commentators who have approached *Dead of Night* by way of Freud's concept of repression include Alan Burton and Tim O'Sullivan, who argue that the film describes a "serial conflict between Freudian psychoanalysis and the uncanny manifestation of the paranormal [...] superbly rich in interpretive potential with its dramatic fabric of dread, anxiety, foreknowledge, repression and oneiric metaphor."[5] In similar terms, Charles Barr finds that both the Haunted Mirror and the Ventriloquist Dummy segments of the film "are clearly stories of the return of the repressed: elements of the psyche that have been rigidly kept down find their way back to confront the repressor in a monstrous externalized form."[6] Repression also seems central to Jonathan Rigby's claim that Robert Hamer, the director of the film's Haunted Mirror segment, "makes it clear that the sadistic 19th century madman and the neutered post-war accountant are mirror reflections of one another."[7] Barr also highlights the "repressed" nature of Ealing's wartime output in its role as the dominant studio for war-effort production, and *Dead of Night* as breaking new ground by lifting "the lid on forces of sex, violence and fantasy which Ealing's wartime project had kept almost out of sight."[8]

However, what is striking is that these commentators seem to suggest the dilemmas of *Dead of Night*'s beleaguered male figures as resulting from a general tendency in the British male toward being repressed without defining exactly what it is they are repressing, and without placing their male figures' dilemmas within a particular historical context. In contrast, Peter Hutchings locates the problems faced by *Dead of Night*'s male figures soundly within the atmosphere of cultural change that defined the immediate post-war years. While he begins his assessment of the film by emphasizing the self-reflexive elements of the film that encourage the viewer to share

---

[4] Sigmund Freud, "Repression," in *The Standard Edition vol. XIV*, ed. by James Strachey (London: The Hogarth Press, 1957; repr. 1999), pp. 143–58.
[5] Alan Burton and Tim O'Sullivan, *The Cinema of Basil Dearden and Michael Relph* (Edinburgh: Edinburgh University Press, 2009), p. 74.
[6] Charles Barr, *All Our Yesterdays: 90 Years of British Cinema* (London: BFI Publishing, 1986), pp. 17–18.
[7] Jonathan Rigby, *English Gothic: A Century of Horror Cinema* (London: Reynolds & Hearn, 2002), p. 35.
[8] Barr, *All Our Yesterdays*, p. 18.

the uncertainty that its various characters feel about what is subjective and what is objective or what is real and what is fantasy, he continues to outline how certain factors of the Hearse Driver and Haunted Mirror segments proceed from the unstable social setting in which the film came into being. Hutchings states that:

> Grainger's and Peter's visions, and the play of belief and disbelief apparent in them, are associated with a crisis of gender (and especially male) identity. This of course is an anxiety specific to the post-1945 transition from war to peace and the social and representational dislocations that is involved, an anxiety acknowledged throughout this film, in all of its stories.[9]

Hutchings also pertinently points out that how *Dead of Night* addresses the problem of male anxiety is itself problematic in that it offers no sure redress to this dilemma in its various stories and no reassuring closure in its conclusion.

Hutchings's views have been formative to my belief that *Dead of Night* can be read most productively in the context of male anxieties that were pervasive in British society at the time of the film's production in the mid-1940s. What I want to propose is that these anxieties had arisen less from a general tendency in the British male toward being repressed, as Burton and O'Sullivan, Barr, and Rigby have suggested, and more from specific stresses that had been building within the male psyche during the interwar period. *Dead of Night* engages with these stresses obliquely; and it is only by reading between the lines of film form and film narrative, and sometimes outside these lines, that their existence can be revealed.

I look first at how *Dead of Night*'s Hearse Driver story and Linking narrative recirculate discourses surrounding the psychoanalytic ideas of disavowal, displacement, and compulsive repetition to bind the anxieties of its male characters securely to the trauma of the Second World War. Then, I demonstrate how the Christmas Party and Haunted Mirror segments engage with other psychoanalytic discourses connected to sexual difference, sexual development, motherhood, paranoia, and the interplay between subjectivity and objectivity, to lay bare the male anxieties that had erupted from the destabilization of pre-war dominant patriarchal power relations, and to ask whether a return to the "pre-war normality" of female and male relationships is by now even possible.

---

[9] Hutchings, *Hammer and Beyond*, p. 35.

Synopsis of *Dead of Night*

In *Dead of Night*, an architect, Walter Craig (Mervyn Johns), arrives at Pilgrim's Farm, the country house of Eliot Foley (Roland Culver), where he has been invited for the weekend to discuss its renovation. On entering the house, Craig finds Foley's mother (Mary Merrall) serving tea to a group of weekend guests. The group is composed of a racing driver, Hugh Grainger (Anthony Baird), a young girl, Sally O'Hara (Sally Ann Howes), a confident young woman, Joan Cortland (Googie Withers), and a psychoanalyst, Dr. Van Straaten (Frederick Valk). Although Craig claims to have never visited this part of the country before, he says that the house and guests are familiar to him from a recurring dream. All of those present, except for Mrs. Foley, proceed to recount their own extraordinary past experiences, their stories making up the five story segments of the film.

Grainger's tale, the Hearse Driver, begins as he suffers a near-fatal crash in his racing car. One week later, he is being treated in the Park Clinic by Dr. Albury (Robert Wyndham) and a nurse, Joyce (Judy Kelly). Although Grainger shows no sign of physical injuries, he is suffering from frequent high temperatures, and also recurrent dreams in which he relives his accident. However, Grainger soon begins to recover, although he admits to Joyce that he still has "awful bad nightmares." One night, as he prepares to go to sleep, he has a vision of an old-fashioned empty hearse and its driver who looks up at him and says: "Just room for one inside, sir." One week later, immediately after he has been discharged from the clinic, he experiences another similar vision, which has the effect of saving him from being killed in a chance traffic accident.

Now Sally O'Hara begins her tale, the Christmas Party story, in which she recounts her experiences while she and her family were staying in Somerset for Christmas. In the story, Sally is attending a children's costume party given by Mrs. Watson, a friend of her mother's. After hiding with Mrs. Watson's son, Jimmy (Michael Allen) during a game of sardines, Sally discovers a room where she finds a younger boy who is dressed in clothes of a much earlier period. As she comforts him, she learns from the boy that his name is Francis Kent, and that his half-sister would like to kill him. Sally then re-joins the party only to be informed by Mrs. Watson that the boy must be the ghost of Francis Kent, who had been murdered by his half-sister Constance in the house many years before.

The next to speak is Joan Cortland, who recounts the Haunted Mirror story, which begins just after she had become engaged to Peter (Ralph Michael). In her story, she presents Peter with an ornate mirror, in which he starts to see visions of a room quite unlike his own. As the story unfolds, Peter begins to identify with the traumatic experience of the previous owner of the mirror and, believing Joan to be having an affair, he attempts to strangle her before she destroys the mirror and brings the visions to an end.

Eliot Foley now begins his tale, the Golfing Story, which revolves around two friends of his, George Parratt (Basil Radford) and Larry Potter (Naunton Wayne), who share an interest in golf. Both are the stars of their club, and both fall in love with an attractive young woman, Mary Lee (Peggy Bryan). Faced with the dilemma of which of them will marry Mary, they resolve to settle the matter by playing eighteen holes, the loser to "vanish from the scene forever." Parratt wins by cheating, and, because he has lost, Potter drowns himself in a nearby lake. Sometime later, Potter returns as a ghost, and he exacts his revenge by changing places with Parratt and usurping his role with Mary in the marital bedroom on their wedding night.

Finally, Dr. Van Straaten begins the Ventriloquist's Dummy story, in which he recounts an experience of some years before. His story tells of the attempted murder by a ventriloquist, Maxwell Frere (Michael Redgrave), of a professional rival, Sylvester Kee (Hartley Power). The story hinges on Kee's account of the strange relationship that exists between Frere and his dummy, Hugo Fitch. Hugo seemingly operates independently to Frere, humiliating him in public, and threatening to leave him and to go into partnership with Kee. Frere, an alcoholic who suffers from increasingly paranoid delusions, shoots and wounds Kee in a fit of jealousy. Dr. Van Straaten brings Hugo to the prison cell where Frere is being held awaiting trial for the shooting, and in a state of panic Frere destroys the dummy. Some weeks later, Frere has been committed to an asylum having descended into a catatonic trance. Dr. Van Straaten persuades Kee to accompany him when he visits Frere, and now Frere wakes from his trance and recognizes Kee, but he can talk only in the voice of Hugo, his mind having been completely dominated by the part of him that is the dummy.

Back in the living room at Pilgrim's Farm, Dr. Van Straaten breaks his glasses as Craig has earlier predicted that he would, and Craig becomes terrified that a premonition that he has had in his recurring dream is now coming to pass. Dr. Van Straaten recognizes Craig's distress, and, saying that he now accepts Craig's dream, he suggests that the others leave them alone. Craig strangles the psychoanalyst, and then wakes up in his own bed at home, only to receive a phone call from Eliot Foley inviting him down to the country for the weekend. The film ends precisely as it began, with Craig arriving at Pilgrim's Farm, and his nightmare beginning all over again.

Dead of Night's Trauma Narratives: The Linearity of Its Multiple Timelines and Its Non-Linear Uses of the Mechanisms of Disavowal, Displacement, and Compulsive Repetition in the Linking Narrative and the Hearse Driver Story

The narrative structure of *Dead of Night* is complex in that it is made up of multiple narratives and sub-narratives, and one purpose of the Linking narrative, which itself has great importance to the overall meaning of the film, is to tie these narratives together. The actions described by the Linking narrative constitute the film's present, and the stories themselves constitute different points in the film's past. One way that the film defines the temporal relationship that the Linking narrative has with the other stories is by establishing normal temporal continuity during each of the linking sequences, and then re-establishing this continuity when each of the stories is over. *Dead of Night* is made up of five stories, and naturally this means that the Linking narrative is split into six sections, the two that begin and end the film, and the four that separate the stories and link them together. The film establishes temporal continuity within the Linking narrative at various moments by drawing our attention to two clocks in the farm's living room where almost all the action in the Linking narrative takes place. One is a grandfather clock that stands just inside the entrance to the room, and the other is a lantern clock that sits on the mantlepiece.

For example, near the beginning of the film, when Eliot Foley is showing Walter Craig into the living room just as Mrs. Foley is serving tea to the guests, Mrs. Foley stands up and then walks toward him offering her hand in greeting. The camera holds Craig, Foley, and Mrs. Foley on the threshold of the room in a medium shot for a second, before tracking backward into the room and revealing a grandfather clock that stands against the wall to the left of the frame. So, we can read that the time when the Linking narrative begins is half past four. A little later, just before Grainger begins to tell the first story, a wide shot of the interior of the room shows Joan Cortland, Foley, and Dr. Van Straaten listening to Craig as he tells them about his dream in which he has met them all before: "together here—in this room." The grandfather clock is standing in the background of the shot, telling us that the time is now a quarter to five. Similar set-ups are repeated all the way through the six sections of the Linking narrative, marking the time that has elapsed at Pilgrim's Farm while the stories are being told. Finally, near the end of the film, after Dr. Van Straaten's glasses have been broken and as Craig is circling behind him, the grandfather clock is at the back of the frame informing us that the time is now seven o'clock, and that two and a half hours have passed since Craig's arrival.

As in most films that establish temporal continuity in this way, it becomes manifest to the viewer as the film progresses that the film's screen time is shorter than the diagetic time that elapses during the film's narrative. However, while time is elongated during the six linking sequences, the two clocks have told us that the progression of time during these sequences is linear, and this is also true in the stories themselves. The progression of time is also established as causal, in that the past events that are described by the guests in the stories undoubtedly have shaped the opinions that they express at Pilgrim's Farm in the film's present.

The tales that the five guests tell all describe certain events that have occurred in the past; the first four, it seems, in the recent past. For example, Sally O'Hara is explicit in stating at the beginning of her story that her experience occurred only "last year" when she and her family were spending the school holidays in Somerset. Three of the other segments, the Hearse Driver, the Haunted Mirror, and the Golfing Story, also seem to be set in the recent past. We know that the events described in the Ventriloquist Dummy segment take place before and soon after the sixth of February 1938, because this date is clearly shown to us on Sylvester Kee's witness statement, and while this is further in the past than the other stories, Dr. Van Straaten's statement to the guests as he starts his story: "You may remember the case" suggests that the events that he describes exist within the guests' recent memory.

But why is *Dead of Night* so careful to define the moments in the past in which its stories are set, and why does it take such trouble to establish linear and causal temporality within the Linking narrative and between the Linking narrative and the stories themselves?

Dead of Night was shot during the last few months of the war in Europe and released in Britain in September 1945, four months after the war had ended. While we have already established that the Ventriloquist Dummy segment has a pre-war setting, we must conclude that the events described in the other four stories have taken place during the war, and that the Linking narrative takes place in the war's immediate aftermath. However, the war is never referenced at any point in *Dead of Night*'s various narratives, and there are no signs of the existence of the war anywhere in the mise-en-scene of its various stories. The war as a physical event is therefore omitted by the film completely, and this omission can be accounted for by thinking of the film as using the psychoanalytic ideas of *disavowal* and *displacement*.

Freud proposes the idea of disavowal as describing a mode of psychical defense that amounts to a refusal to recognize the reality of a traumatic perception, arguing that this is most frequently found in situations where the male child is confronted by the absence in the woman of a penis. Freud states that: "We know how children react to their first impressions of the absence of a penis. They disavow the fact and believe that they *do* see a penis, all the same."[10] Freud also draws parallels between the process of disavowal and a psychical mechanism that amounts to a state of psychosis:

> A process may set in which I should like to call a "disavowal", a process which in the mental life of children seems neither uncommon nor very dangerous but which in an adult would mean the beginning of a psychosis.[11]

In the same way that Freud defines the absence of a penis in the woman as being traumatic for the male child, and therefore something that must be disavowed, in *Dead of Night* the war as a traumatic event is disavowed and omitted from the film's normal narrative exposition completely. However, the existence of this disavowal becomes gradually clear to the viewer at numerous points in the film. It is obvious, for example, in the absence of military uniforms anywhere in the film's mise-en-scene. It is clear in the Haunted Mirror segment, when at first we do not notice, but—*after some thought*—we do notice Peter and Joan Cortland enjoying an affluent lifestyle in London unconstrained by rationing or the danger of bombing (Figure 3.1), and also at the end of the Linking narrative, when we do not see, but—*if we look closely*—we do see through Walter Craig's bedroom window St. Paul's Cathedral and a London skyline unmarked by any effects of the Blitz (Figure 3.2).

---

[10] Sigmund Freud, "The Infantile Genital Organization," in *The Standard Edition vol. XIX*, ed. by James Strachey (London: The Hogarth Press, 1961; repr. 1999), pp. 143–4.

[11] Sigmund Freud, "Some Psychical Consequences of the Anatomical Distinction between the Sexes," in *The Standard Edition vol. XIX*, ed. by James Strachey (London: The Hogarth Press, 1961; repr. 1999), p. 249.

"The Perpetual Recurrence of the Same Thing" 87

Figure 3.1 *Dead of Night*: Joan and Peter Cortland: "What shall we do tonight? Dress up – spend lots of money?"

Figure 3.2 *Dead of Night*: A London skyline unmarked by the Blitz.

In the context of the time in which *Dead of Night* was made and first shown, the film's disavowal of the war as a physical event is precisely what enables it to create a space that is safe enough for its audiences to begin to think about the detrimental effects of their own wartime experiences. Or, to put this in Laub and Podell's words, the film's disavowal of the war amounts to the creation of an *empty space* that can point toward its audiences' own traumas and anxieties without bringing them into direct representation. However, because *Dead of Night* has taken such trouble to build its complicated narrative structure within a linear and causal temporal framework, the viewer is constantly reminded of this framework, and so constantly reminded of the film's omissions and its state of disavowal. This is perhaps one of the factors that make the experience of watching the film even now so unsettling. But by making its disavowal of the war so obvious to the viewer, the film is also signaling this state of disavowal as being potentially problematic, in that the war as the real cause of the traumas and anxieties that the film is by implication laying out is merely being covered over, and not being addressed *per se*.

While *Dead of Night* certainly disavows the physical existence of the war in its various narratives, the traumatic consequences of war are one of its main concerns, and to reveal how it engages with the war's traumatic effects, we must examine in detail certain motifs that occur in the film but outside normal narrative exposition. One of these can be discovered in the film's opening title sequence.

The titles appear in front of a static shot of a drawing that is not referenced in the titles themselves or in the main body of the film. The drawing is of a figure of indeterminate sex lying on its front; its face is turned toward us, but its gaze is directed downwards at the surface on which it lies. The figure is shrouded from its ankles to its head and bound to the surface by a proliferation of wires, the ends of which seem securely attached to the surface. The figure seems to be pushing upwards and straining its shoulders and toes in a vain attempt to free itself from its bindings, but as it strains away from the surface, it seems to pull the wires ever tighter around its body (Figure 3.3).

The drawing is *Figure in a Shelter* by Henry Moore, one of a series of his works that present abstracted blanketed shelter sleepers squatting or lying on the platforms of underground stations during the Blitz. According to Moore's own account, during the fourth night of the Blitz on the eleventh of September 1940, he saw from the interior of an underground train blanketed shelterers taking refuge from the mayhem that was taking place above ground. This experience

Figure 3.3 *Dead of Night*: Henry Moore's *Figure in a Shelter*.

motivated a body of Moore's work that, according to art historian David Alan Mellor, "would become mythical in their status as documents of British resistance against Nazi aggression."[12] Moore's drawings were commissioned by the coalition government's War Artists Advisory Committee, initially reproduced in the magazine *Horizon*, before being exhibited in the National Gallery in April 1941 and then sent to New York two months later as part of the *Britain at War* exhibition. The art historian Geoffrey Grigson describes the subjects of Moore's shelter drawings in these terms:

> They are figures of life (at least in the tube series), the wonder of which is terrifically threatened. The figures belong to the mass of life; they are below the edge of will. Rather than life vertebrate, active and thinking, they are life to which terrible things are being done.[13]

In placing Moore's *Figure in a Shelter* in the background of its opening titles, *Dead of Night* announces its interest in wartime trauma and anxiety from its

---

[12] David Alan Mellor, "'And Oh! The stench': Spain, the Blitz, Abjection and the Shelter drawings," in *Henry Moore* (London: Tate Publishing, 2010), p. 61.
[13] Geoffrey Grigson, *Henry Moore* (London: Penguin, 1943), p. 14.

outset, and this interest seems to have been obvious to the News Chronicle critic, Richard Winnington, at the time of the film's release when he observed that: "A Henry Moore drawing on the opening title whips us quickly out of our happy peacetime world."[14] While the devastation of the Blitz is *omitted* by the film in the shot of the London skyline that we see through Craig's bedroom window, in the credit sequence the war as a physical event is not omitted as such, but instead *admitted* and at the same time *displaced* onto another representational form that is less threatening. In *The Interpretation of Dreams*, Freud proposes dream displacement as a defensive action of self-censorship—one that strips elements that have high anxietal value of their intensity, creating new elements that have low anxietal value that permit the initial traumatic event to be objectivized and neutralized.[15]

Another example of *Dead of Night*'s use of the psychoanalytic idea of displacement can be found in how the symptoms of war trauma are displaced onto the psychical wounds suffered by the victim of a racing crash in the film's Hearse Driver segment.

The story that Grainger tells hinges on his recollection of three visions that he has experienced while recovering from the effects of a near-fatal racing crash. As Grainger begins his story, a dissolve takes us from the living room at Pilgrim's Farm to a racing track. As the cars speed from right to left, we see that one of them is on fire. The camera pans quickly left to follow it, and we see the car trying to avoid another car and then spinning out of control. The driver is thrown from his seat. Another quicker dissolve transitions to a close-up of Grainger as he lies in a hospital bed; he is unshaven, his eyes are closed, and he is clearly delirious. The camera pulls back to reveal the figure of Dr. Albury standing over Grainger; in his delirium, Grainger says: "Now's my chance. I can't make it. I can't make it. Yes, I can. Now then. This is it" (Figure 3.4). While we are not sure—because we are not shown—what Grainger is experiencing, we must assume from his words that he is re-living the build-up to his crash and the crash itself. We are told that a week has passed since the accident, and Grainger is being attended to by Dr. Albury and a nurse, Joyce, who informs the doctor that the patient's mind had cleared that morning and that she had been able to inform him that the other driver was unhurt. He has apparently slept soundly after this. Dr. Albury says that, while there is no injury to his brain, he is concerned about Grainger's

---

[14] *News Chronicle*, 9 September 1945.
[15] Sigmund Freud, "The Interpretation of Dreams," in *The Standard Edition vol. IV*, ed. by James Strachey (London: The Hogarth Press, 1953; repr. 1991), pp. 305–9.

Figure 3.4 *Dead of Night*: Grainger reliving his trauma.

persistent high temperatures and bouts of delirium. However, only a few days later, Grainger seems to have made a remarkable recovery after being tended to by his wife-to-be Joyce, and his temperature has returned to normal. At this point, Grainger experiences his second vision.

After Joyce has tucked Grainger in for the night, he sits in bed reading. A curtained window next to his bed is open, and we can hear music coming from a radio that is being played somewhere outside. As the camera tracks in slowly toward Grainger we also become aware of a clock ticking. He raises his head and listens intently, and the music fades and Grainger looks toward the window, and then a close shot of the window from his perspective shows the curtains moving slightly in the breeze. Now we hear—as he is undoubtedly also hearing—the sound of a racing car speeding past. He opens the curtains to find daylight outside and sees an old-fashioned horse-drawn hearse and its driver in the street below, and in another shot from his perspective, the camera zooms in very quickly to the face of the hearse driver, who looks up and says: "Just room for one inside, sir."

Grainger's third vision occurs a few days later, just after he has been discharged from the nursing home. He stands in the bus queue outside and when the bus arrives, he starts to step onto it. As the bus conductor turns to face him, the camera zooms forward, and we see that the conductor has the face of the hearse driver from the previous sequence. The conductor says: "Just room for one inside, sir" and Grainger backs away, horrified. Then, he stands watching as the bus swerves to avoid a dust cart and crashes over a bridge.

I have argued in my analysis of *The Halfway House* that the story of Rhys and Gwyneth has a discursive relation to ideas surrounding the concept of traumatic repetition that Freud puts forward in "Remembering, Repeating and Working-Through." It will be remembered that here Freud proposes that repressed elements of patients' earlier conflicts have the tendency to return in visions, dreams, and debilitating obsessional behaviors that occur in their later lives. During the analytic treatment, these elements emerge once again in the dialogue that occurs between the analyst and the patient, and the analyst treats the conflict, which has hitherto been buried by the patient but that is now being repeated, not as something that exists in the past, but as a *present-day force* that is able to be linked to the patient's past experiences. As a result of the demonstration of this linkage to the patient, over time the conflict can begin to be confronted, and so the process of working-through can begin.

Because it seems that in these various visions Grainger is reliving the trauma of his accident, it is logical to think of Freud's concept of traumatic repetition as being just as relevant to how *Dead of Night* lays out Grainger's visions as it is to how *The Halfway House* lays out Rhys and Gwyneth's reliving of the moments before they perished in the inn. But if this is true, then why are all three of Grainger's visions not also mere repetitions of his original trauma?

Unlike in the case of Rhys and Gwyneth, where the trauma is being repeated *ad infinitum*, the severity of what Grainger sees and hears becomes gradually attenuated over the course of his three visions because the level of his anxiety is decreasing. In the delirium of his first vision, Grainger feels himself to be re-living the build-up to the crash and the crash itself, just as he has been re-living these moments repeatedly during the seven days since. But by the time of the second vision, all visual traces of the crash have disappeared, and only aural traces remain in the sound of the racing car that Grainger hears—and we hear—speeding past outside his bedroom window. Unlike in the first vision, he no longer feels that he is re-experiencing the crash itself, and his fear that he has killed another driver has also disappeared because Joyce has already assured him that this was not the case.

After his second vision, Grainger makes it clear to Dr. Albury that all that remains in his mind from the crash is his firm feeling that he has cheated death, and this feeling takes the displaced form in his second vision of a hearse that is empty, and a hearse driver who says: "Just room for one inside, sir" (Figure 3.5)

In Grainger's third vision, no visual or aural traces of the racing crash remain at all, and only two elements remain from the second vision. The figure of the hearse driver is now merely a bus conductor, and the words that are spoken by the hearse driver are now merely the words that might be spoken by any bus conductor on any day in normal life (Figure 3.6). The gradual attenuation of the severity of Grainger's visions calls to mind a successful analysis where the dialogue between patient and analyst has enabled the earlier conflict to be confronted, worked-through, and overcome, and, at the end of the story, when we return to the living room at Pilgrim's Farm, there seems to be no sign of Grainger's trauma remaining at all.

We have already seen how by a process of displacement *Dead of Night*'s opening title sequence has enabled the objectification and neutralization of anxieties that the experience of the Blitz might have motivated in its audiences. In similar terms, the

Figure 3.5 *Dead of Night*: "Just room for one inside, sir."

Figure 3.6 *Dead of Night*: Any bus conductor on any day in normal life.

film's use of displacement in the Hearse Driver story has enabled an objectification and neutralization of an anxiety founded on someone's experience of the closeness of death, and of having killed—or maybe having killed—another person. Grainger's experiences could, therefore, be thought of as the metaphoric representations of the anxieties of any returning and traumatized veteran. But while this segment of *Dead of Night* has encouraged our belief that the repetition of the past may enable a progression from the experience of traumatic events, the ending of the Linking narrative suggests that, tragically, this is sometimes not the case.

Several authors have approached the Linking narrative by trying to ascertain what parts of it are "real" and what parts of it are contained within Walter Craig's recurring dream. Ivan Butler follows this line of reasoning when he analyzes a shot near the end of the film after Craig wakes at home and receives the telephone call from Eliot Foley inviting him for the weekend. During their conversation, the film cuts from showing Craig to a single shot of Foley talking to Craig on the telephone. Butler argues that:

> The film throughout has been seen from Craig's viewpoint. Even the stories, where he was not present, are seen as told to him. Now, suddenly, *we see*

Foley. Craig has not met him. The dream has faded. [...] This time, it is really happening. There will be no waking relief for Craig. This time, he drives to his doom.[16]

(Butler's italics)

Bruce Kawin considers that the ending of the Linking narrative should be viewed in rather more ambivalent terms. He draws our attention to a series of shots that occur soon afterward, when we see Craig arriving again at Pilgrim's Farm:

> We do not know whether the dream, with its inevitable events, has started again or whether this is the real-world event at last, because it would look the same either way. No matter how much Craig tries to escape, there is no escape, whether he is dreaming or finally visiting. The dream or event replays itself without a change, precisely as if it were a film that is starting over. *Dead of Night* is a narrative trap.[17]

I agree with Kawin that the ending of *Dead of Night* provides no escape for Craig and no real conclusion to the film's narrative. But I would like to approach the Linking narrative from a different angle and suggest that what the film is describing in the Linking narrative *in its entirety* amounts to a reccurring nightmare that does not need to be thought of as Craig's at all, but instead as one that could be experienced by any traumatized person as they are condemned merely to repeat the original traumatic event *ad infinitum*.

In *Beyond the Pleasure Principle*, Freud provides examples of traumatized patients for whom the process of working-through is unsuccessful, in that what is simply repetition for most patients becomes instead a *compulsion to repeat* that can ultimately lead to the breakdown of the analysis. Instead of actively working-through past situations and emotions with the analyst, these patients merely

> repeat all of these unwanted situations and painful emotions in the transference and revive them with the greatest ingenuity. They seek to bring about the interruption of the treatment while it is still incomplete; they contrive once more to feel themselves scorned, to oblige the physician to speak severely to them and treat them coldly.[18]

Freud defines the compulsion to repeat as being the force behind neurotic obsessive-compulsive behaviors and ideas, destructive compulsions in dysfunctional

---

[16] Butler, *The Horror Film*, p. 78.
[17] Bruce Kawin, *Horror and the Horror* Film (London, New York and Delhi: Anthem Press, 2012), p. 40.
[18] Sigmund Freud, *Beyond the Pleasure Principle*, in *The Standard Edition vol. XVIII*, ed. by James Strachey (London: The Hogarth Press, 1955; repr. 1981), p. 21.

relationships, and repetitive visions and dreams of the traumatized, and he describes victims of the compulsion to repeat as giving the impression of being pursued by a malignant fate and possessed by a "daemonic power."

Because the Linking narrative ends precisely as it began, we are given no sign that Craig is "finally visiting" Pilgrim's Farm or that his dream has "faded" at all. It seems instead that his dream will never end, and that Craig is caught in the grip of a force that is driving him—as he himself describes it at the end of the film—"towards something unspeakably evil." His dream therefore has the quality of a disastrously failed analysis, where the patient's psychical state does not progress from passive to active by means of the process of working-through, but instead deteriorates from passive to fragmented.

Over the course of the Hearse Driver story, Grainger's mental state has progressed from the passivity of his delirium to the activity of his recovery and his union with Joyce, and his recovery is evidenced by the gradual attenuation of the severity of his visions and his joining Joyce in the Linking narrative. In contrast, within the Linking narrative, Craig's condition deteriorates from one that allows him to listen to the stories of the other guests objectively, to one in which the distinction between the stories and his own inner world collapses entirely. At the end of the film, the structure of the film itself becomes fragmented, and Craig finds himself trapped inside the stories; in Peter Cortland's mirror-image bedroom, then pursuing and striking Sally O'Hara at the Christmas party, and finally in the prison cell with Hugo Fitch. Because *Dead of Night* ends precisely as it began, the Linking narrative is revealed as being concerned less with a description of the serial conflict between Freudian psychoanalysis and the uncanny manifestation of the paranormal, and more with victims of trauma who are so radically traumatized by their experiences that they cannot be helped by psychoanalytic intervention or any other form of intervention at all, as they are merely condemned to relive their traumas repeatedly *ad infinitum*.

The Dread of Woman: Sexual Difference, Female Sexual Development, and Motherhood in the Christmas Party Story

… and what about motherhood? And the blissful consciousness of bearing a new life within oneself? And the ineffable happiness of the increasing expectation of the appearance of a new being? And the joy when it finally makes its appearance and one holds it for the first time in one's arms? And the deep pleasurable feeling of satisfaction in suckling it and the happiness of the whole period when the infant needs her care?[19]

While it has become obvious that many of the narrative strands of *Dead of Night* are influenced by psychoanalytic discourses surrounding psychical trauma, the film is also subject to other discourses that had emerged in the 1920s and 1930s from the turn in psychoanalysis away from the father and toward the mother. These surface in *Dead of Night* in the close attention that the film pays particularly in its second, third, and fourth segments to ideas of sexual difference, sexual development, feminine psychology, and motherhood. They are one of the motivational forces behind the problematic relationship between Joan and Peter Cortland in the Haunted Mirror story, and they are central to the dilemmas posed by the fraught three-way romantic liaison between Mary Lee, George Parratt, and Larry Potter in the Golfing Story. They also influence how the figure of Sally O'Hara is ordered in the Christmas Party story, and how her character relates to the story's two male characters: her young suitor Jimmy Watson and the phantom Francis Kent.

Sally O'Hara introduces her story by stating that she and her family had spent the previous Christmas in Somerset where she had been invited to a children's party by Mrs. Watson, an old school friend of her mother's. As the story begins, we see a group of children playing "Blind Man's Buff" around a Christmas tree in the hall of a large country house. At the center of the group are Sally and Mrs. Watson's son Jimmy, both seeming somewhat older than the rest of the group. Sally is blindfolded, and, as she gropes around, she catches hold of Jimmy and he kneels in front of her. As she feels his face to work out whom she has caught, Sally grasps Jimmy's nose and says: "No one else could have such a silly nose. It's Jimmy" (Figure 3.7). The group of younger children then propose a game of sardines, choosing Sally as the one to hide.

Sally conceals herself upstairs in a small, curtained-off window seat, but only moments later, she is discovered by Jimmy. We can see that it is snowing outside, and Sally shivers and complains of the cold and Jimmy responds by putting his arm around her. Jimmy then says that he knows a much better place to hide, takes Sally's hand and leads her up a spiral staircase into a dusty attic. Jimmy tells Sally that the house is haunted, and that a murder had been committed there in

---

[19] Karen Horney, "The Flight from Womanhood: The Masculinity Complex in Women as Viewed by Men and by Women," in *Feminine Psychology* (New York and London: W. W. Norton, 1973), p. 60.

Figure 3.7 *Dead of Night*: Jimmy and Sally: "Nobody else could have such a silly nose."

the 1860s by a girl who "must have been crackers, I suppose really. Strangled him and then half cut his head off." The two then proceed to act out imagined elements of the haunting, and then Jimmy pulls Sally toward him saying: "Give us a kiss, Sal." Sally reacts by dragging down a dusty rotten sack from the ceiling onto Jimmy, and he turns away from her coughing and sneezing and smothered in dust. Sally watches him for a moment, a little staggered by the effect of her act, but as soon as she has seen that he is alright, she leaves the room.

Leon Balter describes the Christmas Party story as taking place during Sally's transition from asexual latency to sexual adolescence, arguing that this is suggested graphically at the opening of the story in how she and Jimmy are markedly older than the other guests and obviously already pubescent, and symbolically in their actions during the game:

> In the game of Blind Man's Bluff, she (blindfolded) holds the boy's nose and pronounces it both his and (in adolescent fashion) "silly". And, in case the audience fails to see the boy's nose as a phallic symbol, the elongated nose on his upturned mask points upward at an extremely suggestive angle.[20]

---

[20] Leon Balter, "Dead of Night," in *The Psychoanalytic Quarterly* 79:3 (2010), p. 763.

I agree with Balter that the difference in age between Sally and Jimmy and the younger children makes it clear that they both are at the point of sexual adolescence, and that the sexual nature of their actions in the game reinforces this notion. However, what I want to propose is that the Christmas Party story is concerned more with the *differences* between Sally and Jimmy's nascent sexualities than the similarities, and that these differences have already been indicated to us at the outset of the story by the costumes that Sally and Jimmy are wearing.

As Jez Conolly and David Owain Bates have noted, while the younger children are dressed in a random assortment of costumes, Sally's and Jimmy's immediately signal their connection to each other and also their differences because we recognize them as those worn by two of the stock characters of the *commedia dell'arte*.[21] Sally is wearing the cap, apron, and low-cut "folly dress" of the flirtatious lady's maid Columbina, and Jimmy the randomly patched tight-fitting jacket and trousers of the mischievous manservant Arlecchino. John Rudlin points out that the costumes, gestures, and masks of the *commedia dell'arte* stock characters are expressive of their fixed character traits, and, while within the conventions of Commedia these traits are immutable, they are not in any way reductive because each of the characters contains several paradoxes. According to Rudlin, the character traits of Columbina are that she is "strong and attractive," "autonomous and self-sufficient," but, while she loves Arlecchino, Columbina at the same time "sees through him [...] scolds him, punishes him. Her affections seem to flow through her physically, but she always holds something back." Also, while Columbina seems sexually knowing, she is also sometimes a virgin, when it suits her.[22] As for Arlecchino, "his paradox is that of having a dull mind and an agile body [...] he responds to everything—hunger, love, danger—in a way that is taken to apocalyptic proportions and then forgotten entirely—until next time." He is "in love with Columbina, but his sexual appetite is immediate in terms of any passing woman."[23]

Balter is right to draw our attention to the phallic symbolism of Jimmy's upturned mask that he wears in the first of these two sequences, but what he does not point out is that this mask is not the one usually worn in the Commedia by Arlecchino, but by the boastful charlatan figure Il Capitano. Again, according to Rudlin, the paradoxical character traits of Il Capitano are

---

[21] Jez Conolly and David Owain Bates, *Dead of Night* (Leighton Buzzard: Auteur, 2015), p. 61.
[22] John Rudlin, *Commedia dell'Arte: An Actor's Handbook* (London and New York: Routledge, 1994), pp. 129–30.
[23] Ibid., p. 79.

that while he sees himself as a great military hero, he is really a coward, "easily deflated", and also "threatened [...] by Columbina's plain speaking, especially in matters of sexual conquest."²⁴

In the first of the two sequences I have described, the paradoxical character traits of Columbina (self-sufficient, virginal, and yet sexually knowing) are seen to be Sally's in her standing over Jimmy and feeling his face and grasping his nose, and those of Arlecchino/El Capitano (ardent, boastful, but easily deflated) are seen to be Jimmy's in his kneeling in front of Sally and allowing himself to be made the object of Sally's amusement. While it has certainly been made clear to us that Sally and Jimmy are both at the point of sexual adolescence, what is being emphasized in this sequence is that the nature of this transition is different for each of them, and that the process of this transition has given rise to an asymmetry in the power relations that now exist between them. This idea is developed further in the next sequence.

After Sally has invited Jimmy's attentions in the window seat, and then allowed him to lead her by the hand up into the attic, she listens to Jimmy's tale of the haunting. However, he suddenly breaks off his story saying: "Of course, there's a lot more but you're too young." As he is saying this, the film cuts from a close two-shot with Jimmy on the left of the frame and Sally on the right, to a close shot of Sally as Jimmy is passing behind her. Just as he says: "You're too young," Sally adopts a knowing expression and arches her eyebrow and, moments later, she reacts to Jimmy's asking her for a kiss by pulling the dusty sack down on top of him. The point that being made here is that, while Jimmy thinks that he is the master of the situation, it is Sally who is the one in the position of power and not Jimmy, and it is Jimmy who is left deflated and somewhat humiliated by Sally's actions.

After leaving the attic, Sally passes along a dimly lit corridor and stops at a doorway when she hears what seems to be the sound of a child crying. As she enters the room, Sally pauses for a second on the threshold, and because the camera is observing her slightly from below, she seems very tall, and her form fills the doorway. The room appears to be a nursery, and here Sally discovers a little boy of about eight years old who is dressed in clothes of a much earlier period. The boy explains that he is Francis Kent, and that he shares the room with his older half-sister Constance. He says to Sally that Constance is "grown up, like you," and that "she hates me, she says she'd like to kill me." Sally sits the

---

²⁴ Ibid., pp. 122–3.

boy on her lap, wipes away his tears, and kisses him before tucking him into bed and singing him a lullaby. Only when the boy seems to be about to go to sleep does Sally turn away and leave the room.

Balter proposes that when Sally leaves Jimmy behind in the attic and enters the nursery

> her running away from the associated sexual excitement indicates that she still has some way to go to integrate her already mature sexuality with her still-lingering latency morality. However, crucial to the story, in her running away from this invitation to adult sexuality, *she runs back into the world of children.*[25]
>
> (Balter's italics)

But surely the opposite of this is true. In moving from the attic to the nursery, Sally's transition from asexual latency to sexual adolescence has been confirmed by the film precisely because she has left behind the world of childhood games that she has been playing with Jimmy and entered the world of motherhood in relation to Francis Kent. Sally's actions in comforting Francis in the nursery are obviously motherly. However, what is being emphasized in this sequence is that Sally's transition from sexual latency to sexual adolescence is different to Jimmy's because her transition means that she can now take on the qualities and spirit of *being a mother.*

Sally's transformation to motherhood is first hinted at when she unhesitatingly crosses the threshold into the nursery after she has heard the sound of a child crying. It becomes clearer in her joyful facial expression when she first sees Francis and realizes that he needs her to take care of him (Figure 3.8). It is emphasized moments later in formal terms by the film's use of lighting. While the close shot of Sally in the attic when Jimmy is saying: "You're too young" is lit with a low-key light that renders Sally's image two-dimensional and therefore unreal and subsumed by her surroundings, from the moment when she first sees Francis, Sally is lit with classical three-point lighting with a strong key light and back light that lends her shape and volume and that emphasizes her luminescence and her emergence from her surroundings as an individual and as a woman.

After Sally has returned downstairs and joined the other children at the party, the story ends, and we are returned to Pilgrim's Farm and Sally is taken home by her rather dominating mother to attend Uncle Edwin's birthday party. However, near the end of the film, after Walter Craig has followed his predetermined path

---

[25] Balter, "Dead of Night," p. 764.

Figure 3.8 *Dead of Night*: Sally as mother to the phantom Francis Kent.

in strangling the now-defenseless Dr. Van Straaten, Craig suffers his psychotic breakdown and Sally makes a brief re-appearance in another, shorter, version of the Christmas Party story.

This time it is Craig who is the one chosen to hide, and Sally, Jimmy, and the younger children begin to count. Craig conceals himself upstairs in the same small, curtained-off window seat where Sally had hidden previously, but Sally finds Craig almost immediately. When Sally flings open the curtain, she shouts: "I've got him, I've got him!," and Craig grabs hold of her and covers her mouth with his hand. Now, the camera tilts to forty-five degrees as Craig takes the place that Jimmy has occupied before with Sally on the spiral staircase, but instead of leading Sally by the hand, Craig forces her up the stairs and into the attic, and all the time Sally is screaming. Somehow, Sally manages to wriggle free from Craig's grasp and shouts for help, but Craig punches her savagely on the jaw and Sally staggers back into a rocking chair. Then, from a reverse angle, and with the camera tilted almost to the horizontal, the film overlaps Sally's fall and Craig stands menacingly over her, his fists clenched as if he is going to strike her again. The chair starts to rock, and Sally lies unconscious, her hair streaming back (Figure 3.9).

Figure 3.9 *Dead of Night*: Walter Craig hits Sally "savagely, viciously."

At the beginning of her seminal paper on female psychology "The Flight from Womanhood," Karen Horney observes that:

> In some of his latest works Freud has drawn attention with increasing urgency to a certain one-sidedness in our analytic researches. I refer to the fact that till quite recently the minds of boys and men only were taken as objects of investigation. The reason for this is obvious. Psychoanalysis is the creation of a male genius, and almost all those who have developed his ideas have been men. It is only right and reasonable that they should evolve more easily a masculine psychology and understand more of the development of men than of women.[26]

Horney asks how far the evolution of women as depicted by psychoanalysis has been measured by masculine standards, and whether this picture fails to present accurately the real nature of women. Horney suggests that what has been at the center of attention in psychoanalysis has been the genital difference between the sexes, and what has been left out are the different parts played by women and men in the function of reproduction. While Horney does not deny the

---

[26] Horney, "The Flight from Womanhood", p. 54.

existence of penis envy in women as such, she argues that, in their capacity for motherhood, women have

> a quite indisputable and by no means negligible physiological superiority. This is most clearly reflected in the unconscious of the male psyche in the boy's intense envy of motherhood. We are familiar with this envy as such, but it has hardly received due consideration as a dynamic factor. When one begins, as I did, to analyze men only after a fairly long experience of analyzing women, one receives a most surprising impression of the intensity of the envy of pregnancy, childbirth, and motherhood, as well as of the breasts and of the act of suckling.[27]

Horney proposes the intense masculine envy of motherhood as being a driving force in the establishment of the cultural values that exist between the sexes, and that this male envy of women is often not openly admitted by men but instead sublimated within the male drive toward cultural productivity:

> In the historic times that are known to us, this productivity has undoubtedly been incomparably greater in men that in women. Is not the tremendous strength in men of the impulse to creative work in every field precisely due to their feeling of playing a relatively small part in the creation of living beings, which constantly impels them to an overcompensation in achievement?[28]

Horney asks whether, if we are right in making this connection, we are confronted with the problem of why the envy of the male genital in women is less than the envy of the female genital in men?

In her paper "The Dread of Woman" Horney argues that, while the male child has acquired a conscious knowledge of the female genital by the time when he has reached puberty, he nevertheless comes to dread *something else* in women that he feels to be uncanny and mysterious. Horney concludes that if the male child grows up and continues to regard women in this way, then this feeling must be not of the dread of the female genital itself, but of the whole female sex, in whom he feels there resides a secret that he cannot define, one that can only relate ultimately to one thing: "the mystery of motherhood. Everything else is merely residue of the dread of this."[29]

If we are to think of Horney's work as having a discursive relation to how *Dead of Night* lays out Sally's and Jimmy's respective transitions from sexual latency to

---

[27] Ibid., pp. 60–1.
[28] Ibid., p. 61.
[29] Karen Horney, "The Dread of Woman," in *Psychoanalysis and Male Sexuality*, ed. by Hendrick M. Ruitenbeek (New Haven, CT: College & University Press, 1966), pp. 90–1.

sexual adolescence, then Craig's treatment of Sally at the end of the film must be read as compensating for the dread that her capacity for motherhood has motivated in Jimmy. But if this is true, then how are we to reconcile Craig's act of violence toward Sally with the level of sympathy that we have by now built up for Craig?

A reading of Craig's striking of Sally as an act of compensation for the dread that her ascent to womanhood has inspired in Jimmy—and by extension in the male generally—would define *Dead of Night* as being bound by ideas that are ideologically normative in the extreme. However, because the film defines this act as being performed by Craig and not Jimmy, and because Craig's act exists not within Jimmy's need for retribution for the threat that Sally has posed to him, but within Craig's obvious state of psychosis, this definition is called into question. In this instance, *Dead of Night* should instead be read as operating as an ideological psychoanalytic discourse that is not normative but subversive, in that the film is defining the male need to compensate for women's physiological superiority as only being able to be countenanced within Craig's obvious state of psychosis, and—by extension—only within the vicissitudes of male psychopathology. This idea of psychopathological need for the male to compensate in the face of the threat posed by the reproductive potential of the female is taken up and developed in the next of *Dead of Night*'s stories.

Projection, Introjection, and the Identification with the Aggressor: The Interplay between Subjectivity and Objectivity and Reality and Fantasy in the Haunted Mirror Story

When we have returned to Pilgrim's Farm after Sally's story is over, and just before Joan Cortland begins her story, Joan turns to face the camera and addresses Dr. Van Straaten. She says:

> Doctor, may I hope that you will be able to explain to me a happening which—to put it mildly—has always puzzled me? It started a few weeks after we had become engaged. It was the ninth of April to be exact. I remember the date because it was Peter's birthday. You know how difficult it is choosing presents for a man. They always seem to have everything they want.

The "happening" that Joan refers to is a series of unaccountable visions that Peter experiences while looking into the ornate mirror that Joan has given him for his birthday. Peter's visions occur in two cycles separated from each other by a period of several weeks. The first begins on his birthday and ends just before Joan and Peter's wedding, and the second plays out over the course of a weekend some weeks later. Even at the beginning of the story, Peter's character is defined by his passivity and the high level of his emotional dependency on Joan, and, as his visions begin to take hold, he becomes increasingly listless and unable to differentiate between reality and the other world that he sees in the mirror. The Haunted Mirror story confronts post-war male anxieties that have already been touched on in Christmas Party story; however, they are re-examined here via a specific engagement with psychoanalytic discourses related to the interplay between subjectivity and objectivity. The first part of this section focuses on the changing nature of the relationship between the external reality of the visions themselves and the dynamics of Peter's own internal world, and the second part investigates what is at stake at the end of the story when Joan too, for a moment, sees Peter's vision before breaking the mirror and bringing their visions to an end.

After Joan has introduced her story, a dissolve takes us from the living room at Pilgrim's Farm to the sitting room of Peter's modern London flat. Joan arrives with a large parcel, and Peter asks: "You haven't gone and had your portrait painted, have you?," to which Joan replies: "No, I thought you'd like to look at yourself." It turns out that the parcel contains an ornate Chippendale mirror, which Peter proceeds to fix to the wall behind the dressing table in his bedroom. As he is doing this, Joan sits on his bed and Peter asks her what sort of journey she has had. Joan replies that she has been given a lift to Peter's flat by Guy:

> PETER: Poor old Guy. What will he do when we get married? Hardly the big game shooting type, is he?
> JOAN: Hardly. He nearly put us into a ditch coming up, trying to avoid a rabbit.
> PETER: Fellow feeling, obviously.
> JOAN: You be careful. I'm very fond of Guy.
> PETER: Meaning that it pleases your disgusting female vanity to have him on a string. A spaniel would do just as well.
> JOAN: Mm, but spaniels don't have nice comfortable Bentleys, do they?

Immediately after this exchange, Joan and Peter stand side by side in front of the mirror and gaze at their reflections and Joan pronounces them a "handsome couple," but Peter seems to see something strange in one corner of the mirror that he cannot define. That evening, when Peter is dressing for dinner, he stands in front of the mirror and is amazed when he sees reflected not his own bedroom, but a wood-paneled candle-lit room of a much earlier period with a log fire burning in the grate and a large four-poster bed draped with tapestries and carved with vine leaves (Figure 3.10). Peter closes his eyes, and when he opens them again the reflection has returned to normal.

Later the same day, Joan and Peter dine out together, and she asks him whether anything is the matter. Peter replies that he has seen something strange in the mirror: "When I was dressing this evening, just as I was tying my tie, I suddenly noticed that the reflection was all wrong [...] it wasn't my room I was seeing, it was some other room." After dinner, Peter returns to his flat alone and he sees the vision in the mirror again, but although he closes his eyes tight as he has done earlier that evening, he is horrified when he opens them again and finds that his vision of the other room remains in the mirror.

The couple spend the next few weeks house hunting and they find a house in Chelsea, and while Joan notices that Peter seems preoccupied and a bit jumpy and irritable, she assumes that this is just eve-of-wedding nerves. When Joan arrives at Peter's flat only days before the wedding, the couple argue and Peter

Figure 3.10 *Dead of Night*: Peter's first vision in the mirror.

apologizes, saying that he has not been sleeping well. However, he does admit that he has consulted a doctor because he has been seeing the visions in the mirror with increasing regularity and he is no longer able to control them:

> At first, if I made an enormous effort of will, the reflection used to change back to what it ought to be. But lately, however hard I try, it—it doesn't change any more. The only thing is not to look in it at all. But in a queer sort of way, it fascinates me. I feel as if that room—the one in the mirror—were trying to claim me, to draw me into it. It almost becomes the real room and my own bedroom imaginary, and I know that there is something waiting for me on the other side of the mirror, something evil, monstrously evil—and that if I cross that dividing line, something awful will happen.

Joan then commands Peter to stands with her in front of the mirror, and when she clasps his hand, Peter finds that he can make the vision disappear. A fortnight later, the couple are married, and for a while Peter completely loses his fear of the mirror.

Peter's second cycle of visions begins a few weeks later. Joan leaves to spend the weekend with her mother in Chichester, and Peter stays behind in London because of a big audit that is being rushed through. So, Peter is left in their new house on his own. The accentuation of the severity of Peter's visions that had been gradual in the first cycle now increases markedly, and Peter is no longer able to differentiate at all between the real world and the world that he sees in the mirror.

While it seems at first glance as if Peter's first cycle of visions begins with the arrival of the mirror, this is not the case. After Peter has unwrapped the mirror and Joan has fixed them a drink, Peter pronounces the mirror "a beauty" and "a honey," and the couple raise their glasses to each other and stand contentedly in front of the mirror admiring their reflections (Figure 3.11). In fact, the visions begin a little later, after the conversation that Joan and Peter have in Peter's bedroom about Guy. During this exchange, it becomes clear that Guy has been a long-standing factor in Joan and Peter's relationship, and that Peter has negotiated the presence of Guy in a way that is markedly different to Joan. While Peter feigns to make light of the situation by referring to him as "poor old Guy" and suggesting that Guy must have "fellow feeling" with the rabbit that he has swerved to avoid on the journey to Peter's flat, Joan responds to Peter seriously, and with a warning: "You be careful. I'm very fond of Guy." Thus, the claim that Joan will make at the end of the story that "we've always treated him as a joke" is

Figure 3.11 *Dead of Night*: "Hmmm, handsome couple."

signaled here as being false, and Peter's reply to this: "Yes, I know we've always pretended to", as being nearer the truth.

According to Peter Hutchings, Peter's character has been defined as "inadequate" in the face of Joan's strength from the outset of the story. Hutchings states that: "The episode opens with him seated in his flat waiting for Joan to appear, a position usually reserved—in cinema, at least—for the female half of the relationship," and that

> it is Peter rather than Joan who suffers from the again conventionally feminine eve-of-wedding nerves. [...] This is further underlined by Joan's gift of the mirror to Peter, which emasculates him in two related ways. First, the mirror in art has frequently been used to symbolize female vanity. Second, the male gaze is here associated with a narcissism which signals a fascination evident throughout the film with images of male introspection.[30]

I agree with Hutchings that the story conveys Peter's inadequacy in relation to Joan's strength to the viewer from the beginning, but I would like to go further

---

[30] Hutchings, *Hammer and Beyond*, pp. 31–2.

and propose that the story emphasizes Peter's inadequacy by defining it as a factor that is not only obvious to us, but one that is central to the asymmetric nature of Joan and Peter's relationship. This can be seen most clearly in the sequence that shows them at dinner at the expensive restaurant where Peter has taken Joan after their disagreement about Guy.

After they have finished dancing, the couple return to their table and Peter remarks on the heat, saying: "We ought to have worn our grass skirts." When they have taken their seats, Peter lights Joan's cigarette, and she looks at him seriously at first and asks whether anything is the matter. Then, she observes: "You seem to have been a bit broody all evening," to which Peter replies that he is: "A bit limp with the heat I expect." As Joan is speaking, she is almost center frame and facing the camera and Peter is sitting on the right with his back to the camera, the shot therefore favors Joan. When Joan says that Peter has been "a bit broody," she only just manages to keep a straight face, and when Peter replies that he is "a bit limp with the heat I expect," she laughs openly. Thus, the film's placing of the couple in the frame has drawn our attention to Joan's amusement at Peter's words and not to Peter's expression (Figure 3.1). And, because Peter can only react to Joan's joke about his "broodiness" by making another joke about his being "a bit limp," his words and the formal layout of the shot have the effect of aligning us with Joan's perception of Peter's inadequacy and not Peter's obvious need for Joan's reassurance at the precise moment when he first acknowledges his breakdown.

The asymmetry of power that has come to exist in Joan and Peter's relationship is defined by the story in terms of the high level of Joan's sexual confidence and the high level of Peter's insecurity. But the story also suggests that there is an *economic* asymmetry at work in their relationship, which is in turn amplified by the asymmetry that it implies as existing between Peter and Joan's implied lover, Guy. Joan makes the existence of the first of these asymmetries clear to us when she states to Peter that the mirror was "very expensive" and that she has been "very generous" in giving it to him. The second is made obvious in Joan's assumption that Peter should accept her ongoing relationship with Guy because Guy has a "nice comfortable Bentley," while seconds later defining her use for Peter only in terms of his being "useful about the house." So, Peter's suggestion immediately after this exchange that they should go out on the town, "dress up," and "spend lots of money" can be read as a dual defensive strategy operating against the threat that Joan poses to him, and just as much against the threat posed to him by Joan's relationship with Guy.

The problem of Peter's sexual insecurity in relation to Joan's liaison with Guy and the highly unstable state of Joan and Peter's relationship in general are the backdrop for the visions that Peter begins to see in the mirror. There is no accounting for how Peter's visions come to contain elements of the story of Francis Etherington, which presumably he has never heard, and which will only be told to Joan later by the antique dealer Mister Rutherford during her weekend away with her mother. This is a supernatural element of the story that the viewer accepts without question in the same way as we accept without question the presence of the phantom Francis Kent in the nursery in the Christmas Party story. Setting this element of the segment aside, what I would like to propose is that Peter's visions can usefully be thought of as being ordered around the Freudian psychoanalytic concept of *projection*; a process by which unacceptable internal impulses are externalized and imagined as existing instead outside the self in the character of another.

After spending the early years of his career in the study of hysteria, infantile sexuality, and the psychoneuroses, Freud's attention turned to the psychoses, and particularly to whether there might be a common factor at work in patients suffering from conditions such as paranoia, schizophrenia, and manic depression. In a letter to Ferenczi of February 1908, Freud reports that a female patient of his is enduring a "mature paranoia," and that, while he feels she is probably beyond the limits of therapeutic intervention, he has nevertheless learned one thing from her:

> From a theoretic point of view the case has confirmed what I already knew, namely, that in these forms of paranoia it is a case of detaching the homosexual component of the libido. In consequence of juvenile homosexual fixation, she is attracted to all the women with whom she suspects her husband of being involved. She struggles against this attraction and projects it onto her husband; her libido for her husband is strengthened by being detached from the women.[31]

Later the same year, Freud came across the case of Daniel Paul Schreber, an eminent civil servant and later judge with a long history of depression, persecutory anxiety, narcissism, and paranoia, who had given a graphic account of his various disorders in his autobiography, *Memoirs of My Nervous Illness*. Although Freud never met Schreber, he uses this account as the basis for a case study, proposing that Schreber's illness must have begun with his intense erotic

---

[31] Eva Brabant, Ernst Falzeder, and Patrizia Giampieri-Deutsch, eds., *The Correspondence of Sigmund Freud and Sandor Ferenczi* (Cambridge, MA, and London: The Belknap Press of Harvard University Press, 1992), p. 5.

attachment to his psychiatrist, Professor Flechsig. Freud puts forward the idea that the principal forms of paranoia begin with unacceptable psychosexual wishes that have been repressed by the patient, and that these delusions might usefully be thought of as contradictions of the single proposition: "*I* (a man) *love him* (a man)."[32] As Jean-Michel Quinodoz explains:

> Since that proposition is unacceptable to the individual consciousness, it is transformed into the opposite: "*I do not* love *him—I* hate *him!*" The intolerable feeling of hate is repressed into the unconscious then is projected on to someone in the external world: "*I hate him*" thus becomes "He hates *(persecutes) me, which will justify me in hating him.*" In this way, the unconscious feeling of hate within the individual makes its appearance as though it were an external perception: "*I do not* love *him—I* hate *him, because HE PERSECUTES ME.*"[33]
>
> (Freud's italics and capitals)

In psychoanalysis, projection is defined as the process whereby an internal perception is suppressed, and after undergoing a certain kind of distortion enters the consciousness in the form of an external perception. Freud proposes that projection is the main characteristic of symptom-formation in all forms of paranoia, including persecutory anxiety and delusions of jealousy, and that it must also have a part to play in normal life in connecting our internal consciousness to the external world.

Toward the end of his investigation of the Schreber case, Freud seems to contradict his previous statement that projection is *only* an action that involves the externalization of an unacceptable internal impulse when he states that:

> What forces itself so noisily upon our attention is the process of recovery, which undoes the work of repression and brings back the libido again on to the people it had abandoned. In paranoia this process is carried out by the method of projection. It was incorrect to say that the perception which was suppressed internally is projected outwards; the truth is rather, as we now see, that what was abolished internally returns from without.[34]

What Freud had come to realize was that projection is not simply a matter of the expulsion of unacceptable feelings into the outside world, but a complex

---

[32] Sigmund Freud, "Psycho-Analytic Notes on an Autobiographical Account of a Case of Paranoia (Dementia Paranoides)," in *The Standard Edition vol. XII*, ed. by James Strachey (London: The Hogarth Press, 1958; repr. 1999), p. 63.

[33] Jean-Michel Quinodoz, *Reading Freud: A Chronological Explanation of Freud's Writings* (New York and London: Routledge, 2004), p. 104.

[34] Freud, "Psycho-Analytic Notes on an Autobiographical Account of a Case of Paranoia," p. 71.

interplay of fantasies that also involves the return or *introjection* of these feelings in changed form back into the self. Freud concludes that "the thorough examination of the process of projection which we have postponed to another occasion will clear up our remaining doubts on this subject"; however as his editor notes, there is no trace of any such later discussion existing, and it would remain to object relations theorists such as Klein and Winnicott to expand on this theme in the decades that followed.

While Freud's concept of projection is not taken to a theoretical conclusion, it is nevertheless useful to think of the Schreber case as having a discursive relation to how the Haunted Mirror story connects Peter's sexual insecurities to the visions he sees in the mirror. In the same way that Freud establishes that the principal forms of paranoia all begin with unacceptable psychosexual wishes being initially suppressed and then projected onto the character of another, in the Haunted Mirror story, the basis of Peter's illness is defined as the suppression of his sexual and economic inadequacies in relation to Joan and the projection of these feelings onto the story of Francis Etherington.

The story is told to Joan by the antique dealer Mister Rutherford while she is staying with her mother for the weekend in Chichester. Mister Rutherford's account establishes that Etherington was "a man of dominating character, arrogant, reckless, handsome, and of a violent temper" who married a beautiful heiress, a Miss Pelling:

> The couple retired to Marsden Lacy, where they lived contentedly for a time. Then suddenly, disaster overtook them. Out hunting one day, Etherington was thrown by his horse, which then rolled on him, his spine was injured, and he was never again able to do more than drag himself a few paces from his bed. Unfortunately, the effect of such constraint on a man of his enormous energy was more than his mind could endure. He became morose, embittered, suspicious. Above all, of his wife. Quite without reason, he began accusing the poor lady of betraying him, with his friends—with strangers, with his servants. Had she not been so devoted to him, she certainly would have left him, and, indeed, it would have been better for her had she done so. For one day, in an access of jealous rage, he strangled her, and then sat down in front of the mirror—your mirror—and cut his throat.

In tracing the discursive connection between the Haunted Mirror story and the case of Schreber, we must conclude that what emerges in Peter's visions are aspects of Peter's own internal world that have been initially suppressed by him and then projected onto an external other in different form. In his visions, the listless and avowedly neutered post-war accountant, Peter, is transformed into the enormously energetic, arrogant, reckless, and handsome country squire Francis Etherington. In similar terms, Peter's spartan, cold, modern bedroom is transformed into the Victorian Gothic sensuality of the mirror bedroom, and Joan, who in real life poses such a threat to Peter, is metamorphosed into the devoted and beautiful heiress Miss Pelling. In effect, Peter's visions can be understood as nothing less than a defensive re-ordering of the post-war world of uncertain gender relationships, which takes the form for him of a return to an imagined pre-war *status quo* of dominant masculinity and submissive femininity.

But if we are to assume a discursive connection between the Schreber case and the logic of the Haunter Mirror story, then surely the story should also follow Freud's logic at the end of the Schreber case and define Peter's suppressed and abolished wishes as returning from his projections and re-entering his own psyche?

After hearing the story and realizing the implications that its conclusion has for Peter, Joan rushes home, and when she bursts through the door, she finds Peter sitting in front of the mirror waiting for her. Peter says: "Something gone wrong with your plans for the weekend?" Joan now approaches him, hesitantly at first, but then immediately regaining her composure. She smiles slightly and then takes off her coat, flinging it casually onto the bed saying: "I haven't the faintest idea what you're talking about." But now Peter's character seems to be completely transformed, and in a precise reversal of the shot in the restaurant sequence, with Peter now on the left of the frame facing the camera and Joan with her back to the camera on the right, far from capitulating in the face of Joan's strength as no doubt he would have done before, he instead confronts her saying:

> Well, what's the matter? Why have you come back? No, let me guess. You were enjoying a pleasant weekend with Guy, but he was called away, so you had to come back to me [...] But this time I've had enough, and I'm going to punish you as you deserve to be punished.

As the final sequence of the story builds toward its climax, Peter becomes ever more confident, and Joan ever more apprehensive as she comes to realize that the asymmetry of power that existed up until now in their relationship has been overturned. As the couple struggle in front of the mirror, and as then Peter attempts to strangle Joan to punish her for her "infidelity," Joan, for a second, sees Peter's vision (Figure 3.12). While Peter's own unacceptable character traits have been suppressed, distorted, and then projected outwards onto the fantasy of Francis Etherington, what has returned from without at this moment is precisely Peter's

Figure 3.12 *Dead of Night*: Joan threatened with her extinction.

fantasized figure of Etherington himself, whose character traits have now been introjected by Peter enabling him—if only for an instant—to prevail over Joan.

But why does Joan see the room only now and not before this moment, and what is at stake in the fact that what Joan is now seeing in the mirror seems to us to be the same as what Peter has seen before?

The story carefully underpins the idea that Joan's vision is the same as Peter's by having Joyce state to Dr. Van Straaten after it has ended that "Joan saw the room in the mirror as well as Peter." But if we are to think of the film as laying out Peter's vision as elements of his unacceptable wishes being projected outwards, then what Joan sees cannot be explained as a projection of her unacceptable wishes because she betrays none of Peter's insecurities, and even if she did, then her projections would certainly be configured differently to Peter's.

When we have returned to the Linking narrative after the Haunted Mirror story is over, Dr. Van Straaten accounts for Joan's vision by defining it as "a case of crypto-amnesia. The transmissibility of an illusion by one person to one or more other persons who are emotionally cohesive is well established." While the doctor's words seem to make little sense to the weekend guests at Pilgrim's Farm, his idea that Peter's illusions have been in some way transmitted to Joan recalls Ferenczi's and Anna Freud's idea of how feelings of guilt are transmitted in the aftermath of trauma within a psychical defense mechanism that they term the *identification with the aggressor*.

In his paper "Confusion of the Tongues between the Adults and the Child," Ferenczi describes the aftermath of a sexual attack on a child. Ferenczi states that the child victim's immediate impulse after the attack is one of "rejection, hatred, disgust and energetic refusal," and if these anxieties are allowed to grow and reach a certain level of extremity, they must lead to an introjection of certain elements of the aggressor's psyche:

> *The same anxiety, however, if it reaches a certain maximum, compels them to subordinate themselves like automatons to the will of the aggressor, to divine each one of his desires and to gratify these; completely oblivious of themselves they identify with the aggressor.*[35]

(Ferenczi's italics)

In similar terms, in *The Ego and the Mechanisms of Defence*, Anna Freud argues that, in the moments after a sexual assault, the child

> introjects some characteristic of an anxiety object and so assimilates an anxiety experience which he has just undergone. Here, the mechanism of identification or introjection is combined with a second important mechanism. By impersonating the aggressor, assuming his attributes or imitating his aggression, the child transforms himself from the person threatened into the person who makes the threat.[36]

By means of the identification with the aggressor, therefore, the victim's position is turned from passivity to activity in that both the attack and the attacker cease to exist for the victim as rigid external entities, and so the situation can be controlled. However, this relief often comes at a very high cost to the victim. As Judit Mészáros explains, the use of this defense "brings about a paradoxical situation: it ensures survival but at the price of perpetuating the traumatic situation, that is of allowing the possibility of repetition, taken *ad absurdum*, the aggression becomes acceptable, and the aggressor is tamed."[37]

---

[35] Sándor Ferenczi, "Confusion of the Tongues between the Adults and the Child," in *Final Contributions to the Problems and Methods of Psychoanalysis* (London: The Hogarth Press, 1955), p. 164.

[36] Anna Freud, *The Ego and the Mechanisms of Defence* (London: The Hogarth Press, 1966), p. 113.

[37] Judit Mészáros, "Building Blocks toward Contemporary Trauma Theory: Ferenczi's Paradigm Shift," in *The American Journal of Psychoanalysis* 70 (2010), p. 336.

In that it is only at this moment that Joan sees her vision in the mirror, and in that the vision that Joan sees seems to be the same as Peter's, Ferenczi's and Anna Freud's idea of the identification with the aggressor seem aligned with how the Haunted Mirror story lays out its final moments. Threatened with her extinction, Joan has no other course but to identify with her aggressor, Peter, and to introject his fantasy in an unconscious defensive action that subordinates her vision to his and so her survival is assured. But if we are to accept the relationship between these psychoanalytic ideas and the layout of the film's narrative to be true, then why does Joan only seconds later smash the mirror and obliterate her introjection of Peter's vision and so abandon her defense against Peter's aggression?

Charles Barr argues that the final moments of the Haunted Mirror story are characterized by a high level of ambivalence in that:

> It is by her sudden insight and strength that [Joan] saves [Peter] from re-enacting the violence stored in the mirror world and in himself: she struggles with him and smashes the mirror. But the effect is to restore the *status quo*, this time definitively. He no longer remembers the nightmare, and they are free to go back to being a charming young couple, which is what they presumably will do. It is like a lobotomy.[38]

While I agree with Barr that Joan's breaking of the mirror is a demonstration of her strength and her understanding of the threat that Peter poses to her, Joan's action should be interpreted not as having the effect of restoring the *status quo* but absolutely rejecting it. Seen in Ferenczi's and Anna Freud's terms, by breaking the mirror and bringing the visions to an end, Joan is defined as deciding at this point that the situation that she finds herself in with Peter must be ended, and that there must be no possibility of the situation ever happening again. In effect, by breaking the mirror, she has declined the possibility of any further relationship with Peter because she has rejected her subordination to Peter's fantasy entirely.

At the conclusion of the Hearse Driver story, Grainger and Joyce are re-united in the present of the Linking narrative and their reproductive potential has been ensured by his return to health and their union in marriage. In some ways, the ending of the Haunted Mirror story predicts the ending of the Linking narrative when Craig strikes Sally as an act of retribution that is shown to exist within his obvious state of psychosis. So, in the final analysis, the Haunted Mirror story

---

[38] Charles Barr, *Ealing Studios* (London: Studio Vista, 1993), pp. 56–7.

must be read as the counterpoint to the Hearse driver story in that it defines the *status quo* of pre-war dominant masculine and submissive feminine sexual relationships as only being able to be defined within the deluded distortions of paranoid male fantasy. And when the Haunted Mirror story has ended, far from going back to being a charming young couple, Peter disappears from *Dead of Night*'s narrative completely and he is never mentioned again, and the strong and independent figure of Joan emerges as the only survivor of her story.

4

"What Does a Woman Want?"

Childhood Trauma, Female Desire, and Female Subjectivity in *The Seventh Veil* and *Madonna of the Seven Moons*

Introduction to *The Seventh Veil*

As Sue Harper has pointed out, the outbreak of war in 1939 meant that the fabric of everyday British life was transformed. Two major changes that affected women's lives during the Second World War were that

> they could be conscripted, and there were more opportunities for sexual freedom. The film industry dealt with these changes in an extremely nervous and selective way. For the first time, films were made which foregrounded female employment: *Millions Like Us* and *The Lamp Still Burns* were released in 1943. The sea-change in women's sexual behaviour was examined in an indirect form in melodramas about female desire, such as *Madonna of the Seven Moons* (1944) and *The Seventh Veil* (1945)[1]

The independent Sydney Box production *The Seventh Veil* was enormously successful both commercially and critically in Britain and America following its release in the winter of 1945/6, and it would be one of the official British entries at the Cannes Film Festival and Muriel and Sydney Box would win the Academy Award for best original screenplay the following year. The film has many of the qualities of the contemporary melodrama, but it is unusual in that the romance between its two main characters, Francesca and Nicholas, is rendered fraught during much of the film by their respective neurotic obsessions. The film makes it clear that their neuroses have resulted from traumatic events they have suffered

---

[1] Sue Harper, *Women in British Cinema: Mad, Bad and Dangerous to Know* (London and New York: Continuum, 2000), p. 30.

during their childhoods such as parental loss, physical abuse, and childhood abandonment, and toward the end of the film a psychoanalyst, Dr. Larsen, helps Francesca to address her various dilemmas, enabling her to re-enter the world of functioning human relationships.

Gainsborough's *Madonna of the Seven Moons*, released a few months before *The Seventh Veil* in January 1945, followed *The Man in Grey* and *Fanny by Gaslight* as the third in the series of highly profitable melodramas produced by the studio between 1943 and 1947. These proved to be the antidote to the mainly realist films made in the early years of the war such as *The Bells Go Down* and *In Which We Serve*, which had furthered the war effort by promoting ideas of community, duty, and social responsibility. According to Marcia Landy, the Gainsborough melodramas represent the heyday of the British woman's film, popular because they included the work of indigenous and imaginative artists, new stars such as James Mason, Margaret Lockwood, and Stewart Granger, and exotic narratives playing out in often remote settings that touched on everyday conflicts concerning women's experience. These films appealed predominantly to female audiences, portraying women as being divided against themselves and facing conflicting demands:

> The women are either paragons of virtue and respectability or violators of social conventions. In certain instances illness serves as a metaphor for their uneasy relationship to the world of conventional expectation. Such issues as mother-daughter relations are occasionally raised, and in most cases, the uneasy relationship between men and women is resolved through death or marriage. But the resolutions of the films never quite conceal the unresolvable conflicts.[2]

There are many similarities to be found between *Madonna of the Seven Moons* and *The Seventh Veil*, most obviously in how their central female characters are defined by mental traumas suffered as children that render them unable to sustain conventional sexual relationships in later life. In the case of *Madonna of the Seven Moons*, Maddalena's traumas are defined as resulting from the loss of her mother at a young age, and from her rape by a stranger at the convent where she has been sent by her father immediately after her mother's death.

In the first section of this chapter, I assess what is at stake in *The Seventh Veil*'s appropriation of cultural psychoanalytic discourses surrounding early traumatic experiences and the neurotic effects that these experiences cause

---

[2] Marcia Landy, *British Genres: Cinema and Society, 1930–1960* (Princeton: Princeton University Press, 1991), pp. 195–6.

in later life. Then, I investigate how the psychoanalytic setting is used by the film to motivate objective investigation and subjective narration, and how the actions of Dr. Larsen attempt in ideological terms the reproduction of dominant beliefs connected to marriage, the family unit, and productive female sexuality. In the second section, I examine how *Madonna of the Seven Moons* harnesses Maddalena's schizophrenic psychosis as a means of interrogating her transgressive sexuality and defining it as psychopathological, and how the fragmentation of the film's narrative conclusion reveals the opposing ideological systems that influence its ambivalent worldview.

Synopsis of *The Seventh Veil*

At the beginning of *The Seventh Veil*, a brilliant young concert pianist, Francesca Cunningham (Ann Todd), has been placed in the care of a psychoanalyst, Dr. Larsen (Herbert Lom), after she has suffered a neurotic breakdown and attempted to take her own life. While previous attempts to treat Francesca's mental illness have been unsuccessful, Dr. Larsen administers a drug that enables her to recount to him the story of her problematic upbringing and the events in her later life that have led to her breakdown.

During her analysis under narcosis, Francesca reveals the story of her past to Dr. Larsen, and we learn that her mother died when she was six and that she was then sent to a boarding school. Here, she fails to obtain a music scholarship after she has been caned on her hands by the headmistress for a minor misdemeanor. At the age of fourteen, following the death of her father, Francesca is sent to live at the London home of a wealthy older second cousin, Nicholas (James Mason), who is her only relative. Nicholas walks with a limp, and, like Francesca, he has had a troubled upbringing. While Nicholas is distant toward Francesca and prone to fits of violent temper, he begins to encourage her to develop her talents as a pianist, eventually becoming her mentor and arranging for her tuition at the Royal Academy of Music. Soon afterward, she meets Peter Gay (Hugh McDermott), an American saxophonist, and they fall in love and decide to marry. When Francesca announces her intentions to Nicholas, he forbids the marriage and ensures that she is not able to pursue her relationship with Peter by taking her away to Europe, where he oversees her successful career as a concert pianist. Nicholas controls every aspect of Francesca's life, and for seven years they travel Europe together before finally returning to London.

Sometime later, Nicholas arranges for Francesca to have her portrait painted by a famous artist, Maxwell Leyden (Albert Lieven), and after Francesca and Max have become romantically involved, she agrees to live with him outside wedlock in his villa in Italy. When she informs Nicholas of this, he flies into a rage and strikes her hands repeatedly with his walking stick. Francesca flees the house with Max, but as they drive away their car crashes. While the physical effects of the crash on Francesca are limited to superficial burns to her hands, she suffers a mental breakdown and, fearing that she will never be able to play the piano again, she attempts to take her own life. She then descends into a cataleptic trance and is consigned to the care of Dr. Larsen.

When Francesca's narco-analysis is over, the narrative returns to the present. Dr. Larsen declares that Francesca's illness is the result of her past traumatic experiences, and he announces his intention to hypnotize her as he believes that this will remove the fixation that is the barrier to her recovery. While this procedure seems initially unsuccessful, Dr. Larsen is subsequently able to help Francesca to face up to her past traumas and return her to good health. He then assembles her three suitors, Nicholas, Max, and Peter, and announces that Francesca's past is over for her and that she is now able to decide whom she wants to be with. Francesca chooses Nicholas.

The Troubled Pasts of Francesca and Nicholas: Early Detrimental Experiences, the Predisposition to Traumatic Neurosis, and the Beginning of a Way Forward

As we have found in our close reading of certain sections of *The Halfway House* and *Dead of Night*, the narratives of many British trauma films are complicated by their combining events from their characters' pasts with events that are now taking place in their present. This narrative dilemma also exists in *The Seventh Veil*, and it seems useful by way of clarification to split the film's ninety minutes of running time into three sections. The first ten minutes makes up the film's first section; this is set in the present as Francesca wakes in a nursing home, attempts to take her own life by jumping off a bridge, and then begins her analysis with Dr. Larsen. The sixty minutes that follow form the film's second section; this is made up of Francesca's account of her past which she provides to Dr. Larsen during her narco-analysis, beginning when she is fourteen and ending when Francesca wakes again at the nursing home and we see her attempted suicide for the second time. The end of section two therefore slightly overlaps the beginning of section one. Occasionally during this middle section, we are returned from Francesca's account of the past to the present of the analytic setting, and, at several moments, Francesca's voice as she speaks to Dr. Larsen in the present operates as a voiceover for the action that we are shown taking place in the past. The third section of the film plays out over the final twenty minutes within a conventional linear timeline, as Francesca is guided by Dr. Larsen toward her "cure" and her union with Nicholas.

Toward the end of the film's first section, when Francesca has been rendered speechless and practically immobile after her attempted suicide, Dr. Larsen instructs a nurse to administer an injection. Francesca is seated to the left of the frame and Dr. Larsen is on the right and slightly behind her. He checks that she is on the edge of sleep by raising one of her eyelids, and then explains to her that she can now do what she likes and go where she pleases (Figure 4.1). He asks her:

> What would you like to do? Where would you like to go? Would you like to go back to school? You were happy when you were a little girl, weren't you? Would you like to go back and be happy again? Back to school? Listen, you are fourteen years of age now and you are at school.

Figure 4.1 *The Seventh Veil*: Francesca with Dr. Larsen: "Would you like to go back to school and be happy again?"

The three short sequences that follow form the beginning of the film's second section, describing certain events from Francesca's schooldays and then her arrival at Nicholas's house in London.

At the school, after an escapade with her friend Susan, Francesca is summoned to the headmistress's office, where she stands in front of the headmistress who is holding a cane in her hand. Francesca says: "Oh I know I must be punished of course but not on the hands, please not on my hands. Today is the music scholarship and if you cane me my hands will … oh please." The film then dissolves to a closer shot of Francesca as she flinches with pain as she is beaten repeatedly on her upturned hands (Figure 4.2). Another dissolve then transports us to the music room where Francesca is seated at a piano during the examination. In a voiceover, Francesca tells Dr. Larsen in her trance that: "By the afternoon my hands were swollen and blistered. I played so badly that I knew I hadn't a chance. I'd set my heart on that scholarship. Music was the only thing I really cared for even then." For a moment, Francesca continues to play, but then she buries her face in her hands, and then slowly rises from the piano and runs from the room.

Figure 4.2 *The Seventh Veil*: Francesca's childhood traumas.

Sometime later, Francesca is orphaned by the death of her father and sent to live with Nicholas. Having arrived at Nicholas's well-appointed London house, she is shown into his drawing room and stands nervously in the doorway at the rear of the frame while Nicholas sits facing us in the foreground. The huge room dwarfs her, and although perspective dictates that Nicholas must appear much larger than Francesca, his figure is rendered just as small as hers because of his being seated in an oversized armchair (Figure 4.3). As Nicholas addresses Francesca, he looks upwards and to his left at something outside of the frame. He says:

> Listen carefully. This is a bachelor establishment; it means I don't like women about the place. When I came to live in this house, I promised myself that no woman should ever enter it, and so far, none has. You are the first.

A short time afterward, we find that his look had been at a portrait of his mother that hangs above his fireplace, and yet we learn that his mother's name is never mentioned in the house as she has run away with a singer, abandoning Nicholas when he was twelve.

Figure 4.3 *The Seventh Veil*: Orphaned and abandoned: Francesca and Nicholas.

In his autobiography, Sydney Box states that the idea for *The Seventh Veil* grew out of a War Office documentary called *The Psychiatric Treatment of Battle Casualties*. Andrew Spicer, the editor of Box's autobiography, reports that he has been unable to trace this film, but it seems likely that Box is referring to a Ministry of Information documentary produced by Basil Wright and directed by Michael Hankinson called *Neuro Psychiatry 1943*. This was made with the intention of convincing policy makers in North America that effective treatments had been found in Britain for servicemen and civilians who were suffering from traumatic neuroses.[3] *Neuro Psychiatry 1943* opens with a title card:

> In total war the threat of injury or death hangs over the entire population—civilian and soldier alike. In September 1939, Britain organized her medical services to meet this threat. As an integral part of National Defence the Emergency Medical Service organized by the Ministry of Health came into being to provide free medical treatment on a nation wide scale.

The film's narrator informs us that the emergency medical services cover the entire country with a network of hospitals that includes centers for the treatment of a wide variety of physical and psychological injuries. The film makes it clear that the full application of psychological methods at these hospitals is subject to wartime limitations of time and urgency, and so long-term psychotherapeutic procedures are seldom undertaken, and physical methods of treatment are used more frequently. Four of these methods, continuous narcosis, modified insulin treatment, electro-convulsion therapy, and narco-analysis, are demonstrated in the extended sequences that follow. In the last of these sequences, a patient suffering from a severe hysterical stammer following his experiences at Dunkirk lies on a bed, a psychiatrist sits on a chair beside him, and a nurse is in the background. After he has been administered an intravenous barbiturate, the patient gradually relaxes and, according to the narrator, he is "rendered more open to strong suggestions attacking his symptoms. This method of treatment is also used for the recovery of lost memory and the exploration of the psychological causes behind it." The parallels between narco-analysis as presented in *Neuro Psychiatry 1943* and the treatment administered by Dr. Larsen to Francesca in *The Seventh Veil* are obvious, and the formal structure of the sequence that describes this treatment in *Neuro Psychiatry 1943* is reproduced in *The Seventh Veil* with only minor changes.

---

[3] Edgar Jones, "*Neuro Psychiatry 1943*: The Role of Documentary Film in the Dissemination of Medical Knowledge and Promotion of the UK Psychiatric Profession," in *Journal of the History of Medicine and Allied Sciences* 69:2 (2012), p. 300.

In the three sequences from *The Seventh Veil* I have described, the film signals its belief that later neuroses can be traced back to events occurring in childhood, and that the recovery of lost traumatic memories can enable those events to be confronted and understood. In Francesca's case, these childhood events are defined as the loss of both of her parents at a young age and her punishment at school. It is implied that Nicholas's issues are the result of his abandonment by his mother when he was twelve, but, as Andrew Spicer argues, contemporary audiences would also have recognized him

> metaphorically, as a damaged veteran, in need of understanding and compassion. Two other enormously popular films, *I'll be Seeing You* (1944) and *Spellbound*, had focused on this figure, and many others followed; *The Seventh Veil* thus mobilized widely shared concerns, its conclusion registering a general hope for reconciliation and atonement as the war ended.[4]

By the metaphor of defining both Francesca and Nicholas as dominated by their surroundings, the film also suggests that common ground can be found between the damaged veteran and women who are also psychically wounded. To this end, *The Seventh Veil* allocates considerable time to describing Nicholas's symptoms, which take the form of his misanthropy, his misogyny, and his violent outbursts, and Francesca's, which take shape in her obsessive behavior in relation to her hands, her inability to sustain sexual relationships, and her tendency toward self-destruction.

In their paper *Psychoanalysis and the War Neuroses*, Ferenczi, Karl Abraham, and Ernst Simmel address many of the theoretical dilemmas that had emerged from the widespread traumatic experience of the First World War. One important question for psychoanalysis in the inter-war years was why only a minority of men who had served at the front developed traumatic neuroses, while the majority of veterans emerged from their experiences free from any lasting traumatic affect. In addressing this question, the authors propose that:

> It is often necessary to appreciate the relation between a current conflict and an older one, for the real strength and importance of the current one is often due to the fact that it has aroused buried and imperfectly controlled older ones.[5]

---

[4] Andrew Spicer, *Sydney Box* (Manchester and New York: Manchester University Press, 2006), p. 54.
[5] Sándor Ferenczi, Ernst Simmel, et al., *Psychoanalysis and the War Neuroses* (London, Vienna, and New York: The International Psycho-Analytic Press, 1921), p. 51.

In tackling what specifically this older conflict might consist of, the authors follow Freud in declaring that it must be "an unresolved infantile conflict which means that the person has not satisfactorily developed past a given stage of individual evolution."[6] However, they do admit that some dissenters within the psychoanalytic community oppose this view, suggesting instead that the war neuroses might differ to the neuroses of peacetime because "in war the conflict with the instinct for self-preservation and the ego-ideal is enough to lead to neurosis."[7] Thus, whilst at this point the majority of influential psychoanalytic theorists still believed, as Freud had believed since the late 1890s, that the emergence of neurosis reveals fissures that have their psychogenesis in Oedipal fixations, others were beginning to believe that war trauma was different, in that it could emerge from factors beyond the psychical orientations of its victims.

In her assessment of the laying out of *The Seventh Veil*'s trauma narratives, Marcia Landy points to Oedipal fixation as underpinning the film's ordering of both Francesca's and Nicholas's troubled pasts. She suggests that:

> The film is replete with father figures—Francesca's suitors, the psychoanalyst—all competing for Francesca. Mother figures are absent except as they appear in Francesca's childhood in the guise of the schoolmistresses. She is bereft of a female figure with whom she can identify and bond. The doctor is the one who unravels Francesca's oedipal attachment to Nicholas, thus enabling Francesca to return to him not as a child but voluntarily as a woman. Nicholas must work through his negative attachment to his mother. Francesca, who has taken his mother's place in his life, exacerbates his mistrust of women.[8]

But *The Seventh Veil* takes great pains to make it clear that the neuroses suffered by Francesca and Nicholas have their roots not in Oedipal fixations which have established themselves during their early childhoods but in historical traumas that have occurred in later life. The key question is, given the film's ordering of its narrative around broadly psychoanalytic ideas, why is it that the film defines its characters' neuroses as arising from historical traumatic events and not Oedipal fixation at a time when most psychoanalytic theorists were still upholding this view?

The answer to this question can surely be found in the huge popularity that *The Seventh Veil* found with its contemporary audiences. In removing Oedipal

---

[6] Ferenczi, Simmel, et al., *Psychoanalysis and the War Neuroses*, p. 54.
[7] Ibid., p. 55.
[8] Landy, *British Genres*, pp. 225–6.

fixation as the determining factor in Francesca's and Nicholas's later dilemmas, the film defines their neurotic behavior as being caused by external events and not by internal factors motivated by their own psychical dysfunctions. Within this model, the victims of trauma have no need to look within for a reason for their traumatization. In following this line of reasoning, *The Seventh Veil*, like almost all the other British trauma films (the exception, as we will see, is *Mine Own Executioner*), is responding to the British population's own traumatic experience of the war as being formed by their experience of real and not imagined traumatic events. In this way, these films are recreating their audiences' own experiences obliquely, and thus creating safe spaces where the remembrance of their own experiences can occur, and where they can begin to understand the impact of these events on their own lives.

The Processes of Psychoanalysis: Narration, the Reliving of Past Events, and the Reestablishment of "Normal" Sexual Relationships

Near the beginning of *The Seventh Veil*, the psychoanalyst Dr. Larsen confers with two medical doctors, Kendall and Irving, whose attempts at treating the neurotic, suicidal, and now cataleptic Francesca by means of conventional methods have been unsuccessful. Dr. Kendall sits at his desk in his book-lined consulting room, and the more junior Dr. Irving stands slightly behind him. Dr. Larsen approaches and perches casually on a corner of the desk, and, as he does so, he runs his finger along the top edge of a framed photograph that seems to be of General Kitchener as if removing a layer of dust. The disapproving Dr. Kendall demurs that psychiatry "savors a little of prying," and he winces when Dr. Larsen likens the psychoanalytic process of uncovering the unconscious to the method of a surgeon who "does not operate without first taking off the patient's clothes." Dr. Larsen states to Kendall and Irving that:

> The human mind is like Salome at the beginning of her dance, hidden from the outside world by seven veils, veils of reserve, shyness, fear. Now with friends the average person will drop first one veil then another, maybe three or four altogether. With a lover she will take off five, or even six, but never the seventh. Never. You see the human mind likes to cover its nakedness and keep its private thoughts to itself. Salome dropped her seventh veil of her own free will, but you will never get the human mind to do that, and that is why I use narcosis. Five

minutes under narcosis and down comes the seventh veil, and we can see what is actually going on behind it, and then we can really help.

Although *The Seventh Veil* orders its narrative broadly around the psychological problems of both Francesca and Nicholas, the primary object of Dr. Larsen's radically modern investigative technique is Francesca. By administering the narcotic to Francesca, Dr. Larsen returns to her the power of speech, and she is thus able to reveal to him—and to us—her traumatic past. The film presents her account in the form of an extended flashback, and the psychoanalytic setting, along with the figure of Dr. Larsen, recedes into the background as Francesca begins her narrative. The viewer is encouraged to enter Francesca's subjectivity as she re-experiences those events that have motivated her breakdown. The subjective nature of the film's narrative mechanism is striking, bringing to mind moments in other British films of the immediate post-war period such as *Brief Encounter*, *A Matter of Life and Death*, and *Mine Own Executioner* where fundamental elements of their characters' internal worlds are revealed. According to Ann Todd, the original script of *The Seventh Veil* described an even more marked representation of Francesca's subjectivity:

> In this story the girl was the only person who appeared on the screen. The other characters were to be filmed in shadow "voices-off" and reflections in the piano and mirrors—avant-garde and experimental for that time.[9]

Many British films made at this time employ subjective modes of narration to tell their stories in new and interesting ways, quite unlike wartime narratives that were, in the most part, motivated to stress the external links that bound British society together in the face of the common adversary. But by foregrounding the mechanisms of subjectivity, internal monologues, visions, and narratives within the psychoanalytic setting, films of this period are also suggesting that they are revealing essential aspects of their characters that would have remained inaccessible within the limitations of traditional storytelling.

In her assessment of the Hollywood woman's film of the 1940s, Mary Ann Doane argues that many of these films activate a discourse in which the traumas of their troubled female characters are made visible by the intervention of the medical professional. In these films, it is often the role of the psychoanalyst to read the symptoms of these women, and so to reveal the essential kernel

---

[9] Ann Todd, *The Eighth Veil* (New York: Putnam, 1981), p. 13.

of truth which would normally escape the eye of the unqualified.[10] The psychoanalyst is thus often afforded extraordinary powers of vision, through which she or he is able to penetrate the barrier posed by the exterior bodily surface. In the narrative of the woman's film, unlike in the majority of classical Hollywood narratives, "the female body is located not so much as spectacle but as an element in the discourse of medicine, a manuscript to be read for the symptoms which betray her story, her identity."[11] In allocating these powers to their psychoanalyst figures, and in having them use these powers to unveil some fundamental feminine quality, Doane argues that the Hollywood woman's film promotes an ideology that rests on a particularly extreme form of essentialism. Also, by declaring the issues that confront the central female figures as signs of neurosis or psychosis, the proposed subject of these films becomes instead their object, their difficulties becoming organized solely for the purposes of medical observation and cultural recuperation. Within this formulation, the figure of the psychoanalyst becomes readable as an instrument of power and constraint rather than one of liberation.

While *The Seventh Veil* does construct a large part of its narrative around Francesca's subjective account of her own traumatic past, the nature of this subjectivity is only superficial. In his speech to Kendall and Irving, Dr. Larsen describes the human mind as being "like Salome at the beginning of her dance," and that "with friends the average person will drop first one veil, then another … maybe three or four altogether. With a lover she will take off five or even six." In stating that the human mind is "like Salome," and by using a female pronoun, Larsen is defining the object of the psychoanalytic gaze in female terms, and the psychoanalytic process as entailing the male investigation of the female object, and specifically the essence of that object that is the cause of the female's neurotic symptoms. Rather than being aligned with Francesca's point of view during her account, the viewer is encouraged to join Dr. Larsen as detective, listening to and watching Francesca's testimony and investigating what has been the cause of Francesca's dilemmas and what are their effects. The causes of Francesca's wounds, like those of Nicholas, are not defined in relation to infantile Oedipal fixations but to real traumatic events that have occurred in later childhood that have rendered her predisposed to her later traumatic neuroses. But the effects of Francesca's childhood experiences are laid out in terms that are quite unlike the

---

[10] Mary Ann Doane, *The Desire to Desire: The Woman's Film of the 1940s* (Basingstoke and London: Macmillan Press, 1987), p. 40.
[11] Ibid., p. 43.

effects of Nicholas's experiences. While his hysterical symptoms are recognizable by the viewer within the context of shell shock, Francesca's symptoms, without an available link to "acceptable" discourses of war trauma, can only be categorized in the context of her neurotic sexual behavior in relation to her male suitors. It is by means of the transgressive nature of her behavior that the figure of Francesca comes to be aligned by Dr. Larsen with pathological and "unacceptable" female sexuality.

The film enlarges on the idea of Francesca's problematic sexuality after she has agreed to leave Nicholas and live with Max in his villa in Italy. While Francesca is revealing the plans for her new life to Nicholas, both Francesca and Nicholas stand in front of the portrait of Nicholas's mother hanging in his drawing room, and so a parallel is drawn between Nicholas's abandonment by his mother when he was twelve and his present "abandonment" by Francesca (Figure 4.4). In stating that the human mind is "like Salome," Dr. Larsen has brought into play what Lawrence Kramer has termed "everyone's favorite *fin-de-siècle* dragon lady." According to Kramer, the figure of Salome stands as the extreme personification of patriarchal fears of female sexuality, "fears so

Figure 4.4 *The Seventh Veil*: Nicholas and his absent mother.

disruptive that they compulsively play themselves out in a scenario of fetishism and castration."[12] At the beginning of the Salome narrative, she is portrayed as the icon of dangerous female seductiveness, imbued with the power of her own sexuality, but then, by the action of removing the veils that cover her body, her power is gradually diminished. Thus, Salome comes ultimately to appear to her observers not as the personification of castrating feminine sexuality, but as the reverse, a figure for precisely those threatening aspects of the feminine that male power can subjugate. In similar terms, Dr. Larsen's removal of Francesca's "seventh veil," in other words his exposing of her unbounded sexual desire in the analysis, and his defining of those desires as psychopathological, have the effect of diminishing Francesca's transgressive power and enabling the beginning of Francesca's return to a submissive position within the dominant patriarchal order.

At the end of *The Seventh Veil*, Dr. Larsen announces that his analysis has provided a "complete cure," and that Francesca is now "a new and very different person" who has the opportunity of choosing the one she loves. That she chooses Nicholas seems surprising to us given his cruel treatment of her throughout the film; however, on two specific levels the narrative can have no other conclusion. On an industrial level, it is unlikely that a character played by James Mason, the leading British male star of the day, would be marginalized by an ending in which another figure claimed the hand of the female lead. However, the expediency of this conclusion also mobilizes a secondary system of signification that operates on a deeper level of ideological discourse. The relationships that Francesca has had during the film with Peter and Max suggest new "enlightened" modes of sexuality as existing for her outside the strict boundaries of traditionally repressive social behavior. With Peter, despite her initial shyness, Francesca has embraced the possibilities afforded by their romance with an increasing confidence that culminates in her throwing convention aside by proposing marriage to him. In more extreme terms, later in the film, when Max asks her whether she wants them to marry, she replies: "I don't think it matters," and she readily agrees to live with him in his villa in Italy *outside the bounds of matrimony*. In contrast to both examples, Francesca's relationship with Nicholas has been always defined by her subservience to him and her adherence to traditionally accepted modes of sexuality and behavior.

---

[12] Lawrence Kramer, "Culture and Musical Hermeneutics," in *Cambridge Opera Journal* 2:3 (1990), p. 271.

By the process of her being psychoanalyzed by Dr. Larsen, the narrative of *The Seventh Veil* has revealed that Francesca's neurotic breakdown has its roots in the traumas of her childhood, but, crucially, her breakdown has been defined as occurring after she has agreed to live with Max outside the traditional boundaries of marriage, and therefore without recourse to the established patriarchal social formation. By pathologizing Francesca's desire and revealing the existence of this "illness" to Francesca, Dr. Larsen has begun the process of her "cure" and laid the groundwork for her return to this formation (Figure 4.5). In *The Seventh Veil*, as in the Hollywood woman's film, the figure of the psychoanalyst acts as a narrative ideological discourse that is constraining and not liberating, in that the cure that Dr. Larsen has achieved has bound Francesca securely to the dominant devices of power. Just as within the patriarchal logic of the Salome narrative Salome's power is diminished by the removal of her clothes and the revealing of her "feminine essence", in *The Seventh Veil* the threat that Francesca poses is neutralized by the removal of her "neurotic" sexuality. So, in the film's conclusion, Francesca becomes "redeemed" by her choice to marry Nicholas, and this, in turn, enables her re-entry into the *status quo* of "normal"

Figure 4.5 *The Seventh Veil*: Francesca's re-entry into the paternal order.

sexual relationships. Within the film's logic, by means of the "cure" that has been achieved by Dr. Larsen, the family unit has been reproduced, and Francesca has been made fit again to be placed in contact with, as Foucault puts it, the social body, the family space, and—potentially—the lives of children.

And yet, this scenario is rarely convincing for the viewer. In her autobiography, Ann Todd reports her experience of watching the film soon after its release:

> I had the great honor just after the first night in London, of being asked to Marlborough House to a private showing of *The Seventh Veil* for Her Majesty Queen Mary. We were in a tiny cinema and I sat next to the queen in the front row. [...] She had tears in her eyes at the end of the film; she turned to me and said, "Child, you didn't go to that horrid man at the end, did you? I couldn't quite see without my glasses."[13]

While Dr. Larsen's treatment has returned Francesca to health and enabled her redemption in ideological terms by choosing to marry Nicholas, her choice is questionable precisely because Nicholas has shown himself, throughout the narrative, to be capable of extreme cruelty toward her. The queen's observation that she could not quite see whom Francesca had "gone to" at the end of the film is not surprising because of the tentative way that the film lays out its final moments. When the three suitors have gathered in the hallway of Nicholas's house, Dr. Larsen announces Francesca's "complete cure." He tells them:

> The past is over for her, quite over. Her mind is clear, and the clouds have been swept away. She is no longer afraid. [...] She will want to be with the one she loves, or the one she has been happiest with, or the one she cannot be without, or the one she trusts.

A close shot of Nicholas reveals his own doubts as to whether Francesca has elected to be with him; however, moments later, Francesca confirms her choice with a look at one of them. Nicholas then walks in silence to the drawing room, and, in an extreme long shot, Francesca flings open the double doors and joins Nicholas as he stands by the piano. In the film's final seconds, and still in long shot, they embrace (Figure 4.6).

The lack of a close-up at the end leaves even the most observant viewer with some uncertainty as to whether it is indeed Nicholas that Francesca has chosen, and, even if we are certain, then we still have doubts as to whether her

---

[13] Todd, *The Eighth Veil*, pp. 19–20.

Figure 4.6 *The Seventh Veil*: Francesca chooses Nicholas.

choice is the right one. As we have already seen at the end of *Dead of Night*, and as we shall see when we examine the conclusion of *Madonna of the Seven Moons*, this group of films often present solutions to their characters' dilemmas that are immediately called into question by their own narrative conclusions, and thus they display a high level of ambivalence as to whether a return to the pre-war *status quo* is desirable or even possible.

Introduction to *Madonna of the Seven Moons*

Between 1943 and 1947, the British studio Gainsborough Pictures produced a series of films that found commercial success in departing from the social realist subject matter which characterized British cinema during the early years of the war. The Gainsborough melodramas employed glamorous stars, elaborate costumes and sets, and escapist romantic storylines to appeal to their predominantly female audiences, and they paid unusual attention to ideas of female desire and female subjectivity. These films thus acknowledged the numbers of women that made up the majority of the wartime cinema-going public, while at the same drawing on cultural uncertainties that had arisen from the changing role that women had come to play within British society in the post-war period. These uncertainties had been brought about, in part, by the increasingly significant position that women were by now occupying in the workplace. As Anthony Aldgate and Jeffrey Richards note:

> By 1943 90 percent of all single women between 18 and 40 and 80 percent of married women with children over 14 were working. Women were also being conscripted into the armed forces. This did not necessarily result in instant equality. Women were for the most part denied equal pay with men and they got less in compensation for industrial accidents than men. But there was an inevitable increase in their sense of responsibility and independence, their mobility and self-esteem.[14]

However, while acknowledging the importance of women's labor to the war effort, British society was often conflicted in its view toward the consequences of this new sense of women's self-determination.

During the interwar years, there had been increasing apprehension about the falling birth rate and the disintegration of the family unit, and this period saw what one demographer has described as "a considerable literature of immoderate dismay" on these subjects.[15] While the birth rate had been 743,360 per annum in 1930, by 1941 it had fallen to 668,843, and the resulting feeling of despondency and alarm gave rise to a pro-natalist movement that took the solution of the problem to be encouraging women to leave work and to return to their role as wives and mothers in the home.[16] This conservative tendency was compounded, as Sonya O. Rose observes, by a concern about declining female morality that drew on First World War discourses surrounding women and girls who were seen to be "consorting with soldiers."[17] Within the context of the Second World War, this sense of disquiet was stimulated by the growing presence of American GIs in British towns and cities, and newspapers increased the level of anxiety by printing lurid headlines, feature articles, and editorials that deliberated at length on the causes and consequences of women "running wild" or "going out for

---

[14] Anthony Aldgate and Jeffrey Richards, *Britain Can Take It: British Cinema in the Second World War* (London and New York: I.B. Tauris, 2007), p. 161.
[15] Rosalind Mitchison quoted in Denise Riley, "The Free Mothers: Pronatalism and Working Women in Industry at the End of the Last War in Britain," in *History Workshop* 11 (1981), p. 90.
[16] Ibid., p. 90.
[17] Sonya O. Rose, "Sex, Citizenship, and the Nation in World War II Britain," in *The American Historical Review* 103:4 (1998), p. 1149.

a good time."[18] These reports fueled the panic by going into great detail about women's "indiscretions" and exciting both the outrage and the prurient attention of the general public.

The Gainsborough melodramas allocate central roles to female characters who consistently challenge the dominant social order, and the films' use of historical and foreign settings provided their contemporary audiences with safe spaces in which the traditional boundaries of femininity could be interrogated and often transgressed. As Marcia Landy argues, these films "portray conflicts surrounding choice of sexual partners, marriage, and female companionship," while emphasizing "the existence of a dual discourse which, on the one hand, sought to dramatize social changes affecting women while, on the other, maintaining a continuity with traditional values."[19] The Gainsborough melodramas draw on this dual discourse by orientating their narratives around conceptions of female desire and female subjectivity, while at the same time presenting female desire in terms that are often excessive, and sometimes as being symptomatic of mental instability.

Madonna of the Seven Moons, released early in 1945, and therefore occupying a central position in this series of films, appropriates elements of historical psychoanalytic discourses motivated by the idea of schizophrenia, the film making clear its interest in mental illness in its opening title: "This story is taken from life. There was a real Maddalena. The medical world have verified her case and other cases like it." In this section, I demonstrate how the discourse of schizophrenia functions in *Madonna of the Seven Moons* at psychosexual, social, and political levels. First, I examine how *Madonna of the Seven Moons* uses Maddalena's schizophrenia to interrogate and categorize as psychopathological her transgressive and "problematic" sexuality, and how it establishes a particular ordering mechanism for its polarized ideological worldview. I continue to investigate the opposing ideological worldviews that are revealed by the ambivalence and fragmentation of the film's narrative irresolution.

Synopsis of *Madonna of the Seven Moons*

In *Madonna of the Seven Moons* a young girl, Maddalena (Phyllis Calvert), is sent by her father to live in the Convent of the Sacred Heart in Florence; here she is raped by a stranger while out on her own picking flowers in the woods.

---

[18] Ibid., p. 1150.
[19] Landy, *British Genres*, p. 210.

Sometime later, her father sends word that it is time for Maddalena to leave the convent as he has arranged her marriage to a wealthy wine merchant, Guiseppe Labardi (John Stuart). Eight months after the wedding, Maddalena gives birth to a daughter, Angela (Patricia Roc). Several years later, Maddalena is living in great luxury in Rome with her husband, and Angela, now a young lady, arrives home from her boarding school in England where she has been for the last five years. Because of a nervous illness, Maddalena has not been able to visit her daughter at school and so has not seen her all the time she has been away.

While Maddalena is saintly and retiring, her daughter turns out to be an unconventional and high-spirited young woman who wears shorts and high-heels and is confident in the company of men. Maddalena is initially shocked at Angela's appearance and behavior, but she resolves to become a modern woman like her daughter.

The upheaval of Angela's homecoming affects Maddalena strangely. At her birthday party, Angela becomes engaged to Evelyn (Alan Haines), a young man whom she met while stopping over in Cannes on the way from England. Later that evening, Maddalena has a mental breakdown; she dresses in gypsy clothes and travels to Florence taking with her all the jewelry that Guiseppe has given her, leaving behind only a cryptic sign of the "Seven Moons" written in lipstick on her bedroom mirror.

We learn from the Labardi family physician, Dr. Ackroyd (Reginald Tate), that Maddalena has a "dual personality" and that she has been living two separate lives. Maddalena has run off twice before; once immediately after her marriage, and then again following Guiseppe's decision to send Angela to school in England rather than to a convent as Maddalena had wished. Each time Maddalena has become Rosanna, living in the house of the Seven Moons in the "worst part of Florence" as the gypsy lover of Nino Barucci (Stewart Granger), a local gang-leader. Angela resolves to find her mother, and, assuming her mother to have repeated the previous pattern of her affliction, Angela travels to Florence along with her father.

In Florence, Angela enlists the help of Jimmy (Peter Murray-Hill) and Nesta Logan (Dulcie Gray), two artist friends of her fiancé Evelyn, and Sandro (Peter Glenville), a gigolo whom she had met on her journey from England.

Unbeknownst to Angela, Sandro is the younger brother of Nino, and he lures Angela to the Seven Moons with the intention of raping her. A carnival is in progress, and Nino and Sandro are both dressed as Harlequins. Sandro drugs Angela and carries her upstairs. Maddalena/Rosanna sees him bending over Angela and, believing him to be Nino, she kills him, but not before he has mortally wounded her. In a fit of jealous rage, Nino has vowed to kill Guiseppe, whom he assumes to have been Maddalena/Rosanna's lover during the periods they have been apart. Maddalena is taken to the Labardi house in Florence, where she dies after receiving the last rites from a priest. Guiseppe and Angela are broken-hearted, and Nino, watching from outside a window, realizes that Guiseppe is Maddalena's husband and not her lover. As Guiseppe places a cross on her breast, Nino throws a white rose beside it.

The Psychoanalytic Discourse of Schizophrenia and the Pathologization of Female Desire

In the opening sequence of *Madonna of the Seven Moons*, we find Maddalena as a young girl walking alone in the woods. She is dressed in a hooded cloak and her hair is tied in pigtails (Figure 4.7). As she stoops to pick some white flowers, a man appears and stands staring at her. Maddalena takes fright, drops

Figure 4.7 *Madonna of the Seven Moons*: Maddalena as the "sweet little maiden" Red Riding Hood.

her flowers, and begins to run away. As she runs, the man follows her and the camera tracks backward, holding her terrified face in close-up.

Maddalena arrives back at her cell at the Convent of the Sacred Heart; she is in tears and overcome with emotion. On the left of the frame a statue of the Madonna and Child stands on a pedestal attached to the cell wall, and on the right a shaft of light from a window is projected onto the wall, the bars of the window making a pattern like the bars of a prison cell. Sometime later, Maddalena is summoned to the office of the Mother Superior, and she is told of her father's plans for her marriage. Maddalena protests that she wants to stay at the convent forever, but the Mother Superior points out that by doing this Maddalena would be contravening her father's wishes. She then gives a prayer book to Maddalena "for her comfort." The two shots that follow reveal two inscriptions on the flyleaves of the book, presumably written later by Maddalena herself. The first states the date of the gift as being the seventh of July 1919, and the second says: "Married to Guiseppe Labardi October 3rd 1919" and "Angela born June 16th 1920" (Figures 4.8 and 4.9).

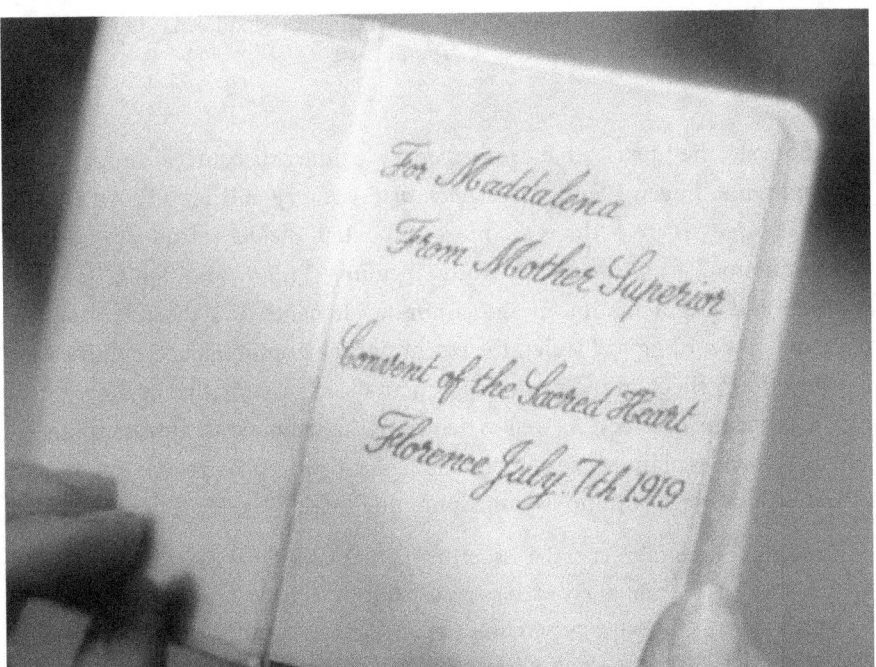

Figure 4.8 *Madonna of the Seven Moons*: "I want you to take this prayer book, for your comfort."

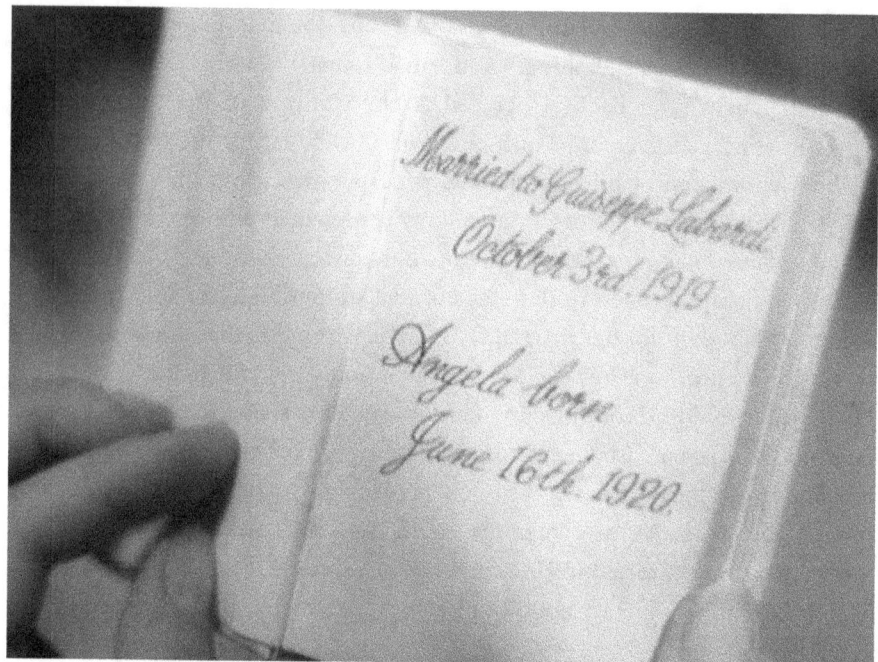

Figure 4.9 *Madonna of the Seven Moons*: The "excess" of Maddalena's libido: The third of October 1919 and the sixteenth of June 1920.

Amongst the texts that informed wartime discourses surrounding schizophrenia, Eugen Bleuler's *Textbook of Psychiatry* and Freud's *An Outline of Psycho-Analysis* are perhaps the most influential. Bleuler introduces the term "schizophrenia," from the Greek words meaning "mind" and "split," to stress splitting and fragmentation as the common elements of a discrete group of psychoses. According to Bleuler, the essence of schizophrenia is the dislocation between the intellectual and emotional functions, a symptom that he describes as the "incongruity of affect," as well as delusions, hallucinations, autistic thinking, and disturbances of the sense of identity. Bleuler also emphasizes the importance of ambivalent states of mind to schizophrenic functioning. He states that:

> The schizophrenic defect of the associative paths makes it possible that contrasts that otherwise are mutually exclusive exist side by side in the psyche. Love and hatred towards the same person may be equally ardent without influencing one another (affective ambivalence). The patients want at the same time to eat and not to eat; they do what they do not want to do as well as what they want to do (ambivalence of the will). In the same moment they think "I am human like

you", and "I am not human like you." God and Devil, parting and meeting are the same to them and fuse into one idea (intellectual ambivalence). In the delusions too, expansive and depressive ideas very frequently mingle in multi-colored confusion.[20]

In *An Outline of Psycho-Analysis*, Freud acknowledges the specificity of schizophrenia and the role that fragmentation plays in its makeup, stating that fragmentation is often preceded by states of anxiety. He argues that anxiety can act as a sign of impending dangers that threaten the cohesion of the ego, a mechanism that operates in a way quite different to repression: "The ego makes use of the sensations of anxiety as a signal to give warning of dangers that threaten its integrity."[21] According to Freud, in cases of schizophrenic psychosis the state of fragmentation is rarely complete because some healthy part of the mind always continues to exist:

> Even in a state so far removed from the reality of the external world as one of hallucinatory confusion, one learns from patients after their recovery that at the same time in some corner of their mind (as they put it) there was a normal person hidden who, like a detached spectator, watched the hubbub of the illness go past him.[22]

Freud also suggests that fragmentation gives rise to two contrary attitudes in the ego that coexist, but when the abnormal gains the upper hand this signals the onset of a psychosis. In cases such as this, one attitude accepts reality and the other rejects it, and Freud terms the latter state of mind a disavowal.[23]

The mise-en-scene of *Madonna of the Seven Moon*'s opening sequence is suggestive. That Maddalena is dressed in a hooded cloak and collecting flowers immediately calls to mind the ancient fairy tale "Red Riding Hood." In the Brothers Grimm version, the "sweet little maiden" Red Riding Hood is warned by her mother not to stray from the path as she walks through the woods to her grandmother's house. Ignoring her mother's advice, she does stray in order to pick some flowers for her grandmother and so is way-laid by the wolf. At the conclusion of the tale, Red Riding Hood is saved along with her grandmother by the huntsman, and she promises herself that "I will never again wander off

---

[20] Eugen Bleuler, *Textbook of Psychiatry* (New York: Macmillan, 1934), p. 382.
[21] Sigmund Freud, *An Outline of Psycho-Analysis* in *The Standard Edition vol. XXIII*, ed. by James Strachey (London: The Hogarth Press, 1964; repr. 1973), p. 199.
[22] Ibid., pp. 201–2.
[23] Ibid., p. 204.

into the forest as long as I live, when my mother forbids it."[24] According to Bruno Bettelheim, the tale "speaks of human passions, oral greediness, aggression, and pubertal sexual desires." Red Riding Hood's

> danger is her budding sexuality, for which she is not yet emotionally mature enough. The person who is psychologically ready to have sexual experiences can master them and grow because of it. But a premature sexuality is a regressive experience, arousing all that is still primitive within us and that threatens to swallow us up.[25]

For Bettelheim, the story of Red Riding Hood is universally loved because "in symbolic form, it projects its central figure into the dangers of her oedipal conflicts during puberty, and then saves her from them, so that she will be able to mature conflict-free."[26] However, in *Madonna of the Seven Moons*, Maddalena, unlike Red Riding Hood, has no huntsman to save her, and it is suggested that her meeting with the stranger ends with her rape and the irretrievable loss both of her "innocence" and her mental integrity, the lasting trauma of the event gradually taking shape in the symptoms of her schizophrenia.

The profound effect of her sexual trauma is indicated in the mise-en-scene of the second sequence, which predicts both Maddalena's future state of mental fragmentation and also the film's polarized ideological worldview. In placing Maddelena between the Madonna and Child and the image of the prison bars, the film proposes that her psyche will be split between the redemptive potential of her Christian faith and the lasting psychical impression of her trauma (Figure 4.10). In the following sequence, the film reveals the dates of Maddalena's leaving the convent, her marriage, and the birth of her daughter. These facts might be missed by even the most observant viewer; however, the implication is that Maddelena's daughter Angela was conceived out of wedlock only two months after Maddalena had met Guiseppe, and a month before their marriage. That Maddalena and Guiseppe seem later to have a caring relationship implies that this act was consensual.

At the outset, the film has suggested that Maddalena's pubertal desire has been held in check by her Catholic belief, this providing a resistance to her

---

[24] Margaret E. Martignoni, ed., *The Illustrated Treasury of Children's Literature* (London and Glasgow: Collins, 1960), pp. 175–7.

[25] Bruno Bettelheim, *The Uses of Enchantment: The Meanings and Importance of Fairy Tales* (London: Penguin, 1991), p. 173.

[26] Ibid., p. 172.

"What Does a Woman Want?" 145

Figure 4.10 *Madonna of the Seven Moons*: The aftermath of Maddalena's rape.

desire which is reinforced by her being physically confined within the convent walls. The film proposes that the trauma of her rape leads to the eruption of an uncontrollable libidinal excess that Maddalena herself recognizes, and so she begs the Mother Superior to be allowed to stay in the convent. Such is the over-abundance of her libido that, despite her strict Catholic belief, within two months of leaving the convent—and a month before her marriage to Guiseppe—Maddalena has become pregnant. According to Guiseppe's later testimony to Angela and Dr. Ackroyd, a few days after the wedding, Maddalena leaves Guiseppe and begins her affair with Nino, staying away for six months. Therefore, the film implies that for the whole time of Maddalena's first affair with Nino she has been pregnant with Angela, and that she only returns to Guiseppe a month before Angela's birth.

In similar terms to *The Seventh Veil*, *Madonna of the Seven Moons* has anchored its narrative in the psychoanalytic concept that traumatic events occurring in childhood can render the victim predisposed to later psychopathologies. The film emphasizes Maddalena's childhood trauma in its opening sequence, and the scenario of her actions after she has left the convent describes Maddalena's resulting libidinal over-abundance in terms so transgressive that this can only be rendered acceptable in the form of her schizophrenia.

Sue Aspinall argues that the Gainsborough melodramas are based on the conflict between two types of women—one representing the virtues of marriage and duty and the other the forces of unrestrained libido.[27] In many of these films, the first type of woman, while suffering for her virtue during the course of the narrative, is rewarded in their conclusions by being given the opportunity to marry. The second is punished for her transgressions and at the end often killed. However, by employing the metaphors of detrimental childhood experience and schizophrenia, *Madonna of the Seven Moons* defines this conflict not as existing between two types of women, but as being internalized within the fragmented inner world of the innocent victim of trauma. Thus, by linking her transgressive desire to her childhood trauma, the film judiciously absolves Maddalena of any guilt, and defines it as a symptom of her mental fragmentation. This symptom is recognized, to an extent, by Dr. Ackroyd, who informs Guiseppe late in the film that Maddalena has a dual personality and that she is living two separate lives:

> In the one she has no knowledge of the other. We know very little of the workings of the human mind. You see, something happened to split her mind in two, it may have been a shock during her childhood. By your showing, it was always after a period of mental strain.

But unlike the psychoanalyst Dr. Larsen in *The Seventh Veil*, who provides a "complete cure" in the form of Francesca's abandonment of her "neurotic" refusal to live within the boundaries of patriarchy, Dr. Ackroyd shows no ability either to interpret Maddalena's symptoms or to suggest a "cure" for her "excessive" libido (Figure 4.11).

In *Madonna of the Seven Moons*, the metaphors of trauma and schizophrenia operate in similar ways to the metaphors of Francesca's trauma and neurosis in *The Seventh Veil*, specifically, as a means by which feminine sexual desire can be pathologized and categorized as deviant and so assimilated into normative structures of patriarchal power. But unlike *The Seventh Veil*, which provides Francesca with the opportunity to return in its conclusion to the dominant social order, *Madonna of the Seven Moons* provides no mechanism by which an "errant" sexuality of this magnitude can be "redeemed."

---

[27] Sue Aspinall, "Sexuality in Costume Melodrama," in *BFI Dossier 18: Gainsborough Melodrama*, ed. by Sue Aspinall and Robert Murphy (London: BFI Publishing, 1983), p. 30.

Figure 4.11 *Madonna of the Seven Moons*: Guiseppe with Dr. Ackroyd: "It may have been a shock during her childhood."

An examination of the *Madonna of the Seven Moon* pressbook reveals how central the idea of schizophrenic psychopathology was to Gainsborough's marketing of the film. For example, it provides an idea for a newspaper article entitled "What Is Schizophrenia?" which states that the film was the first "to be produced with a woman suffering from schizophrenia or dual personality as its central character." Another article claims that the novel by Margery Lawrence, from which the film's screenplay was adapted, drew inspiration from a real case in which an Italian girl "had suffered a shock in her girlhood with the result that she developed the disease known as schizophrenia. She had been treated by the most famous alienists and doctors but could not be cured." A third, entitled "Does Schizophrenia Sound Romantic?," suggests that cinema managers should exploit the "curiosity" of their female customers by asking them: "What Should a Husband Do: His wife is madly in love with him, her home, her child—yet goes away at a mysterious call to the arms of another." The fan magazine *Picturegoer* ran with these ideas in its 23 June 1945 edition by printing an extended piece on schizophrenia entitled "Split Personalities" written by "a psychologist." The article references contemporary films that engage in one way or another with ideas of schizophrenia including *Madonna of the Seven Moons*, *Lady in the Dark* (Mitchell Liesen, 1944), *Murder in Thornton Square* (*Gaslight*) (George Cukor, 1944), and *Hangover Square* (John Brahm, 1945). Schizophrenia is linked in the article to shocks in early life that are often "connected with sex," and schizophrenia is described as causing the "normal personality" to be "blanked out" and "the dark forces of the libido [...] are released."[28] The nature of the articles confirms the claim made by many commentators that the Gainsborough melodramas were mainly aimed at female audiences, and they reveal how, in the case of *Madonna of the Seven Moons*, studio publicists sought to attract those female audiences by linking the idea of schizophrenia to femininity and specifically to female desire.

But how can the extreme conservatism of *Madonna of the Seven Moons*' worldview be squared with its huge popularity with female audiences, and why were these audiences attracted by the film's linkage between female desire and schizophrenia?

The answer to these questions lies in the way in which the film employs the metaphor of schizophrenia. *Madonna of the Seven Moons* appropriates many elements of contemporary psychoanalytic ideas surrounding schizophrenia, in that the ideas of ambivalence of will and affect, disturbances to the sense of identity, anxiety acting as a signal of fragmentation, and healthy parts of the mind continuing to exist within psychosis, are all assimilated into the film's narrative. But, crucially, Bleuler's description of the condition causing the dislocation between the intellectual and the emotional functions and Freud's idea that schizophrenia gives rise within the ego to two contrary attitudes that co-exist come in the film to be transformed into the simplified idea of the schizophrenic "dual" or "split" personality. The Gainsborough melodramas therefore evidence the existence of, and also themselves recirculate, wartime discourses surrounding new ideas of female agency and female desire, which circulated in an environment where the vast majority of women were in full-time employment and enjoying relatively high levels of independence and self-determination. However, in the dynamically changing cultural environment of wartime and post-war Britain, women also found themselves having to square these new ideas, and new freedoms, with other discourses that often configured these as leading

---

[28] *Picturegoer*, June 23rd, 1945, p. 7.

inevitably to irresponsible behavior and even promiscuity. At the same time, women found themselves confronted with the forces of pronatalism, which suggested the solution to the problem of population-fall anxiety to be their leaving work and returning to their pre-war roles as wives and mothers in the home.

By employing the metaphors of childhood trauma and schizophrenia, *Madonna of the Seven Moon* enables the ramifications of these polarized positions to be explored and worked-through by its audiences within the blame-free environment of mental aberration, not as elements that exist within the personalities of "two types" of women, but as contradictory forces that must be assimilated and reconciled within internal psychical mechanisms. In the childhood trauma and "dual personality" of Maddalena/Rosanna, contemporary female audiences could take pleasure in observing the contrary stimuli of marriage and duty on the one hand, and an unrestrained libido on the other, as existing side-by-side within the integrity of the self, at least until the film's conclusion.

The Ambivalent and Fragmented Nature of *Madonna of the Seven Moons*' Narrative Irresolution

The narrative arc of *Madonna of the Seven Moons*, and the way that it presents female desire in terms of polarized opposites, can be traced back to Gainsborough's early wartime output. In the early months of 1943, at the same time as Gainsborough was producing its first melodrama *The Man in Grey*, work was also in progress on another film that would prove popular with the British public whilst adopting a rather different aesthetic. *Millions Like Us* is a documentary-inspired social-realist drama that describes the lives of a socially disparate group of women working at a large armament factory in central England. It focuses particularly on Celia Crowson, the youngest daughter of a closely knit family who live in suburban London. The film's fictional narrative incorporates recent events of the war such as the evacuation of Dunkirk, the Battle of Britain, and the Blitz, and it begins by describing the creeping impact of the war on the working-class Crowson family. The father, Jim, is in the Home Guard; the son, Tom, is serving with the army in Egypt; the eldest daughter, Phyllis, joins the ATS; and near the beginning of the film, Celia receives her call-up papers and reports to the Ministry of Labour and

National Service. As she sits in the waiting-room before her interview, Celia fantasizes about the course that her life is about to take, seeing herself as a WAAF, a WREN, in the ATS, a land girl, and finally a nurse. Instead, Celia is persuaded by Miss Wells to opt for factory work: "The men at the front need tanks, guns, and planes. You can help your country just as much in an overall as you can in uniform these days." Sometime later, Celia arrives at the fictional town of Stockford, where she works in the armament factory and lives in the nearby women's hostel.

In describing Celia's life at the factory and the hostel, the film broadens its focus from the family to the wider community, following Celia's fortunes by tracing her interactions with her fellow factory workers, who come from different parts of the country and different social backgrounds. The main thrust of the narrative traces the romantic fortunes of Celia and of one of her co-workers, the upper-class Jennifer Knowles, and the actions of Celia are contrasted in the film first with those of her elder sister, Phyllis, and then with Jennifer.

While Celia is modest and shy with men, Phyllis is shown in a series of romantic trysts, much to the consternation of her father who, when she announces her intention of joining the ATS, says: "Across my dead body, you're not going to join any woman's army. It may be alright for a girl with her head on her shoulders, but for a daft Nellie like you in amongst all those men …" Phyllis replies: "I can look after myself, I have since I was fourteen." Later, when Celia begins work at the factory she quickly fits in socially and takes easily to the work, whereas the upper-class Jennifer is initially supercilious and antisocial.

The general aesthetic of *Millions Like Us* has a documentary-like quality and much of the film was shot on location at the Castle Bromwich aircraft factory in Birmingham, using real factory workers and members of the armed forces.[29] However, the way that Celia's internal world is presented as she imagines what the future holds for her runs counter to the film's general aesthetic. In her fantasy, Celia imagines herself in several romantic scenarios with members of the armed forces who have the appearance of Hollywood stars, culminating in her being proposed to by a wounded serviceman. The form of the sequence predicts both the presentation and centralization of female desire that would come to characterize the Gainsborough melodramas, and the narrative arc of the sequence anticipates the progression of the "good" figures of many films of the series. Similarly, that *Millions Like Us* is built upon a series of polarized

---

[29] Aldgate and Richards, *Britain Can Take It*, p. 303.

opposites based on the differences of class and sexual codes of conduct that are displayed variously by Celia, Phyllis, and Jennifer predicts the polarized way that both femininity and masculinity would be defined throughout the Gainsborough series. As Sue Aspinall notes, the heroes of the Gainsborough melodramas

> were either good-natured gentlemen, like Stewart Granger in *Caravan* or *The Man in Grey* and Griffith Jones in *The Wicked Lady*, or they were arrogant, domineering and sexy, like James Mason in *The Man in Grey* and *The Wicked Lady*, or Stewart Granger in *Madonna of the Seven Moons*. Similarly, the heroines were either affectionate and naïve, like Phyllis Calvert in *The Man in Grey* or Patricia Roc in *The Wicked Lady*, or they were sexy, unscrupulous and daring, like Margaret Lockwood in *The Wicked Lady* and *The Man in Grey*.[30]

According to Aspinall, the Gainsborough melodramas do not invite unquestioned identification with either one or the other of these polarized opposites, instead provoking what Laura Mulvey has termed "an internal oscillation of desire" that commands an alternate and dynamic identification between two oppositional modes of social identity.[31] For example, in *The Man in Grey*, the pleasures of transgression are motivated by an identification with the actions of the brutish and hedonistic figure of Lord Rohan and the conniving and wanton Hesther, while the film also evokes considerable sympathy for the romantic lovers Clarissa and Rokeby who are destined in its conclusion to enter into a conventional marriage. The Gainsborough melodramas thus "provide both the vicarious pleasures of sexual passion (which cannot lead to married life, in these narratives, because of class incompatibilities), whilst simultaneously offering the pleasures of romantic love as a prelude to marriage."[32]

Madonna of the Seven Moons imports many of these narrative elements, but it departs from this model in how it internalizes its conflict between the family and marriage on one side and libidinal expression on the other within Maddalena's schizophrenic fragmentation. More than this, the film closes off avenues of narrative resolution that in other films of the series are provided by the readmission of their "good" romantic couples to the dominant social order. The dilemma that is created by this process is best illustrated by an examination of the film's final sequence.

---

[30] Aspinall, "Sexuality in Costume Melodrama," p. 33.
[31] Laura Mulvey, "Afterthoughts on 'Visual Pleasure and Narrative Cinema' Inspired by King Vidor's *Duel in the Sun* (1946)," in *Visual and Other Pleasures* (London: Palgrave Macmillan, 2009), p. 39.
[32] Aspinall, "Sexuality in Costume Melodrama," p. 35.

At the end of *Madonna of the Seven Moons*, the wounded Maddalena is carried back to the Labardi house in Florence and she lies close to death in her bedroom. Angela stands with Evelyn at the foot of the bed while Guiseppe kneels at Maddalena's side. Maddalena is attended by Dr. Ackroyd and a priest. After the others have left the room, the priest hears Maddalena's confession and she says: "I have sinned so much Father," to which he replies, "You were in the dark, you couldn't see." When Guiseppe and Angela have returned to the room, the priest administers the Last Communion and Maddalena dies. Then, Dr. Ackroyd ushers Angela out of the room and consigns her to the charge of Evelyn, but, moments later, Nino appears standing at the open window and draws his knife with the intention of murdering Guiseppe. Guiseppe says: "Goodbye Maddalena, my beloved wife. The memory of our life together will always be with me, I wish I had made you happier, forgive me." On hearing that Maddalena was Guiseppe's wife and not his lover, Nino appears shocked and full of remorse, and after Guiseppe has placed a cross on Maddalena's breast Nino puts away his knife and throws a white rose beside it. The nature of Maddalena/Rosanna's transgressions leaves the narrative unable to endorse even a penitent Maddalena, and there is no other option but for the film to conclude with Maddalena's death. In many of the other Gainsborough melodramas, the narrative spotlight now turns to the "good" romantic couple whose marriage provides a satisfactory narrative closure and a return to "normality."

Along these lines, some commentators have interpreted *Madonna of the Seven Moons* as offering normative closure through its shifting of narrative emphasis to its two alternative couples, Maddalena's daughter Angela and Evelyn, and Nesta and Jimmy Logan. Pam Cook, for example, sees the film as turning its attention toward the end away from Maddalena and toward

> the need for a new independent woman, resourceful and courageous, capable of forming egalitarian relationships with men. This 'new woman' is seen to be important to the founding of a new social order based on honesty and democracy, allowing for the woman's freedom of action, unlike the 'old' order based on a religious suppression of women's sexuality.[33]

According to Cook, *Madonna of the Seven Moons* suggests Angela as the new, independent, and resourceful heroine whose potential to bring about this cultural

---

[33] Pam Cook, "Melodrama and the Woman's Picture," in *BFI Dossier 18: Gainsborough Melodrama*, ed. by Sue Aspinall and Robert Murphy (London: BFI Publishing, 1983), pp. 24–5.

change is evidenced by her investigating her mother's secret when her father and Dr. Ackroyd have failed to do so. In similar terms, Sue Aspinall suggests that Angela becomes the focus of the narrative toward the end of the film when she has been lured to the Seven Moons by Sandro. According to Aspinall, the film's conclusion, while being unable to endorse Maddalena, instead proposes the union of Angela and Evelyn and the "mature modern couple," the Logans, as representing new types of marital relationships based on affection, humor, and relatively informal sexual relations.[34]

I agree with Aspinall that in the marriage of Jimmy and Nesta Logan the film does provide an alternative model to the sexually repressed marriage of Maddalena and Guiseppe. However, the Logans are minor figures in the story, disappearing from the narrative some time before the end of the film and therefore excluded from the film's narrative resolution. Also, the timid and accident-prone figure of Nesta is a long way from being the resourceful and independent woman who could fill the void in the narrative left by the death of the complex and magnetic figure of Maddalena/Rosanna. The choreography of the film's final sequence makes it clear that it is not the Logans, but Angela and Evelyn who are proposed as the romantic couple that in so many of the Gainsborough melodramas provide a means of reproducing the productive marital relationship (Figure 4.12). But what is remarkable is that the film's narrative conclusion can be revealed as unresolved because of the flaws that it has already presented as existing in the characters of Angela and Evelyn.

When Angela arrives in Rome after her journey from London, her unconventional dress and high-spirited behavior cause considerable anxiety in the quiet Labardi household, and these elements are at least partly responsible for Maddalena's third breakdown. On the night before her birthday party, Angela questions Dr. Ackroyd in insensitive terms about her mother's illness as Maddalena sits playing the piano, and these questions cause Maddalena's physical and psychical collapse. Later, when she resolves to go to Florence to investigate her mother's disappearance, Angela's attempts to find Maddalena are ineffectual, leading only to her attempted rape by Sandro and indirectly to his death and the death of her mother. As Robert Murphy observes, Angela's behavior is consistently "silly and superficial, a left-over from some thirties British comedy

[34] Ibid.

Figure 4.12 *Madonna of the Seven Moons*: The reproduction of the means of reproduction.

where an ostensibly independent young woman tries to investigate by herself only to reveal that she is weak and helpless and in need of rescue by a strong man."[35] In similar terms, Angela's fiancée Evelyn is very far from the strong and sexually potent male figure that the narrative suggests is needed to replace the flawed figure of Guiseppe.

At the beginning of the film, while Evelyn is driving her to Florence, Angela twice puts her head on Evelyn's shoulder, only for him to rebuff her saying: "I'm taking no risks!," to which she replies: "How very unromantic […] I wonder why I like you so much, you're not at all the sort of person I should expect to like" (Figure 4.13). Evelyn's sexuality is also rendered in ambivalent terms by his having a female name, and, as the Labardi household awaits their arrival, there is considerable confusion as to whether to expect a man or a woman to be accompanying Angela. Finally, when Angela needs him to take the initiative

---

[35] Robert Murphy, *Realism and Tinsel: Cinema and Society in Britain 1939–1948* (London and New York: Routledge, 1989), p. 51.

Figure 4.13 *Madonna of the Seven Moons*: Angela and Evelyn: "I'm taking no risks!"

when her mother has disappeared, Evelyn disappears to London on diplomatic business and takes no part in the investigation.

The Gainsborough melodramas allocate central roles to strong female characters who challenge and often transgress the traditional boundaries of femininity, but just as much as this, the films often present scenarios in which conventional masculinities are rendered problematic. Many of the films describe situations where the paternal function has ceased to operate effectively, or where it acts detrimentally to the social formations that it has been designed to regulate and protect. For example, this can be found in *Fanny by Gaslight*, where Fanny's adoptive father keeps a brothel in the basement of the family house, a situation that leads ultimately to his death and the destruction of his family. However, the perilous situations caused by errant males are generally rectified in the films' conclusions by a reproduction of the patriarchal order made possible by the survival of the romantic "good" couple. In *Madonna of the Seven Moons*, the collapse of paternal responsibility operates in three separate areas of the film's narrative, all of which have destructive consequences for Maddalena. The first is Maddalena's rape at the beginning of the film. The second is Maddalena and Guiseppe's marriage, which is founded not on love or on Maddalena's or Guiseppe's desire but on the proscription of her father. The third is Guiseppe's admission of his failings as a husband as he kneels at his dying wife's side. However, the place of marriage as a defining ideological element of the dominant order is never consciously questioned in the film; in fact, it is emphasized by Nino's reaction to the revelation that Maddalena/Rosanna is the wife of Guiseppe and not his mistress.

The iconography of the film's final sequence is also problematic. The cross that is placed on Maddalena's breast by Guiseppe as she lies dying is the one that he wears on his watch chain, which no doubt has been given to him by Maddalena, and the rose that Nino throws beside it is the one picked by Maddalena in the garden where they lie on the bank together for the last time. However, the significance of both is unclear. The cross could represent Guiseppe's impression of what he has earlier termed Maddalena's general quality of "saintliness," exemplified in her donations to the children's ward in the hospital in Rome. It could also point toward her Catholic belief, which has been the mechanism by which she has regulated the disastrous effects of her childhood trauma. The meaning of the white flower is equally unclear. Pam Cook claims that Maddalena "dies with the two signs of the impossibility of her existence on her body, the red rose (passion) and the cross (saintly love),"[36] but this reading seems suspect in that the flower is white, and white flowers have been prominent elements of the film's mise-en-scene throughout the film. At the beginning, Maddalena is picking white flowers in the woods where she suffers her attack, dropping them as she is being chased by the stranger. This would point to them as being signifiers of Maddalena's purity and innocence. They are also noticeable in the background at the quiet and ordered Labardi family home in Rome, and Maddalena places white flowers next to Angela's bed before she arrives after traveling from England. These instances could point to her motherliness. Conversely, the white flower at the end of the film must stand for the wild sexual abandon of her relationship with Nino, which has been characterized by her rejection of her marriage and her position as a mother, and the rules imposed by her Catholic upbringing (Figures 4.14 and 4.15).

While *Madonna of the Seven Moons* has laid out the problems facing the dominant social order succinctly, it has offered little potential for a return to

---

[36] Cook, "Melodrama and the Woman's Picture," p. 25.

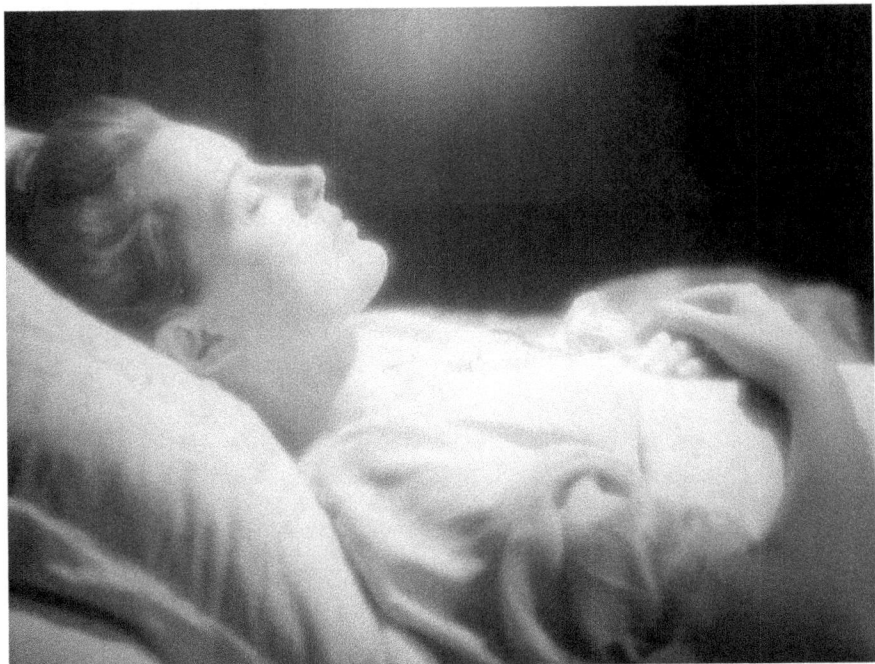

Figure 4.14 *Madonna of the Seven Moons*: The price of Maddalena/Rosanna's transgressions.

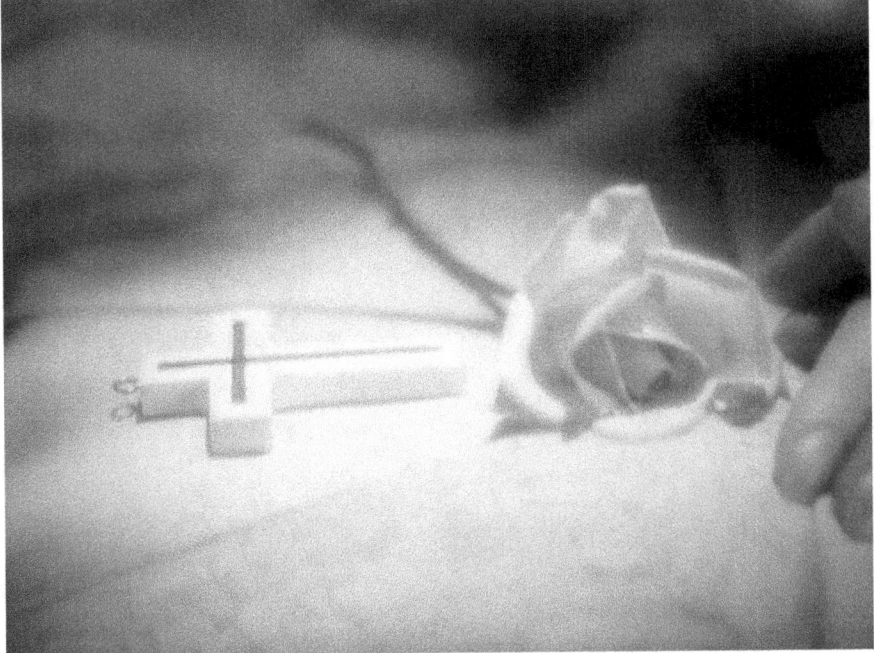

Figure 4.15 *Madonna of the Seven Moons*: "Goodbye Maddalena, my beloved wife."

normality in its surviving romantic couple. Similarly, the uncertainty with which the film lays out the iconography of its final moments denies its audiences any meaningful narrative resolution. The peculiarly oppositional and fragmented nature the film's conclusion tells us much about the uncertain and traumatic time in which the film was made and, as in the ending of *The Seventh Veil*, the high levels of ambivalence that existed at this time about what the social order and the family space should look like in the new post-war Britain.

5

"The World Is Full of Neurotics"

The Traumatized Serviceman, the Collapse of Maternal and Paternal Functions, and the Effects of Post-War Cultural Malaise in *They Made Me a Fugitive* and *Mine Own Executioner*

Introduction to *They Made Me a Fugitive*

Between 1946 and 1948, various British studios produced films that organized their narratives around the activities of the criminal underworld and the figure of the gangster or the black market "spiv." In these films' use of expressionist visual style, their adoption of "hardboiled" conventions of acting and dialogue, their representations of the world as turbulent and often unjust, and their downbeat narrative conclusions, it is possible to find characteristics that are similar to Hollywood film noir, and this has led them to be sometimes grouped together under the heading "British film noir."[1] While acknowledging the importance of tracing the similarities and differences that they display in relation to their American counterparts, in this chapter I am concerned instead with the particularly British nature of these films, and how they come to be influenced by the British experience of the war and by the harsh social and economic realities of the early years of peace. As Robert Murphy has noted:

> Britain had different traditions and a very different experience of the Second World War. The temporary but real solidarity induced by the threat of invasion and the ordeal of the Blitz, the emphasis on communal life, and the drive towards

---

[1] See, for example, William K. Everson, "British Film Noir," in *Films in Review* 38:5 (1987), pp. 285–9; Tony Williams, "British *Film Noir*," in *Film Noir Reader 2*, ed. by Alain Silver and James Ursini (New York: Limelight editions, 1999), pp. 243–69; Robert Murphy, "British Film Noir," in *European Film Noir*, ed. by Andrew Spicer (Manchester and New York: Manchester University Press, 2007), pp. 84–111.

greater equality between men and women, made for a more grimly down to earth atmosphere than in America. Nonetheless Britain suffered a heavy price for the war in terms of lives lost, property damaged, debts incurred, distorted economic development, continued austerity, and a rampant black market.[2]

To this list of factors might be added the uncertainties faced by the more than four million British servicemen who were demobilized between June 1945 and January 1947, the majority of these undoubtedly found the transition to civilian life difficult, the jobs that they had held before the war were often no longer open to them, and the consequent pressures on marriages meant that by 1947 the divorce rate had risen to unprecedented levels.

The individual and collective traumas and anxieties of war and those related to the transition between wartime and peacetime are central to the narrative of *They Made Me a Fugitive*, in which a former R.A.F. serviceman and prisoner of war, Clem Morgan, becomes involved with a gang of black market criminals and its brutal leader, Narcy. The film's adoption of the black market as a central motif is significant. Ina Zweiniger-Bargielowska observes that the use of the black market was extensive in Britain during the war, peaking between 1946 and 1948 and taking the form not only of the theft or receiving of stolen goods, but also the widespread circumvention of regulations that restricted the production and distribution of rationed commodities. The infringement of these regulations thus confronted many of the British public with the prospect of breaking the law for the first time.[3] The discourse of black market activities in *They Made Me a Fugitive* operates as both as a narrative device and as a metaphor that serves to reveal how the transgressions of the marginalized figure of the gangster or spiv can be broadened out and suggested as having relevance to society as a whole.

The first section of this chapter begins by examining how *They Made Me a Fugitive* uses the opposite but complementary figures of Clem and Narcy as the basis for a dialogue that explores contemporary discourses surrounding the effect of trauma and individual and collective moral responsibility. In the second section, I expand my view to explore how the film introduces other characters that function within wider societal discourses that, taken together, describe a neurotic collapse of both paternal and maternal functions in the atmosphere of Britain's post-war cultural malaise.

[2] Murphy, "British Film Noir," p. 89.
[3] Ina Zweiniger-Bargielowska, *Austerity in Britain: Rationing, Controls, and Consumption 1939–1955* (Oxford: Oxford University Press, 2000), pp. 151–3.

Synopsis of *They Made Me a Fugitive*

In *They Made Me a Fugitive*, Narcissus (Griffith Jones), known as Narcy, is the brutal leader of a gang of Soho criminals who deal in stolen black market goods and who use the Valhalla Undertaking Company as a front for their illegal activities. Also influential in the gang is Narcy's mother, Aggie (Mary Merrall). Clem Morgan (Trevor Howard) is a former R.A.F. serviceman and prisoner-of-war with a fine war record. He is invited to join the gang by Narcy because he has "class" and also because Narcy has romantic designs on Clem's fiancée, Ellen (Eve Ashley). Clem thrives in the racket until he discovers that Narcy is dealing in drugs. He strongly disapproves and so confronts Narcy, but the situation is diffused by Aggie. Clem confides to Ellen that he intends to leave the gang after one more job, although he suspects Ellen and Narcy of having begun a relationship. After Clem and Narcy have robbed Hedley's Warehouse, Narcy deliberately sets off the alarm with the intention of entrapping Clem, and as he and Clem flee the scene in a getaway car driven by another of the gang members, Soapy (Jack McNaughton), Narcy directs Soapy to run down a policeman who is attempting to stop them. The policeman is killed, and Narcy knocks Clem unconscious. Narcy and Soapy make good their escape, but Clem is arrested by Inspector Rockliffe (Ballard Berkeley), and he is later found guilty of the murder of the policeman and sentenced to fifteen years in Dartmoor Prison.

Clem is visited in prison by Narcy's girlfriend, Sally Connor (Sally Gray), who informs him that Narcy has begun a relationship with Ellen. Sally declares that she has decided to leave Narcy, and that she is considering persuading Soapy to turn King's Evidence and so provide justice for Clem, but Clem does not believe her. Some days later, at the Music Box club in the West End of London, the theatre where Sally works as a chorus girl, Sally appeals to Soapy's girlfriend, Cora (Rene Ray), to help her effect Clem's release from prison by influencing Soapy to testify on Clem's behalf. Later that same evening, Narcy, who has found out about Sally's visit to Clem, arrives at the Music Box and brutally beats her. Clem escapes from prison, and travels toward London with the intention of clearing his name. On the journey, he is shot and wounded, and he later enters a secluded villa where a woman, Mrs Fenshaw (Vida Hope), provides him with food and clothing, and seeks to persuade him to murder her husband. After Clem has left the house in her husband's clothes, Mrs Fenshaw shoots and kills her husband in cold blood.

Having arrived in London, Clem follows Sally to her flat with the intention of persuading her to reveal Soapy's whereabouts. Clem convinces Sally that he is innocent of the murder of Mr. Fenshaw, and after Sally has removed the shotgun pellets from his back, they form a romantic bond. When Narcy and Inspector Rockliffe arrive at the same time at the flat looking for Clem, Sally helps him to escape. Sally is kidnapped by some of Narcy's gang members, and she is taken to one of the gang's hideouts where she finds Cora, who has also been captured. Cora is threatened with a beating by one of Narcy's henchmen, Jim (Michael Brennan), and she is forced to reveal that Soapy is in hiding at the Hotel Nelson. Clem is then arrested by Inspector Rockliffe but immediately released so he can act as bait to entrap Narcy. Soapy is found at the Nelson by Jim, who stabs him to death.

In the film's final sequence, Clem heads for the Valhalla, where Narcy and his gang have taken Sally against her will. Clem and Sally manage to overpower several of the gang members, and Clem and Narcy then fight on the roof. In attempting to escape, Narcy falls and is mortally wounded. As Narcy lies dying on the pavement both Clem and Sally entreat him to reveal Soapy as the killer of the policeman, but he declares that they can both "rot in hell." After Narcy has died, Inspector Rockliffe says that he will get all the facts before he is through. Sally states that she will wait for Clem, and, after he has been led back to prison, the film closes with Sally walking the streets of London alone.

The Opposite and Complementary Figures of Clem and Narcy, and the Discourses of Traumatic Affect and Moral Responsibility in the Post-War Period

Near the beginning of *They Made Me a Fugitive*, we find Narcy at the Valhalla Undertaking Company with Aggie and several of his henchmen. After they have opened a coffin to reveal that it is packed with cartons of black market cigarettes, Narcy stands filing his fingernails with a large metal rasp that seems more suited for woodwork or metalwork (Figure 5.1). He announces to the group that he has arranged to meet a potential recruit called Clem Morgan, "a bloke out of the R.A.F." who has "found life a bit tame since being demobbed," and who has "class." Narcy says, "we need a bit of that in our business," and, while he states that he has class as well, he admits that Clem was "born into it." When one of the

Figure 5.1 *They Made Me a Fugitive*: Narcy and his henchmen at the Valhalla.

gang, Bert, says that Clem "sounds like trouble," Narcy replies: "I'm ashamed of you, Bert, standing in the way of a job for an ex-serviceman."

Later that evening, Narcy arrives at the club where they have arranged to meet, Clem is already at the bar with his fiancée Ellen, and he is drunk. Clem introduces Ellen, and for a moment she and Narcy stare into each other's eyes. The three sit together at the bar, and Narcy observes to Ellen that Clem sounds like "he's seven thousand feet up in the air," but Ellen says that Clem is just feeling sorry for himself. Clem admits that, if it wasn't for Ellen, he would be liable to do himself "a mischief and spin-in." Narcy says to Ellen that Clem has "too much animal spirits" and that what he needs is an outlet, to which she replies: "what he needs is another war." Clem repeatedly makes to light his cigarette and then blows out the flame.

These two sequences introduce Clem and Narcy as the film's central figures, and they hint at the oppositional but complementary facets of their characters that will dictate the path of their future relationship. By means of its careful choreography, the mise-en-scene of the second sequence emphasizes the connection that exists between the two that will in some ways be mediated by Ellen. It is split into three set-ups and in each Clem, Narcy, and Ellen occupy

Figure 5.2 *They Made Me a Fugitive*: Clem, the "bloke out of the R.A.F.," with Ellen and Narcy.

different positions in relation to the others (Figure 5.2). Clem is a fundamentally decent ex-serviceman who is finding the adjustment to civilian life difficult, and he finds himself drawn to the criminal world that is offered by Narcy because he hopes it will provide him not just with an income but also with a substitute for the excitement of the war. As he puts it to Ellen: "Is it my fault that I've got too set in my ways?" However, the sequence also suggests that Clem has suicidal tendencies and has been drinking heavily; we learn later that he has rarely been sober since meeting Ellen: "You've never seen me like this before have you baby. Stone cold sober." In order to reinforce the idea of Clem's mental disintegration, the sequence also introduces the first signs of his compulsively repetitious behavior. His constant lighting and then blowing out the flame of his cigarette lighter suggests a mechanism by which he can keep a grip on a world that he feels is outside his control, and this pattern of behavior points toward a later scene in Sally's flat, when his verbal repetitions will enable him to endure her slow and painful removing of the shotgun pellets from his back.

The film's narrative will reveal that what lies behind Clem's mental disintegration is that he has been a prisoner of war for two years, only escaping his captors by killing a German prison guard with a beer bottle. By harnessing the idea of compulsive repetition, the film suggests both the traumatic effect of Clem's wartime experiences and the way that this effect predetermines the path that Clem is fated to follow in civilian life.

As we have found Freud's illustration of the tendency of the traumatized to repeat in *Beyond the Pleasure Principle* to have a discursive relation to *The Halfway House* and *Dead of Night*, it has no less relevance to *They Made Me a Fugitive*. It will be remembered that Freud describes the game in which he observes his grandson to persistently throw away and retrieve a wooden cotton reel after his mother has left him alone. Freud argues that, by means of the game, the child can turn his passive position into an active one, and the repetitive nature of the game enables the child to work-through his experience, and therefore master it. However, Freud also warns that in extreme cases the tendency toward repetition may become compulsive. In cases such as these, according to Freud, the victim gives the impression of being pursued by a malignant fate or possessed by some "daemonic power," and being fated to experience a "perpetual recurrence of the same thing."[4] Thought of in these terms, the narrative of *They Made Me a Fugitive* can be defined as ordering itself around Clem's unconscious and suicidal urge to revisit his previous experiences and also as tracing the consequences for him and for others of his desperate and compulsive repetition of his wartime trauma.

While the film suggests that Clem's character has been shaped by the trauma of war, Narcy's is proposed as the product of the dislocation that characterized elements of wartime and post-war life at home. As Cora says of Narcy, he is "not even a respectable crook, just cheap, rotten, after the war trash." That Narcy is dressed in garish tie, monogrammed shirt, and silk handkerchief differentiates him from Clem in his demob suit and "old school" or regimental tie, and this demonstrates both the success of Narcy's criminal business and his narcissistic self-absorption. Narcy is interested in Clem and by extension in Ellen because he believes that Clem has "class," and he is realistic enough to admit the economic limitations that his lack of being born into class poses for him. As Andrew Spicer observes, Narcy "must have the style, and the woman, which Clem possesses," and yet at the same time "he cannot co-exist with Clem, that contemptible 'noorotic … amerchoor' with his well-bred scruples."[5] Spicer also pertinently points out the connection between the figure of Narcy and

---

[4] Sigmund Freud, *Beyond the Pleasure Principle*, in *The Standard Edition vol. XVIII*, ed. by James Strachey (London: The Hogarth Press, 1955; repr. 1981), pp. 21–2.
[5] Andrew Spicer, *Typical Men: The Representation of Masculinity in Popular British Cinema* (London and New York: I.B. Tauris, 2001), p. 138.

the "cruel, sexy aristocrats of the Gainsborough costume dramas."[6] Like them, Narcy provides pleasures for the audience that are based on his flaunting of normative codes of moral conduct and accepted behavior. Also like the villains of the Gainsborough melodramas, *They Made Me a Fugitive* provides Narcy with a remarkable number of the film's best lines, and an examination of the film's marketing campaign reveals that it often gave precedence to the figure of Narcy over that of Clem. For example, one poster for the film proclaims in a banner over a picture of Narcy pointing a gun at the reader: "They made me a spiv! The whole town's sizzling over Griffith Jones as Narcy the Spiv, sleek as a snake in the screen sensation you've got to be tough to take!" However, whilst the film renders the character of Narcy attractive to its audiences on a superficial level, it then proceeds to radically undermine this position by revealing the reality of Narcy's state of abjection when he brutally beats Sally in her dressing room at the Music Box club.

This complex and textually rich sequence lasts for less than a minute; it is composed of fifteen shots, some of which last only a second. To provide a meaningful analysis of this sequence I describe each shot in detail.

At the start of the sequence, shot one has Narcy entering the room at the rear of the frame and approaching Sally, who is sitting alone at a dressing table in front of a bank of illuminated mirrors. These seem to tilt precariously over her. Narcy says that he knows that Sally has visited Clem in prison, but she affects a surface of defiance. In shot two, Sally sits in the foreground with Narcy standing over her; we see that there is another bank of dressing tables and mirrors behind her. Narcy accuses Sally of revealing to Clem that he is "going with" Clem's fiancée, Ellen, and he pulls Sally to her feet. Shot three is of a mirror's reflection of the chair that Sally has been sitting on; Narcy pulls it away, creating a space on the floor behind her. Shot four has Sally facing Narcy at the front of the frame, behind her a mirror reflects them both, in the reflection we can see his face and Sally's back. Narcy then slaps Sally viciously across the face. Shot five is a close-up version of shot four, but it removes Narcy and Sally from the foreground and shows only their reflection in the mirror. Narcy's face is horribly distorted as if by some impurity in the mirror's surface (Figure 5.3).

Shot six repeats shot four. Sally says to Narcy: "Always the perfect little gentleman." She is still calm, but her composure is beginning to falter. Shot seven repeats shot five, as Narcy slaps Sally across the face for the second time. Shot

[6] Ibid., p. 137.

Figure 5.3 *They Made Me a Fugitive*: Narcy's state of abjection.

eight repeats shot three, and we again see the floor space reflected in the mirror. Sally begins to fall. Shot nine is just a brief flash of Sally's face. Shot ten is a close-up of Cora, who is listening fearfully at the door. In shot eleven, Narcy is seen in medium shot kicking Sally as she lies on the floor. Shot twelve is another close-up of Sally, but the horror of her situation is now obvious to her. She is looking straight into the camera as the viewer is placed directly in the position of Narcy (Figure 5.4). Shot thirteen is similar to shots five and seven. Narcy's face is again seen as distorted in the mirror as we hear him slapping Sally for the third time. Shot fourteen repeats shot twelve, a close-up of Sally's frightened face, but now the surface of the film itself seems to have become corrupted, and the emulsion partly erased. Finally, in shot fifteen, we see Narcy from Sally's perspective. He is kicking her repeatedly, and her view of him begins to spin faster and faster on a central axis, first one way and then the other (Figure 5.5).

This brutal and shocking scene reveals to us, and to Sally, the truth that lies behind Narcy's superficially attractive façade. Up until this point, Sally has felt that she has the measure of Narcy because she feels that she knows "how to take care of herself," as she has earlier stated to Cora: "I'm not frightened of Narcy, he wouldn't try anything on me." This scene is a point of no return for Sally,

Figure 5.4 *They Made Me a Fugitive*: Sally realizes Narcy's capacity for evil.

Figure 5.5 *They Made Me a Fugitive*: Sally's world shifting on its axis.

and she is later forced to admit to Cora that she has had to radically change her view of herself, and of Narcy. But how are we to understand why the sequence is constructed in the way that it is, and what is the mechanism by which the film comes to remove the surface that up until now has colored both our and Sally's view of Narcy?

It is useful at this point to explore how contemporary engagements with Klein's object relational revision of Freudian psychoanalysis might be found to have a discursive relation to this sequence. The theory of object relations proposes that internal objects are the psychical representations of those external objects with which the subject has formed interpersonal connections. According to Klein, internal objects are thought of as being in a constant state of flux as the individual's experience of the external world changes, and the inconsistencies that develop between the subject's internal world and the subject's experience of the world that exists outside lead to a calling into question of the boundaries that exist between subjectivity and objectivity.

In his analysis of this sequence Ian Aitken observes that Cavalcanti, the director of *They Made Me a Fugitive*, often employs mirrors in his films to enable his characters to see themselves "as they really are."[7] Referring to Narcy's distorted reflection, he states that:

> At first, Narcy's reflection appears normal, but, after he has slapped [Sally] for the first time, it becomes inexplicably distorted, as though disclosing the underlying brutality normally masked by his handsome appearance. This shot, achieved through the use of lighting effects, is one of the most literal representations of the naturalist 'inner beast' in all of Cavalcanti's films.[8]

Aitken is implying that the shots in which Narcy's face is distorted can best be understood as existing within a framework of expressionist aesthetics. As Annette Kuhn and Julia Knight have explained, the term "expressionism" as used within film studies refers to "an extreme stylization of mise-en-scène in which the formal organization of the film is made very obvious [...]. The overall effect is to create a self-contained fantasy world quite separate from everyday reality."[9]

However, thinking of the sequence as being organized in object relational terms, at the beginning both we and Sally are united by the state of un-integration

---

[7] Ian Aitken, *Alberto Cavalcanti: Realism, Surrealism and National Cinemas* (London and New York: Flicks Books, 2000), p. 171.
[8] Ibid., p. 171.
[9] Annette Kuhn and Julia Knight, "Weimar Cinema," in *The Cinema Book*, ed. by Pam Cook (London: Palgrave Macmillan, 1999; repr. 2007), p. 208.

that we have allowed to build up between the reality of Narcy as a brutal drug dealer, and our internally constructed figure of Narcy that has been colored by the film's ordering of his superficial attraction. The repeated distortions of shots 5, 7, and 13 reveal this state of un-integration to us, but the fact that the distortions exist only within the expressionist formal structure of the film means that, at this point, Sally is still laboring under her illusion about Narcy's true nature. Shots 9, 12, and 14 plot the rapid trajectory of Sally's realization that she has miscalculated both the level of her own agency and Narcy's capacity for evil, and it is the time delay between our realization and Sally's realization that imbues the sequence with its visceral power. By shot 15, our view of Narcy and Sally's view have again become realigned, and we enter Sally's subjectivity for the first time as the image spins first one way then the other. At this point, we share Sally's perspective of Narcy kicking her again and again, and this view certainly emphasizes the extreme violence of the assault on Sally, but it also signifies that the world that we and Sally thought of as existing before has shifted on its axis. In our forced acknowledgment of our previous disavowal of Narcy's true nature, which we have, up until this point, shared with Sally, we are faced with our complicity in Narcy's lack of moral responsibility, and in his state of abjection.

The film's placing of the viewer in a position of complicity in this sequence is something that will recur with increasing frequency as the narrative progresses. From now on, while Narcy remains at the center of the atmosphere of insidious moral disintegration that the film describes as pervading post-war British society, no one is absolved from some level of implication.

The Collapse of the Paternal and Maternal Functions and the Wider Implications of Britain's Post-War Cultural Malaise

I have already demonstrated how *They Made Me a Fugitive* suggests that Narcy's various crimes have implications for the wider society by highlighting the state of disavowal that the audience has allowed to build up in respect of Narcy's true nature. In this section, I begin by examining other means by which the film widens out the theme of moral responsibility, specifically through its presentation of the actions of three of its female characters, Aggie, Ellen, and Sally, all of whom are part of Narcy's criminal world. I proceed to examine how the film enlarges its perspective still further in describing the members of the broader public whom Clem encounters as he makes his way back to London after his escape from prison. Finally, I investigate what is at stake in the film's conclusion, how it differs from the one intended in the film's shooting script, and how the film can be found to delineate a worldview that suggests a collapse of both paternal and maternal functioning within the atmosphere of Britain's post-war cultural malaise.

Early in the film, we are introduced to Aggie at the Valhalla Undertaking Company as several of Narcy's henchmen carry in a coffin that supposedly contains the mortal remains of Alfred George Dabcock of 21 Poplar Street. Played by Mary Merrall, the British character actor who would have been known to contemporary audiences for her upright matriarchal roles in the Ealing productions *Dead of Night* and *Pink String and Sealing Wax* (Robert Hamer, 1945), Aggie seems at first glance to be the epitome of Victorian era respectability. Always dressed in black and wearing jet mourning jewelry, she acts as the public face of Narcy's business, and she intones that Mr. Dabcock "was playing croquet yesterday, not a care in the world. Sic transit gloria mundi." However, when the coffin is opened to reveal that it is packed instead with cartons of black market cigarettes, Aggie lights a cigar and tells the group to "keep out a couple of hundred for me will you? My boyfriend smokes like a chimney." When Aggie later announces that another criminal gang leader, Limpy, is to deliver a consignment of black market New Zealand mutton, she asks Soapy to "keep me a leg of it, if it's one thing my boyfriend likes it's mutton," to which Soapy replies: "Dressed as lamb …"

In his assessment of the character of Aggie, Ian Aitken sees her as acting as one of several in the film that behave in ways designed to contravene conventional mores: "It is not simply that Aggie is an eccentric older woman here, but that the conventional order of things has, to some extent, been inverted within the world she inhabits with Narcy and the others."[10] Aggie's tendency toward moral transgression is also apparent in a later sequence, when Clem threatens to leave the gang after discovering that a consignment of black market stockings that he has transported has contained a quantity of cocaine.[11] Aggie intervenes in the resulting stand-off between him and Narcy by saying that "Narcy ain't going to

---

[10] Aitken, *Alberto Cavalcanti*, p. 168.
[11] A close-up reveals the drug to be a white powder that is referred to by Narcy as "sherbet," but the film's shooting script specifically defines the drug as cocaine. This reference was removed in the film at the request of the BBFC. The shooting script is held in the BFI's Special Collections, reference SCR-17258.

run this stuff as steady line. He's just passing it through for Limpy, same way as Limpy does for us." Dealing in illegal drugs is, for Clem, a line that must not be crossed, but Aggie's intervention is not a sign of her support for Clem's position, but merely her way of defusing a difficult situation, and expediting the gang's return to their criminal activities. Crucially, neither Aggie, nor Clem's fiancée Ellen, who is a bystander in the scene, exhibits any sign that Clem's moral position has any significance for them at all.

The inversion of the conventional order of things also extends to the way that personal relationships are mostly presented in the film as unconventional, and contingent purely on self-interest and economic advancement. When Clem introduces Ellen to Narcy early in the film, a close-up of her reveals her immediate attraction to Narcy, and she abandons Clem soon afterward purely on the grounds that Narcy seems to her to be a better financial prospect. After Clem has threatened to leave the gang, Narcy seems to be undecided as to what measures to take, but, when Clem privately confides his intention to Ellen, she says to him: "You can't do that now you know too much." After Clem says to Ellen that it might break her heart to tear herself away from Narcy, she playfully draws the fingernails of her clawed hand down the side of his face, and the implication is that it is Ellen who influences Narcy to entrap Clem as they flee in the getaway car from Hedley's Warehouse. In similar terms, Narcy abandons Sally for Ellen, prompting Sally's approach to Clem in prison, an action motivated to a large degree by her desire for revenge on Narcy. All these inversions of the conventional order of things exist within the world that these characters inhabit with Narcy; however, the film proceeds to suggest a more general malaise in the sequence that describes Clem's journey back to London after making his escape from Dartmoor Prison.

A montage of shots reveals Clem's journey over Dartmoor as he is pursued by a large contingent of policemen on foot and on horseback. As night falls, Clem finds himself at a secluded villa, and in an extended point-of-view shot we adopt his position as he crosses the villa's unkempt gardens and enters the house through an open set of French doors. Clem finds himself in a large drawing room, and he is confronted with the owner of the house, Mrs. Fenshaw. In another point-of-view shot we now adopt her position as she stares at Clem, who asks whether she is alone, to which she replies that her husband is asleep upstairs. Mrs. Fenshaw acts as if in a trance; her face is expressionless, her voice monotone, and her eyes stare vacantly (Figure 5.6). She states that she knows

Figure 5.6 *They Made Me a Fugitive*: Mrs. Fenshaw as Ferenczi's "mechanical automaton."

who Clem is and that she has heard about him on the wireless, and she offers him clean clothes, food, and a hot bath, and in return she says that she expects Clem to do her "a service."

After Clem has bathed and shaved, he sits down to the meal that Mrs. Fenshaw has prepared. Now Mr. Fenshaw appears in a dressing gown, he is clearly drunk, and he shows no surprise at Clem's presence, merely saying to him: "Just forget you saw me." While Clem eats, Mrs. Fenshaw says that she has heard that he was in prison for killing someone, and while he denies this, Clem admits that, during the war, he had killed a German prison guard. At this point, the "service" that Mrs. Fenshaw requires becomes clear when she offers to give Clem a gun if he will use it to kill her husband. Clem refuses, saying to her: "You're round the bend," and when he immediately leaves, Mrs. Fenshaw proceeds to murder her husband in cold blood, shooting him six times and continuing to pull the trigger repeatedly as he lies dead at her feet (Figure 5.7). In his assessment of this sequence, Aitken describes it as "one of the most surreal"[12] in the film, and he

[12] Aitken, *Alberto Cavalcanti*, p. 174.

Figure 5.7 *They Made Me a Fugitive*: The barbarities that human beings are capable of: Mrs. Fenshaw murders her husband.

connects it to others in Cavalcanti's films that betray the influence of surrealism in their employment of "the structures of the dream, in which the boundaries between the real world and the dream world merge into each other."[13]

I would like to argue instead that this sequence seems to be structured around a realist aesthetic, which is reminiscent of two scenes from Cavalcanti's 1942 Ealing production *Went the Day Well?* In that film, in order to combat the threat posed by an invasion of German troops in the small English village of Bramley End, the elderly postmistress, Mrs. Collins, is forced to kill a German soldier as he sits in her kitchen. After temporarily blinding him with pepper, she purposefully strides toward her victim before dispatching him with a blow to the head with an axe. Later in the film, as the German soldiers are laying siege to the village's manor house, the vicar's daughter, Nora, shoots and kills Oliver Wilsford, a resident of the village whom she loves, after finding him to be a German spy. Both these sequences show acts of extreme violence that are perpetrated by women, presenting them in an uncompromising way and ending

[13] Ibid., p. 155.

with shots of Mrs. Collins and Nora that display their shocked reactions. In highlighting the realist texture of these scenes James Chapman states that:

> The disturbing quality of *Went the Day Well?* lies in the way in which it depicts [these events] with a degree of brutal realism that is quite shocking. This aspect of the film was emphasized in Ealing's publicity material, which said that "the realism of the picture is such that even the hard boiled, skeptical cinemagoers should fall under the spell of its convincing power."[14]

Aitken's description of the scene in *They Made Me a Fugitive* as being "surreal" is presumably based on the catatonic state that Mrs. Fenshaw inhabits both before and after the murder of her husband. While this is undoubtedly true, the question is how can this fact be reconciled with my claim that the scenes from both films are structured within an equally realist aesthetic? In *Beyond the Pleasure Principle*, Freud proposes the existence within the psyche of a "protective shield against stimuli," which has the purpose of protecting the integrity of the mind against an overload of excitation that attacks it both from inside the self and from the external world. According to Freud, traumatic neurosis is the consequence of an extensive breach in this protective shield, and what causes traumatic affect is not the violence of the shock itself but the "fright and the threat to life" that the shock causes.[15] In his later work *Inhibitions, Symptoms and Anxiety*, Freud states that the subject's spontaneous reaction to trauma is often the mobilization of a state of "automatic anxiety," which is a product of "mental helplessness," and which acts as a mechanism to protect the ego from further damage.[16]

Ferenczi, in his seminal paper on historical trauma "Confusion of Tongues," expands Freud's idea in stating that in the aftermath of trauma the victim is "paralyzed by enormous anxiety." Her thinking becomes dissociated and fragmented, and she often carries herself in a "dream-like state" that recalls that of a "mechanical automaton".[17] As I have already argued, whilst some wartime films certainly describe *events* that have the potential to be traumatic, in the post-war period British cinema becomes more willing to represent the traumatic *effects* of those events in explicit terms. In how *They*

---

[14] James Chapman, *The British at War: Cinema, State and Propaganda 1939–1945* (London and New York: I.B. Tauris, 1998; repr. 2008), p. 228.
[15] Freud, *Beyond the Pleasure Principle*, pp. 29–31.
[16] Sigmund Freud, "Inhibitions, Symptoms and Anxiety," in *The Standard Edition vol. XX*, ed. by James Strachey (London: The Hogarth Press, 1959; repr. 1986), p. 138.
[17] Sándor Ferenczi, "Confusion of the Tongues between the Adults and the Child," in *International Journal of Psychoanalysis* 30 (1949), p. 228.

Made Me a Fugitive presents the figure of Mrs. Fenshaw as murdering her husband whilst within a dream-like state of helplessness and mental paralysis, the film draws on the symptoms of traumatization that Freud and Ferenczi have described. The film therefore constructs the actions of Mrs. Fenshaw not within a surrealist aesthetic but a realist one, and her as the traumatized perpetrator of a crime that finds its motivation in the hellish world within which she is incarcerated. By its use of point-of-view shots, the film also anchors us securely within both Mrs. Fenshaw's and Clem's subjectivity, and it encourages us to recognize the "daemonic" nature and complexity of their different traumatic experiences.

Both the transgressive actions of Mr. and Mrs. Fenshaw during this scene and her later willingness to frame Clem for her crime sit comfortably with the pattern of the whole narrative segment that describes Clem's journey back to London. At the beginning of the segment, Clem is shot in the back by a farmer although Clem poses no physical threat to him and after only the scantest of warnings. Later in the segment, a lorry driver gives him a lift part of the way and observes that "people have got terrible dishonest since the war, I don't know what the country's coming to" before offering to sell Clem black market petrol coupons and seeming to take pleasure in Clem's pain as his wounded back is slammed repeatedly against the hard cabin seat. Thus, the insidious moral disintegration that has up until now been limited in the film to those connected with Narcy's gang is observed to have permeated society as a whole.

Writing about *They Made Me a Fugitive*, Charles Drazin recounts that Cavalcanti had traveled during the last days of the war to a newly liberated Paris and then on to Germany, and that the trip had had a profound effect on him:

> His impression was of a country that had been dislodged from its foundations, of a people whose moral worth the Nazis had systematically undermined. The weeks he went on to spend in a defeated Germany served only to deepen his despair. He returned to England haunted by the ease with which evil could undo civilized values and reduce ordinary people to acts of depravity.[18]

In a short sequence after Clem has arrived back in London, Sally is seen reading the front page of a newspaper dated the fifth of February 1947. Under a headline that says: "Morgan now in London" and alongside articles that appear under the

---

[18] Charles Drazin, *The Finest Years: British Cinema of the 1940s* (London and New York: I.B. Tauris, 2007), p. 131.

"The World Is Full of Neurotics"   177

Figure 5.8 *They Made Me a Fugitive*: Carmen Mory, the "Black Angel" of Ravensbrück.

banners: "Street hold-up bandits foiled" and "Mother and child die in flat," the article announces that "Carmen Mory, the 'Black Angel' of Ravensbrück, four other women, and six men all former members of the staff of the concentration camp, were sentenced to death at the Hamburg war crimes court this afternoon" (Figure 5.8). This image is seen on the screen only for a few seconds but its subliminal conflation of Carmen Mory and the horrors of the Holocaust with contemporary social anxieties surrounding robbery and familial neglect chimes with Drazin's account of Cavalcanti's despair and with his description of the film as being concerned ultimately with "the barbarities that human beings are capable of."[19]

An examination of the shooting script for *They Made Me a Fugitive* reveals that the ending of the film was originally intended to be much less bleak than it turned out. In this version, as Narcy lies dying on the pavement outside the Valhalla after his fall, he says to Inspector Rockliffe: "Soapy killed that copper. I fixed it that way. Morgan's just a bad amateur. If you want me to sign anything,

[19] Ibid., p. 132.

you'd better get cracking." After this, Sally visits Mrs. Fenshaw who admits the murder of her husband and says that she is prepared to make a statement to the police. The script ends with Sally visiting Clem in prison and telling him that Inspector Rockliffe is confident that Clem's sentence will be radically reduced at his retrial. Although the final version of the film provides some hope for Clem in Inspector Rockliffe's words: "It's alright Miss Connor, we'll get all the facts before we're through," it ends with Clem being led back to prison and Sally left alone.

Many British films of this period describe situations in which male subjectivity is problematized and female subjectivity is accentuated, and both of these departures from the norm are defined as contributing to the destabilization of the dominant social formation. By punishing their errant female figures, and redeeming their male figures, these films suggest the potential for a return to normative gender roles in their conclusions. *They Made Me a Fugitive* proposes a post-war British cultural malaise in which both paternal and maternal function has atrophied. Society is fragmented, the rule of law in the form of Inspector Rockliffe, is ineffectual at best and compromised at worst, and both male and female characters are equally morally transgressive. However, although the figures of Clem and Sally are tainted by their relationships with Narcy, they show signs at the end of the film of having the basis of a relationship not clouded by self-interest or economic advancement. While this and Inspector Rockliffe's assurance to Sally provide some shreds of hope for the future, the viewer is certainly not provided with any certainty that justice will be served, and that the return to pre-war "normality" that the film espouses on a surface level can be restored.

Introduction to *Mine Own Executioner*

While British crime films such as *They Made Me a Fugitive* describe the marginalization of the returning serviceman as resulting from his being subsumed by an underworld made viable by the disassociation of post-war society, other British films of this period are concerned with the challenges faced by what Andrew Spicer has termed the "damaged Everyman." According to Spicer, these films are centered on "ambivalent, sensitive, tortured and tormented male protagonists engaged in a moral struggle within their own natures, who are plunged into neurotic self-doubts and a crisis of sexual and social identity."[20] In similar terms, Robert Murphy draws a line between the post-war British crime cycle and what he terms the "doom-laden" series of "morbid films" of this time that differentiate themselves through their "particular interest in psychology and neurosis."[21] Examples of these types of films include *The Upturned Glass* (Lawrence Huntington, 1946), *The October Man* (Roy Ward Baker, 1947), *Mine Own Executioner* (Anthony Kimmins, 1947), *Daybreak* (Compton Bennett, 1948), and *The Small Back Room* (Michael Powell and Emeric Pressburger, 1949). Psychoanalyst figures and the psychoanalytic setting have a presence in a number of British films of the immediate post-war period, but they are often placed on the periphery of the narrative and employed mainly as a means to provide opportunities for the objective investigation and subjective narration of the films' central characters. What sets *Mine Own Executioner* aside, and what makes it particularly worthy of scrutiny, is that it takes as its two main protagonists a psychoanalyst and his patient, and it makes psychoanalytic investigation and remembrance integral both to its narrative and to its wider worldview.

The story of *Mine Own Executioner* traces the path of Felix Milne's analysis of Adam Lucien, a former Spitfire pilot who has been traumatized by his experiences as a prisoner of the Japanese, and the film also makes central the vicissitudes of Felix's own psychopathology, which it defines in relation to the regressive nature of his sexuality. The film draws comparisons between Adam's and Felix's respective mental disturbances, which find expression in the erratic nature of their behavior and thought processes, and also in the dysfunctional quality of their marital relationships. The screenplay for the film was adapted by Nigel Balchin from his own novel of the same name, the third book of a hugely popular trilogy published in Britain between 1942 and 1945. Balchin was one of the best-known British writers of the Second World War, and his biographer Derek Collett proposes that the great success of his novel can be attributed in part to its concentration on the practice of psychoanalysis: "regarded in the media as a new and exciting one, with public interest in it being stimulated and sustained by the movie industry."[22] The film adaptation, released in Britain in

---

[20] Spicer, *Typical Men*, p. 163.
[21] Robert Murphy, "Riff-raff: British Cinema and the Underworld," in *All Our Yesterdays: 90 Years of British Cinema* (London: BFI Publishing, 1986; repr. 1996), p. 304.
[22] Derek Collett, *His Own Executioner: The Life of Nigel Balchin* (Bristol: SilverWood, 2015), p. 166.

November 1947, is similarly interested in the psychoanalytic processes, finding common ground with other British films of this time by making contemporary psychoanalytic discourses central to its narrative themes and narrative and stylistic structures.

I begin my assessment of *Mine Own Executioner* by examining how the film orientates itself around the causes and consequences of Adam Lucien's war trauma, and I investigate what is at stake in the film's unusual suggestion that his Oedipal fixation acts to motivate a predisposition toward his later trauma. I continue to assess the film's linkage of Adam's schizophrenia to Felix's various neuroses with reference to the consequences that their respective psychical crises have for their ability to function within their marital relationships. Finally, I employ Siegfried Kracauer's contemporaneous work on Hollywood cinema to assess whether the vogue for psychoanalysis in Britain at this time can be attributed to a similar lack of adequate systems of social communication.

Synopsis of *Mine Own Executioner*

Felix Milne (Burgess Meredith) is a dedicated psychoanalyst who splits his professional life between the Emily Ward Psychiatric Clinic, where he gives his services for free, and his private practice at his home. Felix is disillusioned because he feels that his private practice is mostly composed of people who are not really ill, but instead are "distressingly normal and want to be cured of it." Felix also has domestic problems; his marriage to Pat (Dulcie Gray) is in trouble, and whilst he claims to love her "more than most men love their wives," he is unresponsive to her sexual advances, and he constantly bullies her and calls her "the rhino" because of what he perceives as her carelessness and clumsiness. He is also infatuated with Bab (Christine Norden), a glamorous and sophisticated childhood friend of Pat's, who is married to Peter. Felix is consulted by Molly Lucien (Barbara White), who asks him to see her husband, Adam (Kieron Moore), a traumatized former Spitfire pilot and prisoner of war in Burma, who has tried to murder her only the day before. Suspecting that Adam is schizophrenic, Felix tells Molly that he feels unqualified to treat him, and that she is taking a great risk living with him. He suggests to Molly that Adam should visit another specialist, but because of Adam's fanatical objection to doctors, he eventually accedes to Molly's request.

When they meet the following afternoon, Adam seems initially unwilling to work with Felix, but he eventually admits trying to strangle Molly, and agrees to attend weekly sessions. During one of these sessions, Adam gives an account of his attack on Molly mainly in the third person. He says that this event took place after she had fallen asleep while he was preparing for bed, and, though he claims that he "wasn't there," he admits that he "saw a good deal of it." He also refers to Molly as "it." Felix discloses his attraction to Bab to a psychiatrist colleague, Dr. James Garsten (John Laurie), and he admits that his marriage to Pat has been unhappy for a long time and that he bullies her. However, Dr. Garsten assures Felix that it is behaviours such as these that enable both of them to "feel other people's troubles," and to therefore understand their patients' anxieties, depressions, and neuroses.

During one of the weekly sessions with Adam, Felix injects him with sodium pentothal in order to lay bare the repressed memories of Adam's experiences as a prisoner of war. Adam again recounts these experiences mainly in the third person, and from his perspective we witness the sequence of events that begins with the crash of his Spitfire in the jungle. Adam is captured by a Japanese patrol and, after being tortured for several days, he breaks and gives his captors all the information that they have demanded. His leg has been broken during his interrogation, but after some weeks of captivity he manages to kill one of his guards by cracking him on the head with a bamboo pole and he makes good his escape.

After the session, Adam professes to have made a full recovery. But the following morning, Felix warns Molly that she is still in grave danger as he fears that another trauma exists within Adam at a much deeper level. Felix spends the evening with Bab and, after they have seemingly had sex, he receives a call from Pat to say that Adam has shot Molly and that she has been taken to hospital. Felix arrives at the hospital to find that Molly is dying from her wounds, and when he later returns home, he finds a clearly deranged Adam waiting for him and holding Pat at gunpoint. When Felix attempts to disarm him, Adam strikes Felix and then flees the scene.

The following morning, Adam is discovered by the police standing on a ledge at the top of a tall building, and Felix, who is scared of heights, volunteers to climb a fireman's ladder and attempts to talk him down. After Felix has climbed to the ledge, Adam asks him whether Molly had suffered, and when Felix assures him that she had not, Adam shoots himself and then plunges to his death. Sometime later, Felix is compelled to appear at the inquest and the coroner, who is himself a doctor, raises questions about Felix's lack of a medical qualification and is initially censorious of his actions; however, he exonerates Felix of any blame after Dr. Garsten has intervened on his behalf.

On returning home with Pat, Felix is ready to abandon his work because he feels that the job "needs a God to do it properly," but Pat persuades him to continue, although Felix states that it will be she who will pay the price for it, and that there will be no end to her suffering.

The Nature of Adam's Affliction and the Place of the Oedipus Complex in *Mine Own Executioner*'s Ordering of the Aetiology of His Trauma

When Molly Lucien visits Felix Milne's consulting room at his home, she describes the behavior that her husband has displayed to her in the weeks preceding his attempt on her life. According to Molly's account, before his capture and imprisonment by the Japanese Adam had been "more than alright," he had been decorated for his fine war record and their marriage had been a happy one. However, since being invalided out of the armed forces and returning to England, Adam has become very quiet, and sometimes when Molly has spoken to him, she feels that "it was as if he wasn't there".

Later, when Adam arrives at his first meeting with Felix his state of dissociation is made obvious. As he walks along the pavement outside Felix's house, he seems oblivious to the world around him, and in the consulting room his demeanor alternates between a condition of detachment and one of defensive rage and suppressed violence. When Felix asks Adam to tell him something about his parents, a close-up emphasizes his complete lack of emotion as he says: "My father was a barrister," yet when he continues: "My mother was his wife" his expression is shown to change immediately to one of serene rapture (Figure 5.9). After Adam has left the consulting room at the end of the session, Felix writes in his psychiatric report that he believes Adam to be suffering from schizophrenia and that a split personality is "clearly indicated" as well as a "conflict in early childhood." What seems clear to Felix is that Adam's wartime experiences have been the precipitating factor in but not the cause of his mental disturbance, and in a later session Felix injects Adam with sodium pentothal in order to enable him to clearly recollect these events, and to narrate them on the analyst's couch.

Figure 5.9 *Mine Own Executioner*: Adam Lucian: "My mother was his wife."

The sequence that follows describes Adam's drug-induced remembrance, repetition, and initial working-through of his traumatic wartime experiences, laying out in detail the shooting-down of his Spitfire over the jungle, his capture by a Japanese patrol, his subsequent torture, and finally his escape after he has killed a guard by cracking his skull. Adam narrates his story mostly in the first person; the film adopts Adam's visual and aural perspective and as a result the spectator is firmly sutured into his subjectivity (Figure 5.10).

This part of the film can be defined as a radical example of many sequences that occur in British films of this period in which the films' narrative and formal structures make visible fundamental elements of the troubled inner worlds of their characters. On several occasions, Adam's narration switches to the third person, particularly when he recounts events of a traumatic nature, and these slippages connect this testimony to the peculiar nature of his previous account of his attempted murder of Molly and they also emphasize the splitting of his psyche that his trauma has initiated.

Figure 5.10 *Mine Own Executioner*: Adam re-living his wartime trauma in the psychoanalytic setting.

When Adam returns to Felix's consulting room the following day, he seems to have been transformed by his experience, and when Felix asks him whether he feels better he replies that he considers himself to be "completely different" and "completely normal now." However, to Adam's profound disappointment, Felix states that he believes that their work together has instead only just started. Felix announces to Adam that:

> What I must do now is dig a bit deeper into your life [...]. It may be that this thing inside you that is causing all the trouble is getting frightened, it can feel us moving the layers away from on top of it, and it is afraid that if we go on it will be found and kicked out.

Felix believes that what is at the root of Adam's schizophrenia is a fixation that has occurred in his early childhood and the film has already made clear the Oedipal nature of this fixation through its scrutiny of Adam's description of his early relationship with his parents. In his assessment of this aspect of the film, psychoanalyst Ira Konigsberg suggests that Oedipal material is evident throughout the film, and he lists several sequences in which the film employs image and sound to reveal the Oedipal nature of Adam's dysfunction. For example, as he is seen sitting in the cockpit of his plane at the beginning of his drug-induced remembrance of his trauma, Adam can be heard whistling the tune of the nursery rhyme "Rockabye Baby" and as he makes his way home just before he fatally wounds Molly, the refrain occurs two more times, first within the diagesis being played by a boy on a mouth organ and then on the film's soundtrack. Similarly, in this sequence we see Adam walking in a stupor and then lashing out at two boys with his walking stick after they have run into him and he then proceeds to tear furiously at a poster for Nestlé's Milk, which shows the figure of a naked male baby holding a ball (Figure 5.11). Finally, after Adam has broken into Felix's house, and he is holding Pat at gunpoint, he seems to be referencing his Oedipal fantasy directly when he says to Felix: "Look, I know about women. It's quite clear now, in some ways it's a pity that it wasn't clear before, but I was only a child at the time," and when he tells Pat that she can leave the room he adds: "But she'll ring up the police. They're all the same. No principles."[23]

Figure 5.11 *Mine Own Executioner*: Adam's Oedipal fixation.

[23] Ira Konigsberg, "Does It Work? Mine Own Executioner and Psychoanalytic Interpretation," in *Contemporary Psychoanalysis* 46:2 (2010), pp. 194–5.

In its suggestion that it is Adam's Oedipal fixation that motivates his predisposition toward his later trauma, *Mine Own Executioner* is appropriating an historical psychoanalytic discourse that had come to circulate soon after the end of the First World War. In September 1918, a congress of psychoanalysts was convened in Budapest, attended by official representatives of the governments of Austria, Germany, and Hungary, and intended to engage with the increasing appreciation of the part played by war neuroses in military strategy.[24] Leading psychoanalysts of the time including Ferenczi, Karl Abraham, Ernst Simmel, and Ernest Jones presented papers at the conference, and these were published in a collected volume by the International Psycho-Analytic Press in 1921. In their papers, the authors consistently draw parallels between the neuroses of peacetime and those that have been caused by those traumatic events experienced on the battlefield, and they claim that these neuroses can be traced back to unresolved infantile conflicts at one of the stages of libidinal evolution. For example, Simmel declares that:

> The fact that in the midst of [the occurrences of war] one soldier remains well while another becomes a neurotic may, so far as my experience goes, be very well connected with the psycho-sexual constellation of the particular person. The systematic investigation of the dream-life of the soldier, even after the removal of the war neurotic symptoms, has indeed made it possible to recognise quite frequently threads that lead down to the primordial network of infantile sexuality.[25]

British films of the immediate post-war period generally take great pains to make it clear that the neuroses and psychoses of their central figures have their roots not in Oedipal fixations that have established themselves in their early childhoods but in real historical events that they have experienced in later life such as rape and physical abuse, parental loss, or abandonment. By their removing Oedipal desire as the determining factor in trauma these films define the later psychopathological behavior of their characters as being caused by exogenous events that lie outside the victim's control, and not by endogenous factors that have been motivated by their own psychical dysfunctions. Within this model, these films suggest that the victim of trauma has no reason to look within for the underlying causes of traumatization, with all the implications

---

[24] Peter Gay, *Freud: A Life for Our Time* (London: Max Press, 2006), pp. 375–6.
[25] Sándor Ferenczi, Ernst Simmel, et al., *Psycho-Analysis and the War Neuroses* (London, New York, and Vienna: The International Psycho-Analytic Press, 1921), p. 31.

of sexual guilt that this implies. In the aftermath of the Second World War, the general tendency for British cinema to adopt this model must have been liberating for its contemporary audiences, who had themselves often been exposed to trauma through their experiences of evacuation, the Blitz, and other factors.

The key question is, why does the narrative of *Mine Own Executioner* run precisely counter to this general rule?

In his assessment of this aspect of the film, Tony Williams suggests that the film's proposition that the aetiology of Adam's psychopathology may be traced to "violent Oedipal aggressive feelings against [his] mother who has betrayed his father" can be understood as a disavowal of "the real causes which lead [him] to murder his wife."[26] Williams is proposing that because of the film's assertion that Adam's trauma has its origin in his Oedipal fixation and not in his wartime experience, it finds itself unable to confront the idea that the horrors of war can form the root cause of trauma. However, Williams goes on to concede that "enough evidence remains in both novel and film to suggest that war trauma plays a major role here."[27]

I would like to argue instead that *Mine Own Executioner* is unique in British cinema at this time in finding itself able to address the trauma of war in explicit terms, *and* in being able to position war trauma within a rigorous contemporary psychoanalytic framework. The other films that have been discussed in this book have been shown as being able to address traumatic experience only by engaging with the subject by displacing it onto other events and other cinematic modes of expression within the generic frameworks of the horror film, the romantic fantasy, the melodrama, or the crime film.

Rather than being thought of as disavowing the "real causes" of Adam's psychosis as Williams suggests, *Mine Own Executioner* should be considered instead as the first British film that is able *not to disavow* both the traumatic events themselves and the psychoanalytic belief that those events are rendered problematic because of the fissures that lie within the archaic network of the victim's own infantile sexuality. The film also widens out these ideas of catastrophic primary fantasy and traumatic predisposition in how it describes Felix's dysfunction and the effects that Adam's and Felix's afflictions have for their ability to function within the system of dominant patriarchal beliefs.

---

[26] Williams, "British *Film Noir*," p. 259.
[27] Ibid., p. 259.

The Broadening of the Scope of Male Affliction, and the Consequences of the Psychopathological Impulse toward Destruction and Self-Destruction

I have described how in *They Made Me a Fugitive* the black market is employed as a metaphor that demonstrates how the transgressions of the gangster or spiv can have relevance to a wider society marked by its dissolution and social fragmentation. While in *Mine Own Executioner* the implications of Adam's wartime trauma occupy the central space of the narrative, I would like to argue that the film takes a similar route to *They Made Me a Fugitive* in broadening the relevance of Adam's affliction by making connections between Adam's distressed mental state and that of Felix. In this way, the film is able to make a wider point about the challenges faced by masculinity in the post-war period, one that defines neurotic self-doubts and crises of social and sexual identity as affecting a broader range of male victims than only the traumatized war veteran.

Early in *Mine Own Executioner*, Felix is in his home consulting room having finished an analytic session with Lady Maresfield, one of his wealthy private patients whom he dismisses as having too much money and too little to do. He is tired and irritable, but he is informed by his nurse that his wife Pat has taken it upon herself to arrange for him to see one more patient. When he emerges angrily from his room, he meets Pat as she is walking downstairs having accidently broken a glass tumbler. Felix confronts her and she is immediately defensive, explaining to him that "I couldn't help it, it did it on purpose," to which he replies with barely concealed venom: "Look darling I don't mind you smashing tumblers, even rather nice ones, but don't do a baby-mine about it, there's a good girl." In the following sequence, it becomes clear that only the night before Felix has threatened to walk out on Pat, putting her "under notice," but now Felix attempts to make light of the matter by calling Pat his "own personal rhinoceros" and assuring her that they will "get it sorted out" when they "have more time." It seems that Felix finds Pat irritating; he also finds himself unable to respond to her sexual advances, and he constantly bullies her and calls her "the rhino" because of what he perceives as her carelessness and clumsiness. Later that evening, Pat and Felix entertain two friends to dinner, Bab, a glamourous and sophisticated childhood friend of Pat's, and her husband, Peter.

During the dinner, Felix makes little attempt to conceal his attraction to Bab, and, when Pat later confronts him about his infatuation, Felix seeks to excuse his behavior by laying before her the conclusions of his self-analysis:

> You realize it hasn't anything to do with Bab *as* Bab. You see there's a bit of me that has never quite grown up, it stays at the mental age of about fourteen. Of course, most of me is very grown up indeed, if it wasn't I couldn't do this job. But outside the job I run up against this 'thing'. It takes all sorts of forms, teasing and bullying you for instance, you know some of them, don't you? This business about Bab, the bit of me that finds her attractive is all part of this 'thing', it is a deliberate childish wantonness.

Whilst Felix is shown to be incapable of controlling both his sadistic impulses toward Pat and the destructive aspects of his regressive sexuality, he does seem to recognize the extent of the detrimental effect that his behavior is having on his marriage. He seeks the advice of his psychiatrist colleague, Dr. Garsten, who assures Felix that it is within his power to change his behavior. However, Dr. Garsten also warns him that this will involve eradicating the very neuroses that enable Felix to "feel other people's troubles" and to understand his patients' anxieties, depressions, and neuroses.

Felix is provided with the opportunity to pursue his infatuation with Bab by the inadvertent actions of her husband, Peter. Toward the end of the dinner party, Peter takes Felix aside and asks him to talk with Bab on a professional basis because he believes her to be "a very queer girl, very queer in many ways," and he suggests to Felix that Bab may have "a bit of a sex complex." After a preliminary examination in his consulting room, Felix announces to Bab: "I wouldn't take you on as a patient if it was all that stood between me and the workhouse" because he is "a darned site too interested" in her. Nevertheless, he later suggests that they meet when he is not acting in a professional capacity.

A few days afterward, Felix takes Bab out on date, and after drinks and dinner at a nightclub, they go back to Bab's house, Peter being away for a few days on business. In Bab's drawing room Felix lies on his back on her couch, Bab is leaning over him, and they hold each other in an intimate embrace (Figure 5.12). Although they are clothed, a close-up has revealed that Bab is barefoot, and the atmosphere of the scene suggests a post-coital languor. Bab then gently suggests to Felix that he should speak his mind and tell her the truth as he is always making his patients do. She says to him: "Close your eyes, and talk, anything that comes into your head," and although he is initially reluctant, he gradually begins

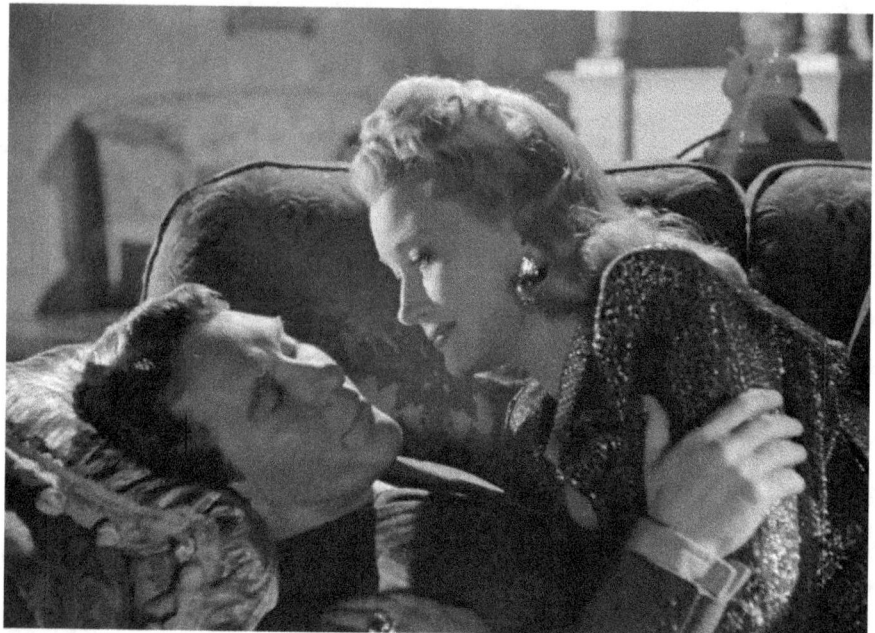

Figure 5.12 *Mine Own Executioner*: Felix on Bab's couch: "Close your eyes, and talk, anything that comes into your head."

to free associate. His words reveal his concern about Adam and his innate desire to forget Adam, and also his fears of his own mortality. He says: "Now he's forgotten, everything forgotten. Kissing and forgetting. Seconds are shorter than ever, hang on to this time."

That this sequence positions Felix on Bab's couch in the place of the analysand echoes Felix's analysis of Adam and it also suggests that they have similar needs, and that common ground might exist within their respective psychopathologies. Similarly, as Ira Konigsberg has noted, the specific way that the film's editing pattern has connected this scene to the one before insinuates the notion that the erratic natures of their lives have become fatally entwined.[28] Just before this sequence, we have seen Adam with Molly in their apartment dressing in preparation for a night on the town. It is made clear that Adam's schizophrenic psychosis now motivates a vision in which his visual impression of Molly is confused with a traumatic memory of the Japanese guard that he has killed during the war (Figures 5.13 and 5.14). Adam immediately fetches a gun from his bedroom and pointing it directly at the camera he shoots Molly five times,

[28] Konigsberg, "Does It Work?", p. 191.

Figure 5.13 *Mine Own Executioner*: "Don't let him see you as a vague or shadowy figure." Molly in the apartment.

Figure 5.14 *Mine Own Executioner*: Deeply buried elements of the traumatic event return in dreams and waking visions.

and the sound of the shots is accentuated on the soundtrack as the sparks fly from the gun's muzzle. A jump-cut then takes us directly to a close-up of a log exploding in the fireplace of Bab's drawing room.

The similarities between Adam's and Felix's afflictions are also reinforced by their respective use of language. After Adam has implied to Felix that Molly has rejected him by going to sleep as he was preparing for bed, Adam finds himself only able to describe her by use of the term "it," a strategy that has the effect of depersonalizing her and therefore enabling him to bring his assault on her into language. In similar terms, Felix's referring to Pat as "the rhino" can be read as a tactic by which he seeks to depersonalize her, and he is only able to admit the existence of his regressive sexuality to Pat by referring to it as "the thing." Through its use of these narrative, formal, and linguistic strategies *Mine Own Executioner* draws together Adam's schizophrenia, which has been found to have been precipitated by his wartime experience, and Felix's neurotic-sadistic impulses and his regressive sexuality, which have been defined as originating within the vicissitudes of everyday life.

However, the defining common ground that *Mine Own Executioner* proposes as existing between Adam and Felix is the compulsively repetitive and destructive behavior that they display toward themselves and their marital relationships. That the novel and the film adaptation of *Mine Own Executioner* both begin with a quotation from John Donne's "Meditation XII" has received no critical attention. The slightly shortened version of the quotation that appears in the film reads thus:

> There are too many Examples of men, that have been their own executioners, and that have made hard shrift to bee so; .... some have beat out their braines at the wal of their prison, and some have eate the fire out of their chimneys; but I do nothing upon my selfe, and yet am mine owne Executioner.

As the literary critic Donald Ramsay Roberts has pointed out, the idea of a death wish that is clearly conveyed in this quotation is a factor that persisted in one form or another throughout Donne's published works. Roberts attributes this to the fact that an urge for self-destruction was a permanent and constant element in Donne's own life. He argues that Donne's essay is a clear anticipation of the concept of the death drive that Freud would put forward in *Beyond the Pleasure Principle* in order to account for the aggressive and self-destructive tendencies that he believed had been revealed by the slaughter of the First World War.[29] The death drive, the urge to return the self to the inorganic state that precedes life, is tied securely by Freud

---

[29] Donald Ramsay Roberts, "The Death Wish of John Donne," in *PMLA* 62:4 (1947), pp. 968–70.

to cases where the neurotic is "daemonically" compelled to repeat over and over the very event that has motivated the initial problem, until the anxiety caused by traumatic tension is eventually reduced to the zero-point of oblivion.

The inclusion of Donne's words at the beginning of *Mine Own Executioner* signals the discursive influence of Donne's and Freud's concept of the death wish or death drive on the particular way that the film has ordered the actions of Adam and Felix. The film defines their respective repetitive-compulsive and destructive tendencies as having their roots in their very different mental afflictions, but they have been shown as rising to the surface within the context of their similar inability to fulfill the role that is expected of them within their marriages. In the same way as it defines Peter as being compelled to project his particular sexual repression onto Bab by creating the fantasy of her "sex complex" in an attempt to disavow his own apparent sexual inadequacy, the film defines both Adam and Felix as seeking to protect themselves from their sexually motivated dilemmas by repetitively turning them outwards and re-directing them toward the destruction of their marital relationships. In its suggestion that there is common ground between Felix's regressive sexuality and Adam's trauma-induced emergence of his Oedipal fixation, the film proposes that insufficiencies such as theirs may emerge just as easily within the vicissitudes of everyday post-war life as within the traumatic experience of the war itself.

The film's suggestion that Adam's and Felix's respective crises as emerging simultaneously within the context of their distressed marital relationships points toward the existence of a more general inability of the male subject to come to terms with the position that he now occupies in the new power system of post-war society. As I will show in the following section, *Mine Own Executioner* proposes that a factor that has accentuated this dilemma is a breakdown in satisfactory systems of social communication. However, it also suggests that a solution to this dilemma may be found within the interpersonal processes of psychoanalysis.

The Post-War Vogue for Psychoanalysis: Fears for the Future and Hope for the Re-instatement of Cultural Systems of Communication

In a series of essays written during the quarter of a century that he spent in America after fleeing Nazi-occupied Europe, the film and cultural theorist Siegfried Kracauer evokes the social developments of the period as well as affording insights into contemporary Hollywood cinema. In "Psychiatry for

Everything," Kracauer addresses the contemporary vogue for psychiatry and particularly psychoanalysis and he argues that, while before the Second World War this had been confined to the intellectual minority, after the war it found such traction within the popular consciousness that it came to achieve the status of a mass phenomenon.[30] What Kracauer finds particularly symptomatic of this vogue are the many "psychological films" being produced in Hollywood at this time, a trend that had begun around 1944, and that at the time remained "unparalleled in other countries, with the exception perhaps of England, where it [had] made only a hesitant beginning."[31] The purpose of Kracauer's essay is to explain this popular fascination and he points toward the proliferation of neurosis amongst people in all walks of life as being one of its motivating factors.

However, while Kracauer suggests that the natural impulse of the popular imagination is to turn from its neurotic symptoms toward measures that might provide some means of redress such as the reform of society or environmental change he observes that the spotlight remains turned inward:

> History teaches us that this shift of emphasis from outer to inner conditions is usually provoked by the impact of drastic social change and crisis. The vogue for psychiatry in my opinion owes its existence to two attitudes forced upon us by the present pressures of American civilization. One attitude amounts to an evasion. The other results from an attempt to compensate for the lack of what I would call emotional behaviour patterns.[32]

Kracauer describes how these two attitudes had arisen within the all-pervasive atmosphere of menace and danger that had emerged in the post-war period from developments such as the atomic bomb, social change, economic uncertainty, and the onset of the Cold War. He suggests the "evasion" as occurring within the context of the "spiritual crisis" that had come to pass; people feeling lost and therefore compelled to improvise day-to-day decisions, and, gripped by uncertainty about the system of values in which these decisions had been rooted, evading them by retreating from society toward the individual. Kracauer proposes the second impulse, the inability to compensate for the lack of emotional behavior patterns, to be based on an absence of adequate systems of interpersonal communication able to provide outlets for these pressures. He

---

[30] Siegfried Kracauer, "Psychiatry for Everything and Everybody: The Present Vogue—and What Is behind It," in *Siegfried Kracauer's American Writings*, ed. by Johannes von Moltke and Kristy Rawson (Berkeley, Los Angeles, and London: University of California Press, 2012), p. 62.
[31] Ibid., p. 63.
[32] Ibid., p. 64.

concludes that, while the fascination for psychiatry has its roots in contemporary anxieties, elements of hope nevertheless present themselves in that people are becoming increasingly aware of the vacuum that exists around them. They are drawn to the idea of psychiatry in the hope that it might provide an alternative means of communication.[33]

In the light of Kracauer's conclusion, the key question that presents itself at this stage is whether this can be found to have relevance to the particular way that psychoanalysis is configured in British cinema at this time. Or, put this more specifically, can psychoanalysis be found to operate in *Mine Own Executioner* not only as a mode of expression that functions to describe and compare Adam's and Felix's particular dysfunctions but as a means of redress for the fears of society as a whole?

Mine Own Executioner defines its two main male figures in terms of their respective psychopathologies, and by various means it draws these together to reveal them as being symptomatic of the wider dilemmas that confront masculinity in post-war society. Other male figures are suggested by the film as suffering from similar psychical dysfunctions. For example, Peter projects his repression onto Bab by creating her "sex complex," and Dr. Garsten acknowledges the similarity between himself and Felix when he admits that they are both "neurotics who know exactly what it feels like to make fools of themselves."

However, whilst the main narrative thrust of the film employs psychoanalytic ideas to trace the path of these various male inadequacies, the film also develops the idea of there being common ground between the mode of communication that defines the psychoanalytic setting, and the systems of communication that exist in everyday life. As Charles Rycroft observes, psychoanalytic theory conceives of mankind

> as a social animal, who, in addition to his drive to self-preservation and self-awareness, is also continuously concerned to maintain himself in a reciprocal, adaptive interrelationship with his objects and which sees psychodynamics as the study of the development of the capacity for interpersonal relations, and psychopathology as the study of the ways in which this capacity may break down.[34]

---

[33] Ibid., pp. 64–72.
[34] Charles Rycroft, "An Enquiry into the Function of Words in the Psycho-Analytic Situation," in *The British School of Psychoanalysis: The Independent Tradition*, ed. by Gregorio Kohon (New Haven and London: Yale University Press, 1986), p. 238.

This concept of a linkage existing between psychoanalysis and day-to-day interpersonal communication is introduced in humorous terms near the beginning of *Mine Own Executioner*, when Felix and Pat are attending a cocktail party given by Bab and Peter. Bab introduces Felix to an advertising agent who describes himself as being in the "same line of business" as Felix, and after declaring advertising to be "psychology, pure psychology" he proposes that Felix should work with him to find the psychological angle on selling cream cheese.

The idea that psychoanalysis can be found to have something to contribute to the way that people communicate in the course of everyday life comes to have increasing significance during the course of the film. It is announced at various times, in the words and actions of Felix's patient Lady Maresfield, in Bab's relationship with Felix, and at the conclusion of the film in Pat's pledge to support Felix's work as a psychoanalyst.

Early in the film, Felix makes clear his lack of sympathy for his list of fee-paying patients in a conversation at the Emily Ward Clinic with his psychiatrist colleague Dr. Garsten. When Felix is asked whether he has a busy afternoon ahead he replies: "Only the usual bunch of private patients, too much money, too little to do." Dr. Garsten observes that these patients pay for Felix's time, and Felix replies wryly: "Listen to Harley Street, relieve their wallets and you'll relieve their minds." In the following sequence, we find Felix in his home consulting room as his long-standing private patient Lady Maresfield is leaving at the end of their session. While Felix helps her on with her coat, he points out to her that she might be finding their meetings unproductive and that she is paying him fees "just to talk." Overcome with emotion, Lady Maresfield replies: "I don't mind that at all, it's worth it. It's worth more than I can tell you for your sympathy and understanding." Again, when Bab is leaning over Felix as he lies on her couch, she senses his despair and invites him to speak his mind and tell her the truth as he is always making his patients do. While Felix is initially hesitant to do this because "the subconscious is notoriously unreliable in these matters," he proceeds to reveal to her his concern for Adam and his fear of his own mortality. Also, at the end of the film, Pat finds herself able to countenance a future with Felix in which there will be no end to her suffering because the price of her *not* staying with him would be Felix's abandoning his work and depriving patients like little Charlie Oaks of the interpersonal connection with Felix that provides hope for their return to normal life (Figure 5.15).

What Lady Maresfield seems to gain from her sessions with Felix and what Bab offers to Felix in her invitation that he should reveal his innermost thoughts

Figure 5.15 *Mine Own Executioner*: Pat and Felix: "It will always be you who will suffer for it."

to her are not psychoanalytic interpretation as such but the functioning reciprocal object relationship that Rycroft describes as being fundamental to the psychoanalytic setting *and* to normal interpersonal relationships. Rycroft states that the drive of the patient who enters analysis is the wish

> which has previously been frustrated in so far as he has been ill and therefore isolated, to have a relationship within which he can share experience. The analytic situation enables the patient to communicate, share, and bring into relation with an object, feelings, memories, and thoughts which have previously been either repressed and unconscious or split-off and only experienced in states of dissociation.[35]

Rycroft is suggesting that the purpose of psychoanalysis can be defined by its intention to increase the patient's capacity to build and maintain object-relationships that in the healthy individual *would have been established by normal and reciprocal communication*. By declaring that she needs Felix's sympathy and understanding, Lady Maresfield is describing the importance to her of

[35] Ibid., p. 243.

just this sort of functioning reciprocal object relationship. In emphasizing the desperation of its characters to communicate with others and to be supported by them *Mine Own Executioner* suggests the same state of post-war crisis and isolation as existing within British society as Kracauer describes as existing in America. However, when it highlights in its conclusion Pat's willingness to sacrifice her own happiness for the greater goal of enabling Felix to continue helping patients such as little Charlie Oaks, *Mine Own Executioner* proposes there to be hope for the establishment of systems of communication that will enable society to at least begin the process of healing the wounds of the war and of its painful aftermath.

Concluding Remarks

I know from other analyses that a part of our personality can 'die', but though many parts can survive the trauma, it wakes up with a gap in its memory, actually with a gap in the personality, since this is not just a memory of the actual death struggle that has selectively disappeared or perhaps has been destroyed but all the associations connected with it as well.[1]

It strikes us more and more that the so-called day's (and as we may add, life's) residues are indeed repetition symptoms of traumata [...] Thus instead of 'the dream is a wish fulfilment' a more complete definition of the dream function would be: every dream, even an unpleasurable one, is an attempt at a better mastery and settling of traumatic experiences.[2]

(Ferenczi's italics)

Throughout this book, my interest in the psychoanalytic elements of these films has been based not on psychoanalysis as psychoanalysis but on psychoanalysis as ideology and psychoanalysis as discourse. My interest has been in how these films re-interpret and recirculate psychoanalytic concepts, and not in the truth or otherwise of the psychoanalytic concepts themselves. I have used a critical theory framework to understand how the ideological beliefs expressed by these films psychoanalytically, and the psychoanalytic discourses embedded within these films, inform their engagements with the psychical consequences of the war. The main purpose of this book has been to discover what is at stake in these engagements, specifically, to understand how these films are molded by ideology and discourse in a way that enables them to address the emotional fallout of the

---

[1] Sándor Ferenczi, *The Clinical Diary of Sándor Ferenczi*, ed. by Judith Dupont (Cambridge, MA: Harvard University Press, 1988), p. 179.
[2] Sándor Ferenczi, "Notes and Fragments," in *Final Contributions to the Problems and Methods of Psycho-Analysis* (London and New York: Karnac, 1994), p. 238.

war at the same time as proposing what the structures of power should look like in a new post-war Britain.

The part that psychoanalysis plays in these films is often complex and sometimes oppositional. On the most obvious level, psychoanalysis provides these films with a language that enables them to describe the psychical consequences of the war and form safe spaces wherein their contemporary audiences could begin to process and come to terms with their own wartime experiences. It could be argued that the process of mastering and settling wartime experiences that these films helped to initiate also made possible the radically different accounts of the war that would be provided by British cinema in the decade that followed. By the end of the 1950s, war films had become easily the biggest single group of British films, often derided by the critics, but nevertheless hugely popular with their contemporary audiences precisely for their sense of nostalgia and their ability to treat the war as pure entertainment. On another level, psychoanalysis operates toward the reinforcement or restoration of the dominant relations of social, political, or sexual power. Both of these functions operate toward a restoration of the pre-war *status quo*, but at other times these films operate in ways that call into question the *status quo* itself, a tendency most often found in the unresolved nature of these films' narrative scenarios and conclusions. As we have discovered by analyzing these films closely, the relationship they have with psychoanalytic knowledge is often extremely ambivalent and difficult to define.

Throughout this book, the contemporary psychoanalytic discourses which influence these films' narrative themes and narrative and formal structures are termed either narrative psychoanalytic discourses, cultural psychoanalytic discourses, or ideological psychoanalytic discourses. Narrative psychoanalytic discourses—psychoanalysis appearing *in* a text by means of its direct representation of psychopathologies, psychoanalyst figures, or the psychoanalytic setting—appear in all six films, tentatively at first in *The Halfway House* and then gradually more directly as the series progresses. This wide-ranging presence can be explained, in part, by the undoubted popularity that psychoanalysis had at this time with the general public. These discourses open up possibilities for these films to use psychoanalysis as a narrative device in a number of ways. They enable them to define their characters in terms of the stresses or aberrations they seek to normalize, as is the case in *The Halfway House*'s laying-out of Alice Meadows' traumatic bereavement, or in how *The Seventh Veil* and *Madonna of the Seven Moons* address Francesca's and Maddalena's respective libidinal "excesses". They also enable the use of internal monologues and spoken narratives in the analytic setting, which allows the films' central characters to reveal aspects of their selves that would have remained inaccessible within the limitations of traditional storytelling. Thus, in *The Seventh Veil*, Francesca is able to provide an account of her childhood trauma and the consequences this has had on her ability to form loving relationships in later life. Similarly, in *Mine Own Executioner*, Adam is able to admit his breaking under torture while a prisoner of war, and also his attempted murder of his wife, Molly.

In some of the films these discourses also motivate the use of flashbacks, which have the effect of exposing the distressed internal worlds of their characters, and also of firmly suturing their viewers into their characters' subjectivities. These identifications, in turn, enable audiences to be able to identify with their characters as they work-through their traumatic experiences and ultimately find some sort of closure. In doing this, these films—and many others made at this time—enable, as Laub and Podell have suggested, a repetition and so a mastery and settling of their audiences' own traumatic experiences.

When psychoanalyst figures appear as narrative discourses, as they do in all the films except *The Halfway House* and *They Made Me a Fugitive*, they operate in two distinct ways. First, to enable an articulation of the contemporary fascination with psychoanalytic ideas and psychopathology in general. Thus, in *Dead of Night*, Dr. Van Straaten defines Joan Cortland's sharing of Peter's vision as "a case of crypto-amnesia," and Dr. Ackroyd in *Madonna of the Seven Moons* and Felix in *Mine Own Executioner* introduce the idea of Maddalena's and Felix's respective early childhood traumas and the consequences these have on their later schizophrenic psychoses. Second, by virtue of how their comparatively one-dimensional characteristics are laid out, the psychoanalyst figures serve to emphasize the stratified complexity of the central figures. This is the case in *Dead of Night*, *The Seventh Veil*, and *Madonna of the Seven Moons*, but not in *Mine Own Executioner*, where the character of the psychoanalyst, Felix, is as developed as that of the patient, Adam.

Cultural psychoanalytic discourses—those formed when psychoanalytic concepts are used within the narrative themes and narrative and formal structures of texts—operate extensively in all these films in a number of ways. First, they provide them with a particular filmic language that enables the films to represent trauma indirectly and thus begin the formation of their safe spaces. The nature of these spaces changes markedly over the period, for example, in the films made toward the end of the war and in the months following the war—*The Halfway*

House, Madonna of the Seven Moons, Dead of Night*, and *The Seventh Veil*—the strategies of disavowal and displacement are used more often than in the later ones. So, in *The Halfway House* and *Dead of Night* the traumas they describe are, to an extent, masked by their being defined as supernatural phenomena, and in *Madonna of the Seven Moons* by their melodramatic excess. In similar terms, *Dead of Night* omits the physical devastation of the Blitz completely from a view of the London skyline but admits—but then displaces—the psychical effects of the Blitz when it places Henry Moore's *Figure in a Shelter* behind its opening titles. Again, in *Dead of Night*, the trauma that afflicts Grainger is a racing car accident, and, in *The Seventh Veil*, Nicholas's trauma is defined in terms of his abandonment by his mother when he was twelve. However, the way the symptoms of these events are presented in narrative terms renders both Grainger and Nicholas clearly recognizable as metaphorical representations of traumatized war veterans. In the later films—*They Made Me a Fugitive* and *Mine Own Executioner*—as the trauma of war becomes contextualized within a historical narrative, the seat of the trauma becomes clearer, and it is often the revisiting of this moment that becomes the driving force of their narratives and the basis of their remedial processes.

Cultural psychoanalytic discourses also operate formally in all these films' extensive uses of point-of-view shots, which enables them to accentuate the fragmented internal worlds of their central characters. Think, for example, of how *They Made Me a Fugitive* reveals Sally's traumatized subjectivity as she is being beaten by Narcy, or how *Mine Own Executioner* presents Adam's reliving of his torture, or how Walter Craig's psychotic breakdown is displayed in the radical discontinuity of the conclusion of *Dead of Night*.

Cultural psychoanalytic discourses are also key to how these films shape their storytelling around certain psychoanalytic ideas. For example, the concepts of traumatic repetition and the compulsion to repeat the trauma *ad infinitum* are employed formally and narratively in all six films. These motivate the circular and elliptical narratives of *The Halfway House* and *Dead of Night*, and also Francesca's series of failed romantic relationships and self-destructiveness in *The Seventh Veil*. In *Madonna of the Seven Moons*, the compulsion to repeat is found in Maddalena's repetitively being drawn away from her marriage to Guiseppe and toward her adulterous relationship with the gypsy robber, Nino. In similar terms, in *They Made Me a Fugitive* and *Mine Own Executioner*, it shapes not only Clem's and Adam's speech patterns and physical mannerisms, but also their self-destructiveness and their destructive attitudes toward their relationships.

Ideological psychoanalytic discourses—those that serve to express texts' various positions, opinions, and worldviews—operate extensively in all the films. When psychoanalysis operates in the films ideologically it is usually as a normative force; however, we have found that this is often countered by *subversive discursive forces* that seem immanent to the films themselves. As Foucault argues, it must not be assumed that the sovereignty of the state—or the media—is the only form that power takes at any given moment; instead, power must be understood as emerging from the multiplicity of force relations *immanent* to the sphere in which they operate. In other words, for Foucault, power emanates not only from the hierarchical structures of coercion that Althusser has described, but also from within, toward other ends, and often in ways that run counter to those determining structures.

Subversive discursive forces are immanent in these films when they operate in ways that oppose their stated ideological aims, and they are easily discovered in the ambivalence of many of these films' scenarios and conclusions. This immanence is evident, for example, toward the end of *The Seventh Veil*, where Francesca seems to have been returned to productive sexuality and the dominant patriarchal configuration. However, at the same time, the viewer is left with a sense of doubt that Nicholas is capable of fulfilling the role that is laid out for him within this configuration in any meaningful way. The conclusions of some of *Dead of Night*'s stories are similarly inconclusive, as are endings of all the later films in the series. As has been demonstrated, the films' engagements with psychoanalysis are complex, and the messages that they convey to their audiences often run counter one to another.

In the four films where psychoanalyst figures appear as narrative ideological discourses, *Dead of Night*, *The Seventh Veil*, *Madonna of the Seven Moons*, and *Mine Own Executioner*, their purpose is always to return the transgressive central characters to a state of "normality" by their re-admission to the dominant social order, sexual productivity, and the family unit. In the case of these films' female characters, their transgressive natures are described in terms of their unusual agency, their hypersexuality, and their refusal to live within the bounds of patriarchy. In contrast, the male characters' transgressions are defined by their listlessness, their sociopathic behaviors, and their sexual insufficiency. The general assumption of all these narratives is that the traumatic experience of the war has caused traditional gender roles to have been in some ways reversed, and both maternal and paternal functions to have ceased to function adequately.

However, the psychoanalyst figures have varying levels of success in restoring these figures to what the films propose as a pre-war state of mental health. In *Dead of Night*, for example, Dr. Van Straaten concurs with Dr. Albury's view that Grainger's racing car crash is a "psychological crisis" that can be, and is, satisfactorily remembered, worked-through, and consigned to the past. Grainger is thus permitted to join his new wife Joyce in the Linking narrative. In *The Seventh Veil* and *Madonna of the Seven Moons*, it is the objective of Dr. Larsen and Dr. Ackroyd to return the errant Francesca and the even more libidinally "excessive" Maddalena/Rosanna to their appointed positions within functioning and productive sexual relationships. In *The Seventh Veil*, Dr. Larsen's categorization of Francesca's sexuality as psychopathological—and his exposing of her unconscious sexual desires within the context of the Salome narrative—has the effect of diminishing Francesca's transgressive powers and thus affording her the opportunity of returning to the dominant order by choosing Nicholas. However, in *Madonna of the Seven Moons*, whilst Maddalena's sexual transgressions are defined as psychopathological by Dr. Ackroyd, he is unable to suggest a "cure" for the overabundance of her libido. Similarly, in *Mine Own Executioner*, although Felix is able to help Adam work-through his war trauma, he fails completely to restore him to a position of male sufficiency within his marriage.

Just as psychoanalysis has been found within these films' discourses to be often ineffective in returning the transgressive central characters to a position of "normality," the films' narrative conclusions are often united by their sense of doubt. In *Dead of Night* this is just as much true in the individual stories as it is in the film's final conclusion. Thus, by smashing the mirror and refusing her subordination to Peter's vision at the end of the Haunted Mirror story, Joan rejects any rational or irrational male control over her world, and Peter simply disappears from the film's narrative. Similarly, at the end of *Dead of Night*, Dr. Van Straaten's "ingenious theories"—as Walter Craig terms them at the beginning of the film—are found to be ineffectual in providing an explanation for his recurring trauma dream and it merely begins all over again.

In *The Seventh Veil*, Francesca is returned to health and redeemed in ideological terms by her choice to marry Nicholas, but the probity of this choice is itself called into question by the fact that Nicholas has shown himself, throughout the narrative, to be capable of extreme cruelty toward her. In similar terms, *Madonna of the Seven Moons* casts doubt on the possibility that Angela and Evelyn will be any more able to function as a couple than Maddalena and Guiseppe. *They Made Me a Fugitive* proposes a British social malaise in which both maternal and paternal functions have similarly atrophied. At the end of the film, although Clem and Sally show signs of having a relationship that is not clouded by self-interest, both have been tainted by their previous relationships with Narcy, and the viewer is provided with no certainty that justice will be done or that their future is assured. The conclusion of *Mine Own Executioner*, while being the most upbeat of the six films in that it provides some hope that the systems of social communication may be re-established, also makes it clear that the profound unhappiness of Pat and Felix's marriage will be the price that has to be paid for this scenario.

In consistently presenting solutions to their characters' various dilemmas that are immediately called into question by their own narrative conclusions, these films display a high level of ambivalence as to whether a return to the pre-war *status quo* is desirable or even possible. It seems, therefore, as though the traumatic aftermath of the war that is their historical context renders these films incapable of describing how the future could potentially be free from the traumatic effect of the past. In this respect, these films seem to orientate themselves around the psychoanalytic concepts of automatic anxiety and signal anxiety. It will be remembered that the former refers to the response of the individual to a previous traumatic situation, while the latter refers to an alerting mechanism that forewarns the individual of impending danger. In all these films, the automatic anxiety they describe as having been triggered as a response to the experience of the war is met by a signal anxiety motivated by the impending danger posed by the onset of peacetime and all the uncertainty this entails. The indelible impression left by viewing these films today is that they describe a society fixed at a point of crisis, one defined both by the immediate traumatic past and also by their inability to countenance a future that they can define in any rational way.

An understanding of the ambivalence and irresolution of these films lays bare in very clear terms the concurrent workings of the hierarchical and discursive elements of their ideological discourses. Psychoanalysis is certainly the mode of expression most often used by these films' authors to enunciate the trauma of the war and the consequent breakdown of dominant social formations. Psychoanalysis is also the instrument deployed by these films with the intention of restoring the dominant beliefs and practices of the ruling ideology and the *status quo* of sexual difference. However, in the final analysis, this restoration is rarely achieved in a way that is convincing.

Whilst psychoanalysis as a normative ideological force is certainly imposed consciously onto the films' characters and scenarios from above by the films' authors, this coercive force is countered by a subversive discursive force that seems to be immanent to the films themselves. Thus, both in the pronouncements of the films' psychoanalyst figures and in the films' fragmented and ambivalent scenarios and conclusions, the reproduction of the dominant order is consistently undermined by the hesitancy with which these films lay out the means of its reproduction. In this respect, the films reveal much about the historical context within which they were made. But more than this, they also make profound statements about the intractability of trauma itself, and the amount of time and working-through that is required to consign traumatic experience to the past so that society can be able to look toward a future that might provide hope for the next generation.

Bibliography

Aitken, Ian, *Alberto Cavalcanti: Realism, Surrealism and National Cinemas* (Trowbridge: Flicks Books, 2000).
Aldgate, Anthony, and Jeffrey Richards, *Britain Can Take It: British Cinema in the Second World War* (London and New York: I.B. Tauris, 2007).
Althusser, Louis, "Ideology and Ideological State Apparatuses," in *Lenin and Philosophy and Other Essays* (New York: Monthly Review Press, 2001), pp. 85–126.
Aspinall, Sue, "Sexuality in Costume Melodrama," in *BFI Dossier 18: Gainsborough Melodrama*, ed. by Sue Aspinall and Robert Murphy (London: BFI Publishing, 1983), pp. 29–39.
Balter, Leon, "Dead of Night," in *The Psychoanalytic Quarterly* 79:3 (2010), pp. 753–83.
Barr, Charles, ed., *All Our Yesterdays: 90 Years of British Cinema* (London: BFI Publishing, 1986; repr. 1996).
Barr, Charles, *Ealing Studios* (London: Studio Vista, 1993).
Barr, Charles, "Introduction: Amnesia and Schizophrenia," in *All Our Yesterdays: 90 Years of British Cinema* (London: BFI Publishing, 1986; repr. 1996), pp. 1–29.
Bell, David, "Projective Identification," in *Kleinian Theory: A Contemporary Perspective*, ed. by Catalina Bronstein (London: Whurr Publishers, 2001), p. 126.
Bettelheim, Bruno, *The Uses of Enchantment: The Meanings and Importance of Fairy Tales* (London: Penguin, 1991).
Bleuler, Eugen, *Textbook of Psychiatry* (New York: Macmillan, 1934).
Borde, Raymond, and Etienne Chaumeton, *A Panorama of American Film Noir* (San Francisco: City Lights Books, 2002).
Borossa, Julia, *Hysteria* (Cambridge: Icon Books, 2001).
Box, Sydney, *The Lion That Lost Its Way*, ed. by Andrew Spicer (Lanham, MD, Toronto, and Oxford: The Scarecrow Press, 2005).
Brabant, Eva, Ernst Falzeder, and Patrizia Giampieri-Deutsch, eds., *The Correspondence of Sigmund Freud and Sandor Ferenczi* (Cambridge, MA, and London: The Belknap Press of Harvard University Press, 1992).
Breuer, Josef, and Sigmund Freud, *Studies on Hysteria* in *The Standard Edition vol. II*, ed. by James Strachey (London: The Hogarth Press, 1955; repr. 1957), pp. 1–251.
Burton, Alan, and Tim O'Sullivan, *The Cinema of Basil Dearden and Michael Relph* (Edinburgh: Edinburgh University Press, 2009).
Butler, Ivan, *The Horror Film* (London: A. Zwemmer, 1967).
Caldwell, Lesley, and Angela Joyce, eds., *Reading Winnicott* (London and New York: Routledge, 2011).

Chapman, James, *The British at War: Cinema, State and Propaganda 1939–1945* (London and New York: I.B. Tauris, 1998; repr. 2008).
Churchill, Winston, *The Second World War Volume IV: The Hinge of Fate* (London: Penguin Books, 1985; repr. 2005).
The Cinema News and Property Gazette, December 31, 1947.
Clarke, T.E.B., *This Is Where I Came in* (London: Michael Joseph, 1974).
Collett, Derek, *His Own Executioner: The Life of Nigel Balchin* (Bristol: SilverWood, 2015).
Connolly, Jez, and David Owain Bates, *Dead of Night* (Leighton Buzzard: Auteur, 2015).
Cook, Pam, "Melodrama and the Woman's Picture," in *BFI Dossier 18: Gainsborough Melodrama*, ed. by Sue Aspinall, and Robert Murphy (London: BFI Publishing, 1983), pp. 14–28.
Daily Telegraph, September 10, 1945.
Daily Telegraph, May 20, 1946.
Daily Telegraph, November 24, 1947.
Dixon, Wheeler Winston, "The Halfway House," in *Liberal Directions: Basil Dearden and Postwar British Film Culture*, ed. by Alan Burton, Tim O'Sullivan, and Paul Wells (Trowbridge: Flicks Books, 1997), pp. 108–15.
Doane, Mary Ann, *The Desire to Desire: The Woman's Film of the 1940s* (Basingstoke and London: Macmillan Press, 1987).
Downing, Lisa, *Michel Foucault* (Cambridge, New York, Melbourne, Madrid, Cape Town, Singapore, São Paulo, Delhi, Tokyo, and Mexico City: Cambridge University Press, 2008).
Downing, Lisa, *The Subject of Murder: Gender, Exceptionality, and the Modern Killer* (Chicago: University of Chicago Press, 2013).
Drazin, Charles, *The Finest Years: British Cinema of the 1940s* (London and New York: I.B. Tauris, 2007).
Durgnat, Raymond, "Paint It Black: The Family Tree of the *Film Noir*," in *The Film Noir Reader*, ed. by Alain Silver (New York: Limelight, 2004), pp. 37–51.
Durgnat, Raymond, "Some Lines of Enquiry into Post-war British Crimes," in *The British Cinema Book*, ed. by Robert Murphy (London: BFI Publishing, 2001), pp. 135–45.
Everson, William K., "British Film Noir," in *Films in Review* 38:5 (1987), pp. 285–9.
Ferenczi, Sándor, *The Clinical Diary of Sándor Ferenczi*, ed. by Judith Dupont (Cambridge, MA: Harvard University Press, 1988).
Ferenczi, Sándor, "Confusion of the Tongues between the Adults and the Child," in *Final Contributions to the Problems and Methods of Psychoanalysis* (London: The Hogarth Press, 1955), pp. 156–67.
Ferenczi, Sándor, "Notes and Fragments," in *Final Contributions to the Problems and Methods of Psycho-Analysis* (London and New York: Karnac, 1994), pp. 216–79.

Ferenczi, Sándor, "Trauma and Striving for Health," in *Final Contributions to the Problems and Methods of Psycho-Analysis*, ed. by Michael Balint (London and New York: Karnac, 1994; repr. 2002), pp. 230-1.

Ferenczi, Sándor, Ernst Simmel, et al., *Psycho-Analysis and the War Neuroses* (London, Vienna and New York: The International Psycho-Analytic Press, 1921).

Foucault, Michel, *The Archaeology of Knowledge* (London and New York: Routledge, 1972; repr. 2002).

Foucault, Michel, *Discipline and Punish: The Birth of the Prison* (New York: Pantheon, 1977).

Foucault, Michel, "The Order of Discourse," in *Untying the Text: A Post-Structuralist Reader*, ed. by Robert Young (Boston, London, and Henley: Routledge, 1981), pp. 51-78.

Foucault, Michel, *The Will to Knowledge: The History of Sexuality* (London: Penguin Books, 1978; repr. 1998).

Freud, Anna, *The Ego and the Mechanisms of Defence* (London: The Hogarth Press, 1966).

Freud, Anna with Dorothy Burlingham, *Infants without Families: Reports on the Hampstead War Nurseries* (New York: International Universities Press, 1973).

Freud, Sigmund, "The Aetiology of Hysteria," in *The Standard Edition vol. III*, ed. by James Strachey (London: The Hogarth Press, 1962; repr. 1999), pp. 191-221.

Freud, Sigmund, *Beyond the Pleasure Principle* in *The Standard Edition vol. XVIII*, ed. by James Strachey (London: The Hogarth Press, 1955; repr. 1981), pp. 7-64.

Freud, Sigmund, "The Economic Problem of Masochism," in *The Standard Edition vol. XIX*, ed. by James Strachey (London: The Hogarth Press, 1961; repr. 1999), pp. 155-70.

Freud, Sigmund, "'From the History of an Infantile Neurosis' (The 'Wolf Man')," in *The Standard Edition vol. XVII*, ed. by James Strachey (London: The Hogarth Press, 1955; repr. 1991), pp. 1-123.

Freud, Sigmund, "On the History of the Psycho-Analytic Movement," in *The Standard Edition vol. XIV*, ed. by James Strachey (London: The Hogarth Press, 1957; repr. 1999), pp. 7-66.

Freud, Sigmund, "The Infantile Genital Organization," in *The Standard Edition vol. XIX*, ed. by James Strachey (London: The Hogarth Press, 1961; repr. 1999), pp. 141-5.

Freud, Sigmund, "Inhibitions, Symptoms and Anxiety," in *The Standard Edition vol. XX*, ed. by James Strachey (London: The Hogarth Press, 1959; repr. 1986), pp. 87-175.

Freud, Sigmund, "The Interpretation of Dreams," in *The Standard Edition vol. IV*, ed. by James Strachey (London: The Hogarth Press, 1953; repr. 1991), pp. 1-338.

Freud, Sigmund, *Introductory Lectures on Psycho-Analysis* in *The Standard Edition vol. XVI*, ed. by James Strachey (London: The Hogarth Press, 1963).

Freud, Sigmund, "Lecture XXXII: Anxiety and Instinctual Life," in *The Standard Edition vol. XXII*, ed. by James Strachey (London: The Hogarth Press, 1964), pp. 81-111.

Freud, Sigmund, "Mourning and Melancholia," in *The Standard Edition vol. XIV*, ed. by James Strachey (London: The Hogarth Press, 1957; repr. 1999), pp. 243–58.

Freud, Sigmund, "On Narcissism," in *The Standard Edition vol. XIV*, ed. by James Strachey (London: The Hogarth Press, 1957; repr. 1999), pp. 73–102.

Freud, Sigmund, *An Outline of Psycho-Analysis* in *The Standard Edition vol. XXIII*, ed. by James Strachey (London: The Hogarth Press, 1964; repr. 1973), pp. 141–207.

Freud, Sigmund, "Psycho-Analytic Notes on an Autobiographical Account of a Case of Paranoia (Dementia Paranoides)," in *The Standard Edition vol. XII*, ed. by James Strachey (London: The Hogarth Press, 1958; repr. 1999), pp. 3–82.

Freud, Sigmund, "Remembering, Repeating and Working-Through," in *The Standard Edition vol XII*, ed. by James Strachey (London: The Hogarth Press, 1958; repr. 1999), pp. 145–56.

Freud, Sigmund, "Repression," in *The Standard Edition vol. XIV*, ed. by James Strachey (London: The Hogarth Press, 1957; repr. 1999), pp. 141–58.

Freud, Sigmund, "The Sexual Theories of Children," in *The Standard Edition vol. IX*, ed. by James Strachey (London: The Hogarth Press, 1959; repr. 1973), pp. 207–26.

Freud, Sigmund, "Some Psychical Consequences of the Anatomical Distinction between the Sexes," in *The Standard Edition vol. XIX*, ed. by James Strachey (London: The Hogarth Press, 1961; repr. 1999), pp. 248–58.

Freud, Sigmund, *Three Essays on Sexuality* in *The Standard Edition vol. VII*, ed. by James Strachey (London: The Hogarth Press, 1953; repr. 1986), pp. 125–245.

Freud, Sigmund, "The Unconscious," in *The Standard Edition vol. XIV*, ed. by James Strachey (London: The Hogarth Press, 1957; repr. 1999), pp. 159–205.

Gay, Peter, *Freud: A Life for Our Times* (London: Little Books, 2006).

Gomez, Lavinia, *An Introduction to Object Relations* (London: Free Association Books, 1997).

Greenberg, Jay, and Stephen A. Mitchell, *Object Relations in Psychoanalytic Theory* (Cambridge, MA, and London: Harvard University Press, 1983).

Grigson, Geoffrey, *Henry Moore* (London: Penguin, 1943).

Guerrier, Simon, "Those Horrible Nightmares Again and Again," in *The Lancet* 2:10 (2015), pp. 873–5.

Harper, Sue, *Picturing the Past: The Rise and Fall of the British Costume Film* (London: BFI Publishing, 1994).

Harper, Sue, *Women in British Cinema: Mad, Bad and Dangerous to Know* (London and New York: Continuum, 2000).

Harper, Sue, and Vincent Porter, *Weeping in the Cinema in 1950: Reassessment of Mass-Observation Material* (Mass-Observation Archive, University of Sussex Library, 1995).

Harrington, Ralph, "The Railway Accident: Trains, Trauma, and Technological Crises in Nineteenth-Century Britain," in *Traumatic Pasts: History, Psychiatry and Trauma in the Modern Age, 1870–1930*, ed. by Mark S. Micale and Paul Lerner (Cambridge: Cambridge University Press, 2001), pp. 31–56.

Harrington, Ralph, "On the Tracks of Trauma: Railway Spine Reconsidered," in *The Journal of the Society for the Social History of Medicine* 16:2 (2003), pp. 209–23.

Hinshelwood, Robert, "Psychoanalysis in Britain: Points of Cultural Access, 1893–1918," in *Psychoanalysis and Its Borders*, ed. by Giuseppe Leo (Lecce: Frenis Zero Press, 2012), pp. 239–89.

Holtzman, Ellen, "The Pursuit of Married Love: Women's Attitudes toward Sexuality and Marriage in Great Britain, 1918–1939," in *Journal of Social History* 16:2 (1989), pp. 39–51.

Horne, Karen, and David Katz, "The Surrender of Tobruk in 1942: Press Reports and Soldiers' Memories," in *Scientia Militaria* 44:1 (2016), pp. 190–208.

Horney, Karen, "The Dread of Woman," in *Psychoanalysis and Male Sexuality*, ed. by Hendrick M. Ruitenbeek (New Haven, CT: College & University Press, 1966), pp. 83–96.

Horney, Karen, *Feminine Psychology* (New York: W. W. Norton, 1973).

Horney, Karen, "On the Genesis of the Castration Complex in Women," in *The International Journal of Psychoanalysis* 5 (1924), pp. 50–65.

Hutchings, Peter, *Hammer and Beyond: The British Horror Film* (Manchester and New York: Manchester University Press, 1993).

Jameson, Fredric, Introduction to *Lenin and Philosophy and Other Essays* (New York: Monthly Review Press, 2001), pp. vii–xiv.

Jones, Edgar, "*Neuro Psychiatry 1943*: The Role of Documentary Film in the Dissemination of Eedical Knowledge and Promotion of the UK Psychiatric Profession," in *Journal of the History of Medicine and Allied Sciences* 69:2 (2012), pp. 294–324.

Jones, Ernest, *Sigmund Freud: Life and Work* (London: Hogarth Press, 1953).

Kaplan, E. Ann, "From Plato's Cave to Freud's Screen," in *Psychoanalysis and Cinema*, ed. by E. Ann Kaplan (New York and London: Routledge, 1990), pp. 1–23.

Kaplan, E. Ann, and Ban Wang, Introduction to *Trauma and Cinema: Cross-Cultural Explorations*, ed. by E. Ann Kaplan and Ban Wang (Hong Kong: Hong Kong University Press, 2008), pp. 1–22.

Kawin, Bruce, *Horror and the Horror Film* (London, New York, and Delhi: Anthem Press, 2012).

Kendall, Gavin, and Gary Wickham, *Using Foucault's Methods* (London, Thousand Oaks, and New Delhi: Sage Publications, 1999; repr. 2000).

King, Pearl, "Activities of British Psychoanalysts during the Second World War and the Influence of Their Inter-Disciplinary Collaboration on the Development of Psychoanalysis in Great Britain," in *International Review of Psycho-Analysis* 16:15 (1989), pp. 15–33.

Klein, Melanie, "A Contribution to the Psychogenesis of Manic-Depressive States," in *The International Journal of Psycho-Analysis* 16 (1935), pp. 145–74.

Klein, Melanie, *Contributions to Psychoanalysis 1921–1945* (London: Hogarth Press, 1948).

Klein, Melanie, "The Importance of Symbol Formation in the Development of the Ego," in *The International Journal of Psycho-Analysis* 11 (1930), pp. 24–39.

Klein, Melanie, "Notes on Some Schizoid Mechanisms," in *The International Journal of Psycho-Analysis* 27 (1946), pp. 99–110.

Klein, Melanie, *The Psychoanalysis of Children* (London: The Hogarth Press, 1980).

Kohon, Gregorio, Introduction to *The British School of Psychoanalysis: The Independent Tradition*, ed. by Gregorio Kohon (New Haven and London: Yale University Press, 1986), pp. 19–80.

Konigsberg, Ira, "Does It Work? *Mine Own Executioner* and Psychoanalytic Interpretation," in *Contemporary Psychoanalysis* 46:2 (2010), pp. 185–202.

Kracauer, Siegfried, "Psychiatry for Everything and Everybody," in *Siegfried Kracauer's American Writings*, ed. by Johannes von Moltke and Kristy Rawson (Berkeley, LA and London: University of California Press, 2012), pp. 62–72.

Kracauer, Siegfried, "Those Movies with a Message," in *Siegfried Kracauer's American Writings*, ed. by Johannes von Moltke and Kristy Rawson (Berkeley, LA and London: University of California Press, 2012), pp. 72–81.

Kramer, Lawrence, "Culture and Musical Hermeneutics," in *Cambridge Opera Journal* 2:3 (1990), pp. 269–94.

Krutnik, Frank, *In a Lonely Street: Film Noir, Genre, Masculinity* (London and New York: Routledge, 1991).

Kuhn, Annette, and Julia Knight, "Weimar Cinema," in *The Cinema Book*, ed. by Pam Cook (London: Palgrave Macmillan, 1999; repr. 2007), pp. 208–11.

Kynaston, David, *Austerity Britain 1945–51* (London: Bloomsbury, 2007).

Landy, Marcia, *British Genres: Cinema and Society, 1930–1960* (Princeton: Princeton University Press, 1991).

Laplanche, Jean, and Jean-Bertrand Pontalis, *The Language of Psychoanalysis* (London: Karnac Books, 1973; repr. 2006).

Laub, Dori, and Daniel Podell, "Art and Trauma," in *International Journal of Psychoanalysis* 76 (1995), pp. 991–1005.

Lawrence, D.H., *Psychoanalysis and the Unconscious* (Mineola, NY: Dover Publications, 2005).

Martignoni, Margaret E., ed., *The Illustrated Treasury of Children's Literature* (London and Glasgow: Collins, 1960).

Mass-Observation, "Atomic War?," in *Peace and the Public* (London, New York, and Toronto: Longmans, Green and Co., 1947), pp. 8–13.

Mass-Observation, *Britain and Her Birth-Rate* (London: John Murray, 1945).

Mass-Observation, *The Journey Home* (London: John Murray, 1944).

Mass-Observation, *Peace and the Public* (London, New York, and Toronto: Longmans, Green, 1947).

Matus, Jill, "Trauma, Memory, and Railway Disaster: The Dickensian Connection," in *Victorian Studies* 43:3 (2001), pp. 413–36.

Mellor, David Alan, "'And Oh! The stench': Spain, the Blitz, Abjection and the Shelter Drawings," in *Henry Moore* (London: Tate Publishing, 2010), pp. 52–63.

Mészáros, Judit, "Building Blocks toward Contemporary Trauma Theory: Ferenczi's Paradigm Shift," in *The American Journal of Psychoanalysis* 70 (2010), pp. 328–40.

Mills, Sarah, *Michel Foucault* (London and New York: Routledge, 2003; repr. 2004).

Mitchell, Juliet, *Psychoanalysis and Feminism* (New York: Basic Books, 2000).

Muir, Stephanie, *Studying Ealing Studios* (Leighton Buzzard: Auteur, 2010).

Mulvey, Laura, "Afterthoughts on 'Visual Pleasure and Narrative Cinema' Inspired by King Vidor's *Duel in the Sun* (1946)," in *Visual and Other Pleasures* (London: Palgrave Macmillan, 2009), pp. 31–40.

Murphy, Robert, "British Film Noir," in *European Film Noir*, ed. by Andrew Spicer (Manchester and New York: Manchester University Press, 2007), pp. 84–111.

Murphy, Robert, "Riff-raff: British Cinema and the Underworld," in *All Our Yesterdays: 90 Years of British Cinema* (London: BFI Publishing, 1986; repr. 1996), pp. 286–305.

Murphy, Robert, *Realism and Tinsel: Cinema and Society in Britain 1939–1948* (London and New York: Routledge, 1989).

Naremore, James, *More Than Night: Film Noir in Its Contexts* (Berkeley, Los Angeles, and London: University of California Press, 1998).

News Chronicle, September 4, 1945.

News Chronicle, September 9, 1945.

News Chronicle, May 18, 1946.

News Chronicle, November 22, 1947.

Nowell-Smith, Geoffrey, "Minnelli and Melodrama," in *Screen* 18:2 (1977), pp. 113–18.

Oudart, Jean-Pierre, "Cinema and Suture," in *Screen* 18:4 (1977), pp. 35–47.

Pegg, Samantha, "Madness Is a Woman: Constance Kent and Victorian Constructions of Female Insanity," in *Liverpool Law Review* 30 (2009), pp. 207–23.

Picturegoer, June 23, 1945.

Piotrowska, Agnieszka, ed., *Embodied Encounters* (London and New York: Routledge, 2015).

Pirie, David, *A New Heritage of Horror* (London and New York: I.B. Tauris, 2008).

Porlock, Kit, *The Seventh Veil* (London: World Film Publication, 1946).

Quinodoz, Jean-Michel, *Reading Freud* (London and New York: Routledge, 2004).

Rabinow, Paul, Introduction to *The Foucault Reader*, ed. by Paul Rabinow (London: Penguin Books, 1984; repr. 1991), pp. 3–29.

Rachman, Arnold, "The Suppression and Censorship of Ferenczi's Confusion of Tongues Paper," in *Psychoanalytic Enquiry* 17 (1997), pp. 459–85.

Rapp, Dean, "The Reception of Freud by the British Press: General Interest and Literary Magazines, 1920-1925," in *Journal of the History of the Behavioural Sciences* 24 (1988), pp. 191-201.

Report of the War Office Committee of Enquiry into "Shell-Shock" (London: Imperial War Museum, 2004).

Rees, John Rawlings, *The Shaping of Psychiatry by War* (New York: W. W. Norton, 1945).

Rhode, John, *The Case of Constance Kent* (London: Geoffrey Bles, 1928).

Richards, Anthony, "The British Response to Shell-Shock: An Historical Essay," in *Report of the War Office Enquiry into "Shell-Shock"* (London: Imperial War Museum: 2004), pp. i-v.

Richards, Graham, "Britain on the Couch: The Popularization of Psychoanalysis in Britain 1918-1940," in *Science in Context* 13:2 (2000), pp. 183-230.

Rigby, Jonathan, *English Gothic: A Century of Horror Cinema* (London: Reynolds & Hearn, 2002).

Riley, Denise, "The Free Mothers: Pronatalism and Working Women in Industry at the End of the Last War in Britain," in *History Workshop* 11 (1981), pp. 58-118.

Roberts, Donald Ramsay, "The Death Wish of John Donne," in *PMLA* 62:4 (1947), pp. 958-76.

Rose, Sonya O, "Sex, Citizenship, and the Nation in World War II Britain," in *The American Historical Review* 103:4 (1998), pp. 1147-76.

Rudlin, John, *Commedia Dell'Arte: An Actor's Handbook* (London and New York: Routledge, 1994).

Rycroft, Charles, *A Critical Dictionary of Psychoanalysis* (London: Penguin Books, 1968; repr. 1995).

Rycroft, Charles, "An Enquiry into the Function of Words in the Psycho-analytic Situation," in *The British School of Psychoanalysis: The Independent Tradition*, ed. by Gregorio Kohon (New Haven and London: Yale University Press, 1986), pp. 237-52.

Sabbadini, Andrea, *Moving Images: Psychoanalytic Reflections on Film* (London and New York: Routledge, 2014).

Santos, Marlisa, *The Dark Mirror* (Lanham, Boulder, New York, Toronto, and Plymouth, UK: Lexington Books, 2011).

Schneider, Irving, "Images of the Mind: Psychiatry in the Commercial Film," in *The American Journal of Psychiatry* 134:6 (1977), pp. 613-20.

Schrader, Paul, "Notes on Film Noir," in *Film Comment* 8:1 (Spring 1972), pp. 8-13.

Silver, Alain, and Elizabeth Ward, *Film Noir: An Encyclopedic Reference to the American Style* (New York: The Overlook Press, 1979).

Silver, Catherine B., "Womb Envy: Loss and Grief of the Maternal Body," in *Psychoanalytic Review* 94:3 (2007), pp. 409-30.

Silverman, Kaja, "Historical Trauma and Male Subjectivity," in *Psychoanalysis and Cinema*, ed. by E. Ann Kaplan (New York and London: Routledge, 1990), pp. 110-27.

Silverman, Kaja, *Male Subjectivity at the Margins* (New York and London: Routledge, 1992).
Sklar, Jonathan, *Landscapes of the Dark: History, Trauma, Psychoanalysis* (London: Karnac, 2011).
Smith, Grafton, and Tom Pear, *Shell Shock and Its Lessons* (Manchester: Manchester University Press, 1917; repr. Memphis, TN: General Books, 2010).
Spicer, Andrew, ed., *European Film Noir* (Manchester and New York: Manchester University Press, 2007).
Spicer, Andrew, *Film Noir* (Harlow, Essex: Longman/Pearson Education, 2002).
Spicer, Andrew, *Sydney Box* (Manchester and New York: Manchester University Press, 2006).
Spicer, Andrew, *Typical Men: The Representation of Masculinity in Popular British Cinema* (London and New York: I.B. Tauris, 2001).
Spillius, Elizabeth Bott, et al., *The New Dictionary of Kleinian Thought* (London and New York: Routledge, 2011).
Street, Sarah, *British National Cinema* (London and New York: Routledge, 1997).
Thompson, Nellie L., "Early Women Psychoanalysts," in *International Review of Psycho-Analysis* 14 (1987), pp. 391–406.
Time and Tide, December 23, 1944.
The Times, June 24, 1942.
Todd, Ann, *The Eighth Veil* (New York: Putnam, 1981).
Whitford, Margaret, "Melanie Klein," in *Feminism and Psychoanalysis*, ed. by Elizabeth Wright (Oxford: Blackwell, 1992), pp. 191–3.
Willcock, H.D., *Mass-Observation Report on Juvenile Delinquency* (London: The Falcon Press, 1949).
Williams, Tony, "British *Film Noir*," in *Film Noir Reader 2*, ed. by Alain Silver and James Ursini (New York: Limelight editions, 1999), pp. 243–69.
Yorkshire Post, June 23, 1942.
Zaretsky, Eli, *Secrets of the Soul: A Social and Cultural History of Psychoanalysis* (New York: Vintage Books, 2005).
Zweiniger-Bargielowska, Ina, *Austerity in Britain: Rationing, Controls, and Consumption 1939–1955* (Oxford: Oxford University Press, 2000).

The British Trauma Film—a Filmography

Films made in the immediate aftermath of the war that deal either directly or indirectly with the neurotic or psychotic *effects* of the war and anxieties emerging from the destabilization of British society's pre-war dominant social formations include:

1944

A Canterbury Tale, dir. by Michael Powell and Emeric Pressburger (The Archers, 1944)
Fanny by Gaslight, dir. by Anthony Asquith (Gainsborough Pictures, 1944)
The Halfway House, dir. by Basil Dearden (Ealing Studios, 1944)
Love Story, dir. by Leslie Arliss (Gainsborough Pictures, 1944)

1945

Blithe Spirit, dir. by David Lean (Two Cities Films, 1945)
Brief Encounter, dir. by David Lean (Cineguild, 1945)
Dead of Night, dir. by Alberto Cavalcanti, Charles Crichton, Basil Dearden, and Robert Hamer (Ealing Studios, 1945)
Latin Quarter, dir. by Vernon Sewell (British National Films, 1945)
Madonna of the Seven Moons, dir. by Arthur Crabtree (Gainsborough Pictures, 1945)
Murder in Reverse, dir. by Montgomery Tully (British National Films, 1945)
Pink String and Sealing Wax, dir. by Robert Hamer (Ealing Studios, 1945)
A Place of One's Own, dir. by Bernard Knowles (Gainsborough Pictures, 1945)
The Seventh Veil, dir. by Compton Bennett (Ortus Films, 1945)
Waterloo Road, dir. by Sydney Gilliat (Gainsborough Pictures, 1945)
The Wicked Lady, dir. by Leslie Arliss (Gainsborough Pictures, 1945)

1946

Appointment with Crime, dir. by John Harlow (British National Films, 1946)
Bedelia, dir. by Lance Comfort (Eagle-Lion Films, 1946)
The Captive Heart, dir. by Basil Dearden (Ealing Studios, 1946)
Caravan, dir. by Arthur Crabtree (Gainsborough Pictures, 1946)
Great Expectations, dir. by David Lean (Cineguild, 1946)

A Matter of Life and Death, dir. by Michael Powell and Emeric Pressburger (The Archers, 1946)
Piccadilly Incident dir. by Herbert Wilcox (Associated British Picture Corporation, 1946)
Wanted for Murder, dir. by Lawrence Huntington (Marcel Hellman Productions, 1946)
The Years Between, dir. by Compton Bennett (Sydney Box Productions, 1946)

1947

Black Narcissus, dir. by Michael Powell and Emeric Pressburger (The Archers, 1947)
Dancing with Crime, dir. by John Paddy Carstairs (Alliance Films, 1947)
Frieda, dir. by Basil Dearden (Ealing Studios, 1947)
Hue and Cry, dir. by Charles Crichton (Ealing Studios, 1947)
It Always Rains on Sunday, dir. by Robert Hamer (Ealing Studios, 1947)
Jassy, dir. by Bernard Knowles (Gainsborough Pictures, 1947)
The Life and Adventures of Nicholas Nickleby, dir. by Alberto Cavalcanti (Ealing Studios, 1947)
Mine Own Executioner, dir. by Anthony Kimmins (London Film Productions, 1947)
The October Man, dir. by Roy Ward Baker (Two Cities Films, 1947)
Odd Man Out, dir. by Carol Reed (Two Cities Films, 1947)
They Made Me a Fugitive, dir. by Alberto Cavalcanti (Alliance Films, 1947)
Uncle Silas, dir. by Charles Frank (Two Cities Films, 1947)
The Upturned Glass, dir. by Lawrence Huntington (Sydney Box Productions, 1947)

1948

Brighton Rock, dir. by John Boulting (Associated British Pictures Corporation, 1948)
Daughter of Darkness, dir. by Lance Comfort (Alliance Films, 1948)
Daybreak, dir. by Compton Bennett (Sydney Box Productions, 1948)
The Fallen Idol, dir. by Carol Reed (London Film Productions, 1948)
Good-Time Girl, dir. by David MacDonald (Sydney Box Productions, 1948)
A Gunman Has Escaped, dir. by Richard M. Grey (Condor Film Productions, 1948)
My Brother's Keeper, dir. by Alfred Roome (Gainsborough Pictures, 1948)
Night Beat, dir. by Harold Huth (British Lion Films, 1948)
No Room at the Inn, dir. by Daniel Birt (British National Films, 1948)
Noose, dir. by Edmond Greville (Associated British Picture Corporation, 1948)
Oliver Twist, dir. by David Lean (Cineguild, 1948)
The Red Shoes, dir. by Michael Powell and Emeric Pressburger (The Archers, 1948)
Saraband for Dead Lovers, dir. by Basil Dearden (Ealing Studios, 1948)

General Filmography

Another Shore, dir. by Charles Crichton (Ealing Studios, 1948)
Appointment with Crime, dir. by John Harlow (British National Films, 1946)
The Bad Lord Byron, dir. by David MacDonald (Gainsborough Pictures, 1949)
The Bells Go Down, dir. by Basil Dearden (Ealing Studios, 1943)
The Best Years of Our Lives, dir. by William Wyler (Samuel Goldwyn Company, 1946)
Beware of Pity, dir. by Maurice Elvey (Two Cities Films, 1946)
Black Memory, dir. by Oswald Mitchell (Ambassador Films, 1947)
Black Narcissus, dir. by Michael Powell and Emeric Pressburger (The Archers, 1947)
Blithe Spirit, dir. by David Lean (Two Cities Films, 1945)
Brief Encounter, dir. by David Lean (Cineguild, 1945)
Brighton Rock, dir. by John Boulting (Associated British Pictures Corporation, 1948)
The Brothers, dir. by David MacDonald (Gainsborough Pictures, 1947)
The Captive Heart, dir. by Basil Dearden (Ealing Studios, 1946)
Caravan, dir. by Arthur Crabtree (Gainsborough Pictures, 1946)
Carnival, dir. by Stanley Haynes (Two Cities Films, 1946)
Christopher Columbus, dir. by David MacDonald (Gainsborough Pictures, 1949)
The Courtneys of Curzon Street, dir. by Herbert Wilcox (Herbert Wilcox Productions, 1947)
Crossfire, dir. by Edward Dmytryk (RKO Pictures, 1947)
Dancing with Crime, dir. by John Paddy Carstairs (Alliance Films, 1947)
The Dark Mirror, dir. by Robert Siodmak (International Pictures, 1946)
Daughter of Darkness, dir. by Lance Comfort (Alliance Films, 1948)
Daybreak, dir. by Compton Bennett (Sydney Box Productions, 1948)
Dead of Night, dir. by Alberto Cavalcanti, Charles Crichton, Basil Dearden, and Robert Hamer (Ealing Studios, 1945)
Fanny by Gaslight, dir. by Anthony Asquith (Gainsborough Pictures, 1944)
Fires Were Started, dir. by Humphrey Jennings (Crown Film Unit, 1943)
The First of the Few, dir. by Leslie Howard (British Aviation Pictures, 1942)
The Flamingo Affair, dir. by Horace Shepherd (Inspiration Films, 1948)
The Foreman Went to France, dir. by Charles Frend (Ealing Studios, 1942)
The Gentle Sex, dir. by Leslie Howard (Two Cities Films, 1943)
The Ghost of St. Michael's, dir. by Marcel Varnel (Ealing Studios, 1941)
The Ghost Train, dir. by Walter Forde (Gainsborough Pictures, 1941)
Gilda, dir. by Charles Vidor (Columbia Pictures, 1946)
Good-Time Girl, dir. by David MacDonald (Sydney Box Productions, 1948)

Great Expectations, dir. by David Lean (Cineguild, 1946)
A Gunman Has Escaped, dir. by Richard M. Grey (Condor Film Productions, 1948)
The Halfway House, dir. by Basil Dearden (Ealing Studios, 1944)
Hamlet, dir. by Lawrence Olivier (Two Cities Films, 1948)
Hungry Hill, dir. by Brian Desmond Hurst (Two Cities Films, 1947)
Henry V, dir. by Lawrence Olivier (Two Cities Films, 1944)
Hue and Cry, dir. by Charles Crichton (Ealing Studios, 1947)
I Know Where I'm Going, dir. by Michael Powell and Emeric Pressburger (The Archers, 1945)
I Live in Grosvenor Square, dir. by Herbert Wilcox (Herbert Wilcox Productions, 1945)
In Which We Serve, dir. by Noël Coward and David Lean (Two Cities Films, 1942)
It Always Rains on Sunday, dir. by Robert Hamer (Ealing Studios, 1947)
It's a Wonderful Life, dir. by Frank Capra (Liberty Films, 1946)
Jassy, dir. by Bernard Knowles (Gainsborough Pictures, 1947)
Kind Hearts and Coronets, dir. by Robert Hamer (Ealing Studios, 1949)
Lady in the Dark, dir. by Mitchell Leisen (Paramount Studios, 1944)
The Lamp Still Burns, dir. by Maurice Elvey (Two Cities Films, 1943)
Latin Quarter, dir. by Vernon Sewell (British National Films, 1945)
Leave Her to Heaven, dir. by John M. Stahl (20th Century Fox, 1945)
The Life and Adventures of Nicholas Nickleby, dir. by Alberto Cavalcanti (Ealing Studios, 1947)
The Locket, dir. by John Brahm (RKO Pictures, 1946)
Love Story, dir. by Leslie Arliss (Gainsborough Pictures, 1944)
The Loves of Joanna Godden, dir. by Charles Frend (Ealing Studios, 1947)
Madonna of the Seven Moons, dir. by Arthur Crabtree (Gainsborough Pictures, 1945)
The Magic Bow, dir. by Bernard Knowles (Gainsborough Pictures, 1946)
The Man in Grey, dir. by Leslie Arliss (Gainsborough Pictures, 1943)
The Man Within, dir. by Bernard Knowles (Gainsborough Pictures, 1946)
A Matter of Life and Death, dir. by Michael Powell and Emeric Pressburger (The Archers, 1946)
Millions Like Us, dir. by Sidney Gilliat and Frank Launder (Gainsborough Pictures, 1943)
Mine Own Executioner, dir. by Anthony Kimmins (London Film Productions, 1947)
My Brother's Keeper, dir. by Alfred Roome (Gainsborough Pictures, 1948)
Neuro Psychiatry 1943, dir. by Michael Hankinson (Ministry of Information, 1943)
Night Beat, dir. by Harold Huth (British Lion Films, 1948)
Nightmare Alley, dir. by Edmund Goulding (Twentieth Century Fox Productions, 1947)
No Room at the Inn, dir. by Daniel Birt (British National Films, 1948)
Noose, dir. by Edmond Greville (Associated British Picture Corporation, 1948)

Now, Voyager, dir. by Irving Rapper (Warner Brothers, 1942)
Obsession, dir. by Edward Dymytrk (Independent Sovereign Films, 1949)
The October Man, dir. by Roy Ward Baker (Two Cities Films, 1947)
Odd Man Out, dir. by Carol Reed (Two Cities Films, 1947)
Oliver Twist, dir. by David Lean (Cineguild, 1948)
One of Our Aircraft Is Missing, dir. by Michael Powell and Emeric Pressburger (The Archers, 1942)
Passport to Pimlico, dir. by Henry Cornelius (Ealing Studios, 1949)
Perfect Strangers, dir. by Alexander Korda (London Films, 1945)
Piccadilly Incident dir. by Herbert Wilcox (Associated British Picture Corporation, 1946)
Pink String and Sealing Wax, dir. by Robert Hamer (Ealing Studios, 1945)
A Place of One's Own, dir. by Bernard Knowles (Gainsborough Pictures, 1945)
Pool of London, dir. by Basil Dearden (Ealing Studios, 1951)
Possessed, dir. by Curtis Bernhardt (Warner Brothers, 1947)
The Red Shoes, dir. by Michael Powell and Emeric Pressburger (The Archers, 1948)
Root of All Evil, dir. by Brock Williams (Gainsborough Pictures, 1947)
San Demetrio London, dir. by Charles Frend (Ealing Studios, 1944)
Saraband for Dead Lovers, dir. by Basil Dearden (Ealing Studios, 1948)
The Seventh Veil, dir. by Compton Bennett (Ortus Films, 1945)
Shoah, dir. by Claud Lanzmann (New Yorker Films, 1985)
The Silver Fleet, dir. by Vernon Sewell (The Archers, 1943)
The Small Back Room, dir. by Michael Powell and Emeric Pressburger (The Archers, 1949)
The Snake Pit, dir. by Anatole Litvak (Twentieth Century Fox Productions, 1948)
Spellbound, dir. by Alfred Hitchcock (Selznick International Pictures, 1945)
Take My Life, dir. by Ronald Neame (Cineguild, 1947)
Temptation Harbour, dir. by Lance Comfort (Associated British Pictures, 1947)
Tender Is the Night, dir. by Henry King (Twentieth Century Fox, 1962)
They Made Me a Fugitive, dir. by Alberto Cavalcanti (Alliance Films, 1947)
They Were Sisters, dir. by Arthur Crabtree (Gainsborough Pictures, 1945)
This Happy Breed, dir. by David Lean (Two Cities Films, 1944)
The Three Faces of Eve, dir. by Nunnally Johnson (Twentieth Century Fox, 1957)
The Upturned Glass, dir. by Lawrence Huntington (Sydney Box Productions, 1947)
Wanted for Murder, dir. by Lawrence Huntington (Marcel Hellman Productions, 1946)
Waterloo Road, dir. by Sydney Gilliat (Gainsborough Pictures, 1945)
The Way Ahead, dir. by Carol Read (Two Cities Films, 1944)
Went the Day Well?, dir. by Alberto Cavalcanti (Ealing Studios, 1942)
White Heat, dir. by Raoul Walsh (Warner Brothers, 1949)
The Wicked Lady, dir. by Leslie Arliss (Gainsborough Pictures, 1945)
The Years Between, dir. by Compton Bennett (Sydney Box Productions, 1946)

Index

Locators followed by "n." indicate endnotes

Abraham, Karl 2, 127, 186
adaptations 36–7, 41, 179, 192
affectivity, theory of 31
Aitken, Ian, *Alberto Cavalcanti: Realism, Surrealism and National Cinemas* 169, 171, 173–5
Aldgate, Anthony 137
Alliance Films 38, 43
Althusser, Louis 1, 18, 20, 22, 24, 203.
    See also "Ideology and Ideological State Apparatuses" (Althusser)
    ideology, idea 15, 25, 64
    state's educational apparatus 1, 18
ambivalence 30–2, 43, 95, 117, 121, 136, 138, 142–3, 148–58, 200, 203, 205–6
Another Shore (1948) 39
anxieties 3–5, 9, 25, 27, 46, 57, 73, 81, 88–90, 92, 116, 137, 153, 193, 195
    automatic 175, 205
    male 81, 106
    objectification and neutralization 93–4
    persecutory 112
    signal 143, 148, 205
    of war 73–7, 160
Appointment with Crime (1946) 38
art of trauma 4–5, 25, 28
Aspinall, Sue 146, 151, 153
Auerhahn, Nanette 70
automatic anxiety 175, 205

The Bad Lord Byron (1949) 36
Balchin, Nigel 26, 179. See also *Mine Own Executioner* (1947)
Balcon, Michael 54
Balter, Leon 98–9, 101
Barr, Charles 25, 27, 29, 45, 49, 61, 80, 117
The Bells Go Down (1943) 27, 46, 50, 120
    Bob Matthews 50
    MacFarlane 50–2
    Ma Turk 51, 53
    Ted Robbins 50, 53
    Tommy Turk 50–3
Bettelheim, Bruno 144
Beware of Pity (1946) 37
Bion, W. R. 15
birth rate, falling 137
Black Memory (1947) 38
Black Narcissus (1947) 37
Bleuler, Eugen 148
    Textbook of Psychiatry 142
Blitz 9, 14, 50, 86, 88, 90, 93, 149, 159, 187, 202
Borde, Raymond, *A Panorama of American Film Noir* 30, 32, 35
Boulting Brothers 38
Box, Muriel 42, 119
Box, Sydney 25–6, 36, 42, 119, 126
Brief Encounter (1945) 37, 39–40, 130
Brighton Rock (1948) 38, 40–1
British Lion Films 43, 51
British National Films 38
British Psycho-Analytical Society 15
British trauma films 26–7, 35, 41, 53, 57, 122, 129. See also specific films
    and film noir 35–43 (See also film noir, Hollywood)
The Brothers (1947) 36
Brothers Grimm 143
Burlingham, Dorothy 14. See also Hampstead War Nurseries
Burton, Alan 49, 80–1
Butler, Ivan 94–5

Cagney, James 32
Calvert, Phyllis 151
Caravan (1946) 36, 151
Carnival (1946) 37
Cavalcanti, Alberto 54, 169, 174, 176–7
Chandler, Raymond 31

Chapman, James 175
Chaumeton, Etienne, *A Panorama of American Film Noir* 30, 32, 35
childhood trauma/sexual trauma 42–3, 201
   Felix (*Mine Own Executioner,* 1947) 201
   Francesca (*The Seventh Veil,* 1945) 40, 42, 124, 132, 146, 201
   Maddalena (*Madonna of the Seven Moons,* 1945) 43, 145–6, 149, 201
Christopher Columbus (1949) 36
Churchill, Winston 75–6
cinematic fragmentation. *See* fragmentation
Civil Resettlement Units 15
Clarke, T. E. B. 54
cognitivism 35
Collett, Derek 26, 179
commedia dell'arte characters 99–100
compulsion to repeat/compulsive repetition 42, 81, 84–96, 165, 202
contemporary melodramas 36–7, 39, 41, 119
Cook, Pam 152, 156
costume dramas 36–7, 39, 41, 166
The Courtneys of Curzon Street (1947) 37
Coward, Noël 51. *See also In Which We Serve* (1942)
crime thrillers 41
critical theory 1, 24–30, 42, 199
cultural appropriation of knowledge 15
cultural psychoanalytic discourses 27, 42, 120, 200–2
cultural values 104
cynicism 31–2

daemonic power 96, 165
Dancing with Crime (1947) 38, 41
Daughter of Darkness (1947) 38
Daybreak (1948) 39, 41, 179
Dead of Night (1945) 1, 35, 37–8, 40, 42, 54, 79, 122, 136, 165, 171, 202–3
   Dr. Albury 82, 90, 93, 204
   Christmas Party story 81–2, 96–9, 102, 106, 111
   disavowal, displacement, and compulsive repetition 42, 81, 84–96, 202
   Eliot Foley 82–4, 94
   female sexual development 81, 96–105
   Francis Etherington 1, 111, 113–15
   Francis Kent 82, 97, 100–2, 111
   George Parratt 83, 97
   Golfing Story 54, 83, 85, 97
   Haunted Mirror story 2, 80–2, 85–6, 97, 106, 113, 115, 117–18, 204
   Hearse Driver story 81–2, 85, 90–4, 96, 117–18
   Henry Moore's *Figure in a Shelter* 88–90, 202
   Hugh Grainger 81–2, 84, 90–4, 96, 117, 202, 204
   Hugo Fitch 83, 96
   Jimmy Watson 82, 97–102, 104–5
   Joan and Peter Cortland 1–3, 82–3, 86–7, 96–7, 105–11, 113–18, 201, 204
   Joyce 82, 90–2, 96, 115, 117
   Larry Potter 83, 97
   linking narrative 81, 84–6, 94–6, 115, 117, 204
   male anxiety 81, 106
   male figures 80
   Mary Lee 83, 97
   Maxwell Frere 83
   motherhood 81, 96–105
   objectivity 3, 42, 81, 105–13
   paranoia 42, 81
   Miss Pelling 113–14
   reality and fantasy 2, 105–13
   Mister Rutherford 111, 113
   Sally O'Hara 82, 85, 96–105, 117
   sexual difference 2–3, 42, 81, 96–105
   subjectivity 3, 42, 81, 105–13
   Sylvester Kee 83, 85
   temporal continuity 84–5
   trauma and traumatic neurosis 42
   traumatic wartime experience 2–4, 83, 88, 94, 96
   Dr. Van Straaten 1, 82–3, 85, 102, 105, 115, 201, 204
   Ventriloquist's Dummy story 83, 85–6
   Walter Craig 82–6, 90, 94–6, 101–3, 105, 117, 202, 204
Dearden, Basil 50. *See also The Halfway House* (1944)

decolonization 10
disavowal 42, 81, 86, 88, 143, 170, 187, 202
displacement 28, 42, 81, 86, 90, 93–4, 202
Dixon, Wheeler Winston 49
Doane, Mary Ann 35, 130–1
  The Desire to Desire 33
Donne, John, "Meditation XII" 192–3
Downing, Lisa 22–3
Drazin, Charles 176–7
Durgnat, Raymond 40–1
  "Paint It Black: The Family Tree of Film Noir" 32

Ealing Studios 1, 29, 36, 38–9, 42, 45, 49–50, 54, 63, 79–80, 171, 174–5
Ellis, Havelock 12
emotional experience (Mass-Observation survey) 6–10
Everson, William K., "British Film Noir" 40, 159
expressionism 169

family units 9, 11, 19, 42, 46, 49, 68–9, 121, 135, 137, 203
Fanny by Gaslight (1944) 36, 120, 155
female desire and subjectivity 33, 42–3, 119, 136, 138, 150, 178
  female agency and 148
  schizophrenia and pathologization 140–9
female employment 119
female morality 137
Ferenczi, Sándor 2, 28, 42, 111, 117, 176, 186
  "Confusion of the Tongues between the Adults and the Child" 70, 116, 175
  Psychoanalysis and the War Neuroses 127
film noir, Hollywood 30–2, 36, 40–1, 159. *See also specific film noir*
  British trauma films and 35–43
  cultural influences 34–5
  influence of psychoanalysis 34–6, 39, 42
  male rationality and patriarchal cultural authority 34
  masculinities 33
  social realism and 41
  tendencies 41
First World War (Great War) 12–14, 72, 127, 137, 186, 192
The Flamingo Affair (1948) 38
Foucault, Michel 1, 135, 203
  cultural infiltration of knowledge 22
  cultural unconscious 22, 25
  discourse, idea 15, 21–2
  immanence 23, 25
  knowledge and discourse 21–2, 24–5
  power, relations (*see* power)
fragmentation 9, 28, 121, 138, 142–4, 146, 148, 151, 188
Freud, Anna 14, 28, 42, 116–17. *See also* Hampstead War Nurseries
  The Ego and the Mechanisms of Defence 116
  identification with the aggressor 42, 116–17
Freud, Sigmund 2–3, 13, 79, 86, 111–14, 128, 148, 169, 176
  attenuation of belief 57, 64
  Beyond the Pleasure Principle 72, 95, 165, 175, 192
  child developmental stages 12
  cynicism 31
  death drive/wish 193
  displacement 28
  extreme traumatic mourning 56–8
  Inhibitions, Symptoms and Anxiety 175
  The Interpretation of Dreams 90
  "Mourning and Melancholia" 56
  An Outline of Psycho-Analysis 142–3
  "Remembering, Repeating and Working-Through" 71–73, 92, 95
  repression 12, 79–80
  Schreber, case of 111–14
  unconscious 12, 21

Gainsborough Pictures 36–9, 41–2, 63, 120, 136, 138, 146–53, 155, 166
The Gentle Sex (1943) 37
German Expressionism 31
The Ghost of St. Michael's (1941) 63
The Ghost Train (1941) 63
Gilda (1946) 31
A Girl in a Million (1946) 37

Gomez, Lavinia 3
Good-Time Girl (1948) 38, 41
Granger, Stewart 38, 151
Great Expectations (1946) 37, 41
Grigson, Geoffrey 89
Guidice, Filippo Del 37
A Gunman Has Escaped (1948) 38

The Halfway House (1944) 2, 35, 37–8, 40, 42, 45, 53, 92, 122, 165, 200–2
   Alice and Harry Meadows 46–9, 54–60, 62, 64, 75, 77, 200
   Captain Fortescue 47, 49, 57–9, 61, 63, 74–5
   David Davies 47, 49, 57–8, 74–5
   early years of the war 48–53
   end of wartime anxiety 73–7
   exact moment, fall of bomb 66, 67
   family unit 42, 46, 49, 68
   ghostly, stories 61–3, 74
   Jim Meadows 46–7, 54–60, 62, 75, 77
   Joanna French 47, 49, 63, 73
   Margaret 47–9
   Morgan and Gwyneth Rhys 46, 48, 54–5, 57, 60–75, 77, 92
   Richard and Jill French 47–9, 57–9, 73–4
   "Rommel approaching Fort Capuzzo" 74–5
   Terence 47, 49, 57, 75
   traumatic wartime events 45–6
   twenty-first of June (1942 & 1943) 73–7
   William Oakley 47, 49, 57–9, 61–3, 73–5
Hamer, Robert 80
Hamlet (1948) 37
Hammett, Dashiell 31
Hampstead War Nurseries 14
Hangover Square (1945) 148
Hankinson, Michael 126
Harper, Sue 6, 8, 119
Hay, Will 63
Henry V (1944) 37
Hinshelwood, Robert 10, 11, 14–15
   cultural locations, psychoanalysis 11–13
historical psychoanalytic discourses 27, 138, 186

Holocaust 5, 9, 177
Horizon magazine 89
Horney, Karen 3
   "The Dread of Woman" 104
   "The Flight from Womanhood" 103–4
Howard, Trevor 38
Hue and Cry (1947) 39–40
Hungry Hill (1947) 37
Hutchings, Peter 80–1, 109

ideological beliefs 17, 24, 199
ideological psychoanalytic discourses 27, 105, 200, 203
"Ideology and Ideological State Apparatuses" (Althusser) 17
   ideological *vs.* repressive state apparatuses 19, 22–3
   infrastructure and superstructure 17–21
   interpellation 20–1
   obviousness 20
   reproduction of labour 18–19
   subordination 24
I Know Where I'm Going (1945) 37
I Live in Grosvenor Square (1945) 37
I'll be Seeing You (1944) 127
Industrial Revolution 10
introjection 113, 116–17
In Which We Serve (1942) 27, 37, 46, 51, 120
   Captain Kinross 51–3
   Shorty Blake 52–3
   Torrin 51–3
   Walter Hardy 52
Isaacs, Susan 3
It Always Rains on Sunday (1947) 38, 40–1

Jameson, Fredric 17
Jassy (1947) 36, 41
Jones, Ernest 186
Jones, Griffith 151, 166

Kawin, Bruce 95
Kind Hearts and Coronets (1949) 41
King, Pearl 14–15
Klein, Melanie 3, 28, 113, 169
Knight, Julia 169
Konigsberg, Ira 184, 190

Kracauer, Siegfried 180, 193, 198
  "Psychiatry for Everything" 193–5
Kramer, Lawrence 132
Krutnik, Frank 35
  In a Lonely Street 33–4
  rationalisation 34
Kuhn, Annette 169
Kynaston, David 9

Lady in the Dark (1944) 148
The Lamp Still Burns (1943) 119
Landy, Marcia 120, 128, 138
language 4, 13, 29, 32, 192, 200–1
Latin Quarter (1945) 38
Laub, Dori 4–5, 25, 28, 70, 88, 201. *See also* art of trauma
Lawrence, D. H. 13
Lawrence, Margery 147
Lean, David 37, 51. *See also specific Lean's movies*
Leave Her to Heaven (1945) 31
The Life and Adventures of Nicholas Nickleby (1947) 37, 41
Lockwood, Margaret 151
The Loves of Joanna Godden (1947) 37
Love Story (1944) 37

Madonna of the Seven Moons (1945) 2, 35, 37, 39, 42–3, 119–20, 136, 200, 202–4
  Dr. Ackroyd 139, 145–7, 152–3, 201, 204
  ambivalent and fragmented nature 43, 149–58
  Angela 139–41, 144–5, 152–6, 204
  dual discourse/personality 138–9, 146–9
  Evelyn 139, 152–5, 204
  Guiseppe Labardi 139–40, 144–7, 152–4, 156, 202, 204
  Jimmy and Nesta Logan 139, 152–3
  libido 111, 142, 145–6, 148–9, 204
  Maddalena/Rosanna 120–1, 138–46, 149, 151–3, 156–7, 200–2, 204
  Mother Superior 141, 145
  Nino Barucci 139–40, 145, 152, 156, 202
  paternal responsibility, collapse 155
  "Red Riding Hood," Maddalena as 140, 143–4
  Sandro 139, 153
  schizophrenic psychosis 43, 121, 138, 140–9, 201
  women's "indiscretions" 137
The Magic Bow (1946) 36
male subjectivity 29, 178
The Man in Grey (1943) 36, 120, 149, 151
The Man Within (1946) 36
Marx, Karl 19
  infrastructure and superstructure 17–21
  Marxisms 17
  means of production 17–18
  state, idea 17
Mason, James 39, 133, 151
Mass-Observation survey 6–10
A Matter of Life and Death (1946) 38, 130
mature paranoia 111
Mellor, David Alan 89
Mészáros, Judit 116
Millions Like Us (1943) 37, 119, 149–50
Mills, John 39
Mine Own Executioner (1947) 2, 26, 35, 38, 40–1, 130, 179, 202–5
  Adam Lucien 179–87, 190, 192, 195, 201–2
  cultural systems of communication 193–8
  destruction and self-destruction 188–93
  Felix Milne 43, 179–82, 184–5, 188–90, 192, 195–8, 201
  interpersonal processes of psychoanalysis 43, 193
  Dr. James Garsten 181–2, 189, 195–6
  Lady Maresfield 188, 196–7
  male affliction 43, 182–93
  Molly Lucien 180–3, 185, 190–2, 201
  Oedipal fixation, Adam's 43, 180, 184–7, 193
  Pat Milne 180, 182, 185, 188–9, 192, 196–8
  Peter and Bab 180–1, 188–90, 192–3, 195–6
  regressive sexuality 189, 192–3
  split personality 182–3

Moore, Henry, *Figure in a Shelter* 88–90, 202
morbid films 36, 38, 40, 179
motherhood 2, 43, 96–105
Mulvey, Laura, internal oscillation of desire 151
Murder in Thornton Square (*Gaslight*) (1944) 148
Murphy, Robert 153, 159, 179
 "British Film Noir" 36, 40–1, 159–60
 Realism and Tinsel (*see Realism and Tinsel* (Murphy))
My Brother's Keeper (1948) 39
Myers, F. W. H. 11

narcissism 12, 109, 165
Naremore, James, *More Than Night: Film Noir and Its Contexts* 34–5
narrative psychoanalytic discourses 27, 200
Neuro Psychiatry 1943 126
neuroses/neurosis 13, 26–7, 42, 72, 119, 126–8, 131, 134, 146, 175, 179, 186, 189, 194
Newton, Robert 39
Night Beat (1948) 38
Niven, David 38
Noose (1948) 38
normality, return to 2, 21, 24, 152, 158, 178, 203–4
Nuremberg Tribunal 9

objectivity 3, 42, 81, 105–13, 169
object relations theory 3, 42, 169, 197–8
Obsession (1949) 39
The October Man (1947) 39, 41, 179
Odd Man Out (1947) 39
Oedipal fixation 43, 128–9, 131, 180, 185–7, 193
Ogden, Peter 49
Oliver Twist (1948) 37
Ostrer, Maurice 36
O'Sullivan, Tim 49, 80–1

paranoia 42, 81, 112–13
The Peaceful Inn 49
Perfect Strangers (1945) 37
Picturegoer magazine 147

Pink String and Sealing Wax (1946) 37, 41, 171
A Place of One's Own (1945) 38
Podell, Daniel 4–5, 25, 28, 88, 201. *See also* art of trauma
pop-Freudian characterizations 27, 35
Porter, Vincent 6, 8
Portman, Eric 39
post-war crisis and isolation 198
post-war films 1, 6–8, 29, 36–8, 41–2, 80, 130, 137, 170, 175, 178, 186. *See also specific films*
 ex-service men, problems 38
 production, immediate 36
power 11, 17, 25, 131, 133, 203
 asymmetry of 110, 114
 daemonic 96, 165
 patriarchal 81, 134, 146
 power systems 33, 35, 193
 relations 19, 21–3, 30, 81, 100
 structures 24, 200
 transgressive 133, 204
pre-war film 7–8, 29, 178, 204
pre-war *status quo* 114, 118, 136, 200, 205
projection 42, 111–15
pro-natalist movement 137
The Psychiatric Treatment of Battle Casualties (War Office documentary) 26, 126
psychoanalysis 1, 4, 22, 31, 33, 39, 42, 79, 96–7, 103, 127, 169, 179, 195–6, 199–200, 203–5
 British culture (twentieth century) 10–15
 interpersonal processes of 43, 193
 new psychiatry 10
 normative ideological force 205
 post-war Britain 24–30, 193–8
psychoanalytic knowledge 15, 21, 25–6, 28, 30, 200
psychogenesis 128
psychological crisis 204
psychological films 194
psychoses/psychosis 13, 26–7, 42–3, 56–7, 86, 105, 111, 117, 121, 131, 143, 148, 186–7, 190, 201

Queen Mary 135
Quinodoz, Jean-Michel 112

Rapp, Dean 14–15
Realism and Tinsel (Murphy) 36, 38, 40–1.
    See also *specific genre films*
    comedies 36, 39
    contemporary melodramas 36–7, 39, 41
    costume drama 36–7, 39, 41
    morbid films 36, 38, 40, 179
    psychologically damaged men, films 41
    spiv films 36, 38, 40
Rees, John Rawlings 15
re-integration 15, 37, 41
repetition 33, 42, 60, 73, 81, 92, 94–5, 116, 164–5, 201–2
    ad infinitum 4, 92, 95–6, 202
Representation of the People Act (1918) 11
repression 12, 19, 79–80, 112, 143, 193, 195
    primal repression 79
    repression proper 79
    sexual 12, 193
Richards, Graham 15
    public's fascination with psychoanalysis 13–14
Richards, Jeffrey 137
Rigby, Jonathan 80–1
Rivers, W. H. R. 12
Roberts, Donald Ramsay 192
Root of All Evil (1947) 37
Rosay, Françoise 54
Rose, Sonya O. 137
Rudlin, John 99
Rycroft, Charles, psychoanalytic theory 195, 197

safe representational spaces 4–5, 29–30, 77, 129, 138, 200–1
San Demetrio London (1944) 27, 45, 50
Saraband for Dead Lovers (1948) 37
schizophrenia/schizophrenic psychosis 34, 39, 43, 142, 147–8, 180, 182, 184, 192
    ambivalence 142–3, 148
    "Does Schizophrenia Sound Romantic?" 147
    fragmentation 143–4, 146, 148
    incongruity of affect 142

    and pathologization 140–9
    "Split Personalities" 147
    "What Is Schizophrenia?" 147
Schreber, Daniel Paul, *Memoirs of My Nervous Illness* 111
Second World War 1, 14–15, 29, 32, 43, 75, 81, 119, 137, 159, 179, 187, 194
semi documentaries 41
The Seventh Veil (1945) 2, 25–6, 35, 37, 39, 119–21, 145, 158, 200, 202, 204
    abondonment 120, 127, 132, 146, 202
    childhood traumas, Francesca's 40, 42, 124, 132, 146, 201
    cultural psychoanalytic discourses 120
    Francesca Cunningham 119, 121–2, 135, 203–4
    Dr. Irving 129, 131
    Dr. Kendall 129, 131
    Dr. Larsen 120–4, 126, 129–35, 146, 204
    Maxwell Leyden 122, 132–4
    narco-analysis 122, 126
    Nicholas 42, 119, 121–2, 132–6, 202–4
    Peter Gay 121
    Salome 129, 131–4, 204
    sexual relationships 120, 127, 129–36, 204
    troubled pasts (Francesca & Nicholas) 122–9
sexual adolescence 98–101, 105
sexual difference 2, 42, 81, 96–105, 205
shell-shock, war trauma 12, 14
Shoah (1985) 5
Sidgwick, Henry 11
signal anxiety 143, 148, 205
Silver, Alan, *Film Noir: An Encyclopedic Reference to the American Style* 32
Silverman, Kaja, male subjectivity 29
Simmel, Ernst 2, 186
    Psychoanalysis and the War Neuroses 127
Sklar, Jonathan, atomization 70
Slaughter, Tod, *The Curse of the Wraydons* 36
The Small Back Room (1949) 39, 41, 179
The Snake Pit (1948) 31
social order 13, 138, 146, 151–2, 156, 158, 203
Society for Psychical Research 11

Spellbound (1945) 31, 127
Spicer, Andrew 2, 34, 41, 126–7, 165
    "damaged Everyman" 178
spiv films 36, 38, 40, 159, 166, 188
Strachey, James 12
subjectivity 3, 33, 42, 81, 105–13, 130–1, 136, 138, 169–70, 176, 178, 183, 202
subversive discursive forces 24, 203, 206
supernatural phenomena/films 28, 38, 202
Surrealism 31
Sutherland, Jock 15
Sydney Box production 119

Take My Life (1947) 39
Temptation Harbour (1947) 39, 41
They Made Me a Fugitive (1947) 2, 35, 38, 39–41, 159, 188, 201–2, 204
    Aggie 161–2, 170–2
    Bert 163
    black market activities 38, 159–62, 171, 176, 188
    Carmen Mory, the 'Black Angel' of Ravensbrück 177
    Clem Morgan 38, 43, 160–73, 176, 178, 202, 205
    Cora 161–2, 165, 167, 169
    dream-like state 175–6
    Ellen 161, 163–6, 170, 172
    Mr. & Mrs Fenshaw 161–2, 172–6, 178
    Inspector Rockliffe 161–2, 177–8
    mechanical automaton 173, 175
    mise-en-scene of second sequence 163, 169
    Narcy 43, 160–72, 171 n.11, 176–8, 202, 205
    paternal and maternal functions, collapse 170–8
    post-war cultural malaise 43, 160, 170–8
    Sally Connor 161–2, 164, 166–70, 172, 176, 178, 202
    Soapy 161–2, 171, 177
    traumatic affect and moral responsibility 162–70
    un-integration, state of 169–70
They Were Sisters (1945) 37
The Third Man (1949) 41
Tobruk, fall of 64, 75–7
Todd, Ann 130, 135

trade union movement 11
transgressions 146, 151–2, 157, 160, 171, 188, 203–4
trauma 25, 27, 46, 53, 61–73, 81, 88–92, 96, 116, 120, 122, 124, 128, 130, 145–6, 160, 201–2, 206. *See also* childhood trauma/sexual trauma
    art of 4–5, 25, 28
    and culture 70–1
    intractability 206
    shell-shock 12, 14
traumatic repetition 92, 95, 202
traumatic war experience 2–4, 29, 43, 46, 54–73, 83, 88, 94, 96, 120, 122, 127, 129, 176, 179, 182–3, 186–7, 192–3, 199–201, 203, 205–6
traumatization 40, 129, 176, 186
Trinder, Tommy 50
Trist, Eric 15
Two Cities Films 37

The Upturned Glass (1947) 39, 179

Vessclo, Arthur 38
Victorian Gothic sensuality 114
Victorian hypocrisy 41

War Artists Advisory Committee 89
Ward, Elizabeth, *Film Noir: An Encyclopedic Reference to the American Style* 32
War Office Committee of Enquiry into Shell Shock 14
wartime film 3, 7–8, 29, 37, 50, 136–7, 175, 200
Waterloo Road (1945) 38
The Way Ahead (1944) 37
Welch, Denton 9
Welfare State 10
Went the Day Well? (1942) 27, 174
    Mrs. Collins 174–5
    Nora 174–5
    Oliver Wilsford 174
White Heat (1949) 32
The Wicked Lady (1945) 36, 151
Williams, Tony 40, 187
Wilson, A. T. M. 15
Winnicott, Clare 14

Winnicott, Donald 3, 14, 113
Winnington, Richard 90
Wittkower, Eric 15
woman's film, Hollywood 33, 120
    cultural environment of wartime 148
    female subjectivity 33, 42, 130–1, 136
    ideology 131, 134
    sexual relationships 120

women in British society 11, 103–4, 137
    "indiscretions" 138
    lives during Second World War 119–20
working-through process 60–73, 92, 95–6, 206
Wright, Basil 126

The Years Between (1946) 37

Zweiniger-Bargielowska, Ina 160

www.ingramcontent.com/pod-product-compliance
Lightning Source LLC
Chambersburg PA
CBHW052036300426
44117CB00012B/1847